N INFORMATION SYSTEMS

Video training courses are available on the subjects of these books in the
James Martin ADVANCED TECHNOLOGY LIBRARY of over 300 tapes and disks,
from Applied Learning, 1751 West Diehl Road, Naperville, IL

Database	Telecommunications	Networks and Data Communications	Society
AN END USER'S GUIDE TO DATABASE	TELECOMMUNICATIONS AND THE COMPUTER (third edition)	PRINCIPLES OF DATA COMMUNICATION	THE COMPUTERIZED SOCIETY
PRINCIPLES OF DATABASE MANAGEMENT (second edition)	FUTURE DEVELOPMENTS IN TELECOMMUNICATIONS (third edition)	TELEPROCESSING NETWORK ORGANIZATION	TELEMATIC SOCIETY: A CHALLENGE FOR TOMORROW
COMPUTER DATABASE ORGANIZATION (third edition)	COMMUNICATIONS SATELLITE SYSTEMS	SYSTEMS ANALYSIS FOR DATA TRANSMISSION	TECHNOLOGY'S CRUCIBLE
MANAGING THE DATABASE ENVIRONMENT (second edition)	ISDN	DATA COMMUNICATION TECHNOLOGY	VIEWDATA AND THE INFORMATION SOCIETY
DATABASE ANALYSIS AND DESIGN	**Distributed Processing**	DATA COMMUNICATION DESIGN TECHNIQUES	TELEVISION AND THE COMPUTER
VSAM: ACCESS METHOD SERVICES AND PROGRAMMING TECHNIQUES	COMPUTER NETWORKS AND DISTRIBUTED PROCESSING	SNA: IBM's NETWORKING SOLUTION	THE WORLD INFORMATION ECONOMY
DB2: CONCEPTS, DESIGN, AND PROGRAMMING	DESIGN AND STRATEGY FOR DISTRIBUTED DATA PROCESSING	ISDN	**Systems In General**
IDMS/R: CONCEPTS, DESIGN, AND PROGRAMMING	**Office Automation**	LOCAL AREA NETWORKS: ARCHITECTURES AND IMPLEMENTATIONS	A BREAKTHROUGH IN MAKING COMPUTERS FRIENDLY: THE MACINTOSH COMPUTER
SQL	IBM's OFFICE AUTOMATION ARCHITECTURE	OFFICE AUTOMATION STANDARDS	SAA: IBM's SYSTEMS APPLICATION ARCHITECTURE
Security	OFFICE AUTOMATION STANDARDS	DATA COMMUNICATION STANDARDS	
SECURITY, ACCURACY, AND PRIVACY IN COMPUTER SYSTEMS		CORPORATE COMMUNICATIONS STRATEGY	
SECURITY AND PRIVACY IN COMPUTER SYSTEMS		COMPUTER NETWORKS AND DISTRIBUTED PROCESSING: SOFTWARE, TECHNIQUES, AND ARCHITECTURE	

IDMS/R

A *James Martin* **BOOK**

THE JAMES MARTIN BOOKS
currently available from Prentice Hall

- Application Development Without Programmers
- Building Expert Systems
- Communications Satellite Systems
- Computer Data-Base Organization, Second Edition
- The Computerized Society
- Computer Networks and Distributed Processing: Software, Techniques, and Architecture
- Data Communication Technology
- DB2: Concepts, Design, and Programming
- Design and Strategy of Distributed Data Processing
- Design of Real-Time Computer Systems
- An End User's Guide to Data Base
- Fourth-Generation Languages, Volume I: Principles
- Fourth-Generation Languages, Volume II: Representative 4GLs
- Fourth-Generation Languages, Volume III: 4GLs from IBM
- Future Developments in Telecommunications, Second Edition
- Hyperdocuments and How to Create Them
- IDMS/R: Concepts, Design, and Programming
- Information Engineering, Book I: Introduction and Principles
- Information Engineering, Book II: Planning and Analysis
- Information Engineering, Book III: Design and Construction
- An Information Systems Manifesto
- Local Area Networks: Architectures and Implementations
- Managing the Data-Base Environment
- Principles of Data-Base Management
- Principles of Data Communication
- Recommended Diagramming Standards for Analysts and Programmers
- SNA: IBM's Networking Solution
- Strategic Information Planning Methodologies, Second Edition
- System Design from Provably Correct Constructs
- Systems Analysis for Data Transmission
- Technology's Crucible
- Telecommunications and the Computer, Third Edition
- Telematic Society: A Challenge for Tomorrow
- VSAM: Access Method Services and Programming Techniques

with Carma McClure

- Action Diagrams: Clearly Structured Specifications, Programs, and Procedures, Second Edition
- Diagramming Techniques for Analysts and Programmers
- Software Maintenance: The Problem and Its Solutions
- Structured Techniques: The Basis for CASE, Revised Edition

IDMS/R
Concepts, Design, and Programming

JAMES MARTIN

with
Richard Derer
Joe Leben

PRENTICE HALL, Englewood Cliffs, New Jersey 07632

Library of Congress Cataloging-in-Publication Data

Martin, James (date)
   IDMS/R: concepts, design, and programming/James Martin, with
Richard Derer, Joe Leben.
     p.   cm.
   "A James Martin book."
   Includes index.
   ISBN 0-13-451212-X: $46.00
   1. Database management. 2. IDMS/R (Computer system) I. Derer,
Richard. II. Leben, Joe. III. Title.
  QA76.9.D3M366 1990
  005.75′4—dc20

                                    89-8846
                                       CIP

Editorial/production supervision: *Kathryn Gollin Marshak*
Jacket cover design: *Bruce Kenselaar*
Manufacturing buyer: *Mary Ann Gloriande*

The publisher offers discounts on this book when ordered
in bulk quantities. For more information write:
Special Sales Prentice-Hall, Inc.
College Technical and Reference Division
Englewood Cliffs, NJ 07632

Printed in the United States of America

10 9 8 7 6 5 4 3 2 1

ISBN   0-13-451212-X

PRENTICE-HALL INTERNATIONAL (UK) LIMITED, *London*
PRENTICE-HALL OF AUSTRALIA PTY. LIMITED, *Sydney*
PRENTICE-HALL CANADA INC., *Toronto*
PRENTICE-HALL HISPANOAMERICANA, S.A., *Mexico*
PRENTICE-HALL OF INDIA PRIVATE LIMITED, *New Delhi*
PRENTICE-HALL OF JAPAN, INC., *Tokyo*
SIMON & SCHUSTER ASIA PTE. LTD., *Singapore*
EDITORA PRENTICE-HALL DO BRASIL, LTDA., *Rio De Janeiro*

CONTENTS

PROGRAMMING WITH NETWORK-STRUCTURED DATABASES

PART **III**

PREFACE

Databases are playing an increasingly important role in supporting an enterprise's information processing requirements. The development of corporate databases will continue to be an extremely important data processing activity for many years to come. Data will be regarded as a vital corporate resource which must be managed so as to maximize its value. Both the quantity of data stored and the complexity of its organization are increasing by leaps and bounds.

Integrated Database Management System/Relational (IDMS/R) is a full-function database management system, fully integrated with a data dictionary subsystem, that is used as the primary database management system in hundreds of IBM mainframe installations. IDMS/R is unique in that it supports network-structured databases using the CODASYL approach to database management and also provides support for the relational database architecture. This book is designed to introduce the main software subsystems that operate in the IDMS/R database managment system environment.

ACKNOWLEDGMENTS   Of paramount importance in any book that depends heavily on computer coding examples is that the examples be accurate and free of coding errors. We were fortunate to have the able assistance of two people from the Aon Corporation in Chicago who painstakingly tested the coding examples for us. We would like to express our appreciation to Robert F. Baldwin, assistant vice-president of database administration, and Warren Cotton, manager of data administration, for their help in testing the computer examples.

James Martin
Richard Derer
Joe Leben

IDMS/R

INTRODUCTION

1 THE IDMS/R ENVIRONMENT

Integrated Database Management System/Relational (IDMS/R) is a software product, marketed by Cullinet Software, that offers capabilities for working with data organized in a variety of forms. IDMS/R is one of a number of software systems that can be classified as a *database management system (DBMS)*. A DBMS is a software subsystem that manages a collection of interrelated data elements, stored in a *database*, that can be accessed in a shared manner by a collection of application programs. On a very conceptual level, we can think of an IDMS/R database as a central reservoir of data that may be accessed by many users. In this book, we will use the term *IDMS/R* to refer to the total collection of software that makes up the IDMS/R product; we will use the term *DBMS* to refer to the portion of the IDMS/R software that handles accesses to the database.

IDMS/R can be described as an *integrated* database management system, in that its components work around a central software subsystem: its *integrated data dictionary (IDD)*. In the IDMS/R environment, all data elements used in application systems are defined in the data dictionary. All application structures such as the logical and physical descriptions of the database, definitions of display screen formats, and application code can also be defined in the data dictionary. Finally, extensive reporting mechanisms work through the dictionary to provide information to data processing professionals concerning IDMS/R application systems and also to produce user-defined application reports.

THE DATABASE ENVIRONMENT

There are many advantages to maintaining, in a central pool, all an organization's data so that it can be shared by a number of application programs. These issues have been discussed at length elsewhere (see James Martin's other general database books listed in the front matter of this book), and it is not our in-

3

tent to examine these advantages at length. However, we will discuss some of the general characteristics of the database approach and examine the personnel roles that are important in the database environment before beginning a technical description of IDMS/R facilities. In general, we can place the advantages of the database approach into two categories:

- Data integrity
- Application development productivity

DATA INTEGRITY   Effective use of a database management system, such as IDMS/R, helps the installation in two ways to control better the *integrity* of the data that is stored in database form. First, a database management system makes it possible to reduce and sometimes eliminate the necessity of storing redundant data. Second, a database management system provides powerful tools for automatically recovering from system failures, restoring the database to its original form, and restarting jobs that were affected by failures.

Reducing Data Redundancy

In the traditional file environment, application programmers design their own data files and establish their own record formats. This makes their programs dependent on the format of those records, and it tends to create a high degree of data redundancy. For example, many different programs in an installation may require access to information about employees. If the records that contain employee information are designed independently, the same piece of employee information may exist in different files, possibly in different forms. Through effective use of database techniques, this redundancy can be better controlled. Ideally, each piece of information is stored only once in the central pool, and all application programs that require the information gain access to it via the database management system. By controlling redundancy in this manner, it is much easier for the installation to ensure that multiple copies of the same data element do not exist in different stages of updating.

Recovery and Restart

When traditional files are used to implement systems, recovery and restart routines must be built into each individual application system. This makes it difficult to implement sophisticated recovery and restart procedures. With a database management system like IDMS/R, recovery and restart procedures can be handled automatically on a systemwide basis using the tools provided by DBMS software.

APPLICATION DEVELOPMENT PRODUCTIVITY

To an application programmer, a major goal of database techniques is to simplify the task of developing an application program and of maintaining the application once it is in production, thus increasing programmer productivity.

Simplified Programming

In the database environment, the job of developing new applications is simplified because the DBMS automatically performs many of the tasks that previously had to be coded into each application program. In a program that uses conventional files, much of the program logic must deal with the way in which files are read and written, and the order in which data is processed. With a database management system, application programs make simple requests for data, and the DBMS performs all the necessary steps to locate the required data. This results in application programs that are less complex than those that work with conventional files.

Reduced Maintenance

A database management system can reduce the amount of program maintenance that is required by making application programs independent of the physical structure of the records they access. In the traditional file environment, application programmers design their application programs based on the functions they must perform and then design the formats of the data records required to perform those functions. This causes application programs to be tied tightly to the formats of files they process. If a record changes in format, all the application programs that access the record must also be modified.

The database approach reverses the role of data design in the development of applications. The data should be designed independently of the application programs that will access it. Since programs do not access data directly, changes can be made to the structure of the database without requiring that application programs be modified.

DATABASE PERSONNEL ROLES

It is now well understood that the personnel roles in the database environment are considerably more specialized than those in the traditional environment. Each person involved in the database environment performs different tasks and views the data differently. The following job functions *must* be performed if database techniques are going to be used successfully:

- Data administrator
- Database administrator

- Systems analysts and designers
- Application programmers
- End users

Box 1.1 briefly describes the five personnel roles that are important in the database environment. In discussing personnel roles, Box 1.1 describes broad job responsibilities; the way in which these responsibilities are assigned to individuals varies widely from installation to installation.

DATABASE ARCHITECTURES   A database management system generally conforms to one of three major database architectures: *hierarchical, network,* or *relational.* In a hierarchically structured database, illustrated in Fig. 1.1, data records are typically connected with embedded pointers to form a tree structure. A network-structured database takes the form of a mesh structure such as that shown in Fig. 1.2, in which dependent records can have more than one parent. With a relational database, data is represented in the form of tables, as shown in Fig. 1.3, and no embedded pointers are required to represent relationships between records.

THE DUAL NATURE OF IDMS/R   The network database model was adopted by the Conference on Data Systems Languages (CODASYL) and accepted by the American National Standards Institute (ANSI) as a national standard on which database management systems could be based. IDMS/R was originally an implementation of the CODASYL architecture but has been enhanced over time beyond the original CODASYL specification. One of the unique features of the IDMS/R product is that current versions successfully combine many of the best features of both the network and the relational database architectures. It should be stated here that it is today generally agreed that the relational approach to database management has many advantages over the older hierarchical and network approaches, but that in many environments, the network and hierarchical approaches still have valid applications.

In many cases database designers must be able to optimize the structure of the database to enhance the performance of well-defined, high-volume transaction processing applications. These types of applications may find that a network-structured or hierarchical database better suits their needs. Other applications are better suited to the versatile relational approach to database management. A user who chooses to view the database as a relational structure looks at the database as if it consisted of a set of two-dimensional tables. This type of database view appeals to users who are interested in controlling their own information processing activities and reducing their dependence on the technical

BOX 1.1 Personnel roles in the database environment

- **Data Administrator.** In today's environment, there must be one key individual who is responsible for the overall centralized control of the organization's data. We refer to this person as the *data administrator*. The job of data administrator is not a technical one. It concerns policy-oriented tasks regarding data strategy and overall data planning. The data administrator is responsible for the actual entities in the business environment that will be represented in the database. The data administrator also works with end users and systems analysts to document the data that will be stored in the database.

- **Database Administrator.** The role of *database administrator (DBA)* is more technical than is that of data administrator. The job of the data administrator is often performed by a single person. Database administration, on the other hand, is often performed by a group of people. However, for simplicity, we will refer to database administration as if it were performed by a single person, the database administrator. The DBA is responsible for designing, controlling, and coordinating the data that is stored in databases. The DBA must perform two very different tasks: the *logical* design and the *physical* design of the organization's databases. In some organizations, both the logical and physical designs are performed by the same individual or group. In other organizations, these tasks are performed by different people.

- **Systems Analysts and Designers.** *Systems analysts* and *designers* analyze and document the needs of the end users. They often work with the data administrator and the DBA in designing the database. In addition, as in conventional system development, analysts and designers typically define the requirements for the application programs that will access the database.

- **Application Programmers.** *Application programmers* write the programs that work with the database and interpret the program requirements specified by the systems analysts and designers.

- **End Users.** End users of the data provide valuable input to the data administrator, DBA, systems analysts and designers, and application programmers. They define what their present data needs are and try to predict what their needs will be in the future. They review the logical structure of the database after it has been documented by the DBA to see if it truly represents their environment. They participate in the testing of the system to insure that the system does what it was intended to do. Finally, they use the system on a daily basis.

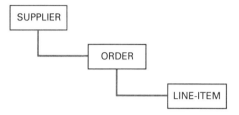

Figure 1.1 A hierarchically structured database typically uses embedded pointers to create a tree configuration in which a dependent record type has one and only one parent.

staff. Combining both network and relational capabilities in one system provides the installation with a versatile tool for meeting both production requirements and the ease-of-use requirements of end users.

The relational and network capabilities of IDMS/R are supported by a single database management system product. This means that data stored in the form of network structures can be accessed by conventional application programs but can also be accessed by the relational facilities for those applications that require a relational view of the network-structured data. In turn, data entered through the relational facility can be used to update the production, network-structured database. In either case, all database access, input/output operations, and space management are performed by the same system components. Figure 1.4 shows the dual nature of IDMS/R.

THE IDMS/R DBMS COMPONENT   The heart of any database product is the software component that manages access to the database. This component is most commonly called the database management system (DBMS). IDMS/R consists of a set of software modules that manage the data elements that are stored in the database and maintains the relationships that exist between them. A major purpose of a DBMS is to isolate application programs from the details concerning how data elements are physi-

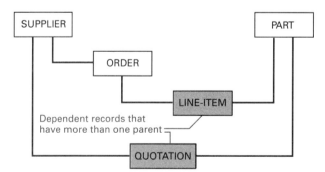

Figure 1.2 A network-structured database typically uses embedded pointers to create a mesh configuration in which a dependent record type can have more than one parent.

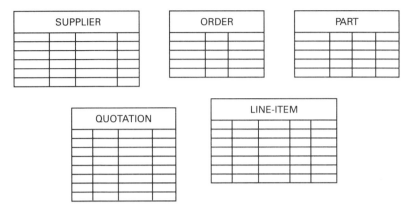

Figure 1.3 A relational database maintains data in the form of tables in which all associations are expressed using values in the stored data rather than with embedded pointers.

cally stored. To this end, the data stored in an IDMS/R database is accessed only by the DBMS and never directly by an application program.

IDMS/R Support for Network Database Structures

IDMS/R support for a network-structured database is provided via two common languages that designers and programmers use to control access to the database: *data description language (DDL)* and *data manipulation language (DML)*. The data description language is used by database designers to describe the logical and physical structure of the database to the DBMS software and to application programs. Application programs use the data manipulation language to specify how the database is accessed. Application programs make requests for access to

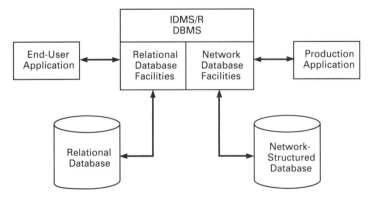

Figure 1.4 IDMS/R combines facilities for working with network-structured databases and with relational databases.

the database by executing DML statements; the DBMS intercepts these requests and performs the required accesses to the database to satisfy these requests.

IDMS/R Support for Relational Database Structures

IDMS/R uses a software subsystem called the *Automatic System Facility (ASF)* to provide users with a relational view of the database. ASF is menu-oriented and relatively easy to use and can be employed both by data processing professionals and by end users. Using ASF, users define their data in the form of tables. ASF automatically generates the supporting physical data structures that are required to implement the tables. Using ASF, many of the time-consuming system design and application development tasks typically required in a database environment can be performed automatically by ASF. We will examine the facilities of ASF in detail in Chapter 19.

SUMMARY   The objectives and advantages of the database approach can be placed into two broad categories: data integrity and application development productivity. Database techniques promote data integrity by reducing redundancy and by providing automatic recovery from system failures. Application development productivity is enhanced by simplifying programming and reducing the need for maintenance. IDMS/R programs issue simple requests for database access using a high-level data manipulation language. Although all database environments share the advantages discussed in this chapter, they do not achieve these advantages in the same manner.

There are three major database architectures: hierarchical, network, and relational. With the hierarchical architecture, the database uses tree structures, database management systems that conform to the network approach use a mesh structure, and relational databases represent data using tables. IDMS/R was originally designed to be an implementation of the CODASYL network database model, but the addition of relational capabilities through the Automatic System Facility has given it a dual nature. Network-structured databases can be used to handle high-volume production demands, while relational databases can be used to accommodate user-generated applications.

PART I

DESIGNING NETWORK-STRUCTURED DATABASES

2 LOGICAL DATABASE STRUCTURE

When we are using a powerful database management system, such as IDMS/R, to manage a central pool of data, we can view the database on a number of different levels. At the highest level is the *application environment,* where we discuss the nature of the *entities* that we are representing in the database. Entities consist of those objects, people, or ideas about which we are storing data. On a lower level we are concerned with *software,* where we describe the *logical structure* of the database that we are using to represent information about entities in the database. On a still lower level is the *hardware,* where we describe the *physical structure* of the database and the way in which logical records are implemented in computer storage. Our focus in this chapter will be on the entities about which we are storing information and the logical structure of the database we are using to represent these entities.

THE BASEBALL DATABASE

Throughout this book we will be using a hypothetical baseball database that might be used to maintain information about baseball players in a baseball league. The database will store information about the following entities:

- **Team.** Information about baseball teams in the league.
- **Player.** Information about the players on each team.
- **Game.** Information about each of the games the teams play.
- **Salary.** Salary history for each player.
- **Bonus.** Bonus history information for each player.

ATTRIBUTES AND RELATIONSHIPS

In discussing entities, we can discuss the *attributes* that an entity has and the *relationships* that exist between the entities.

Entity Attributes

An attribute is a particular piece of information that is associated with an entity. For example, possible attributes for the Team entity are as follows:

- Team name
- Team phone
- Team city

Entity Relationships

We can identify a number of *relationships* between the entities about which we are storing information. For example, the Team and Player entities participate in a one-with-many relationship. Each player belongs to *one* team, but each team has *many* players. The Team and Game entities form another one-with-many relationship. If we define each game as either a home game or an away game, then a given game entity is associated with *one* team, and each team plays *many* games. Player and Salary and Player and Bonus also form one-with-many relationships. We may store many sets of salary information for a player as a player's salary changes and each player may receive many bonuses. However, a given set of salary or bonus information is associated with a particular player. The Player and Game entities form a many-with-many relationship. One player can play in many games, and each game has many players.

ENTITY-RELATIONSHIP DIAGRAMS

We can represent the relationships between our entities using an *entity-relationship diagram*. An entity-relationship diagram for our baseball team information is shown in Fig. 2.1. Each entity is represented by a square-cornered box. We use cardinality symbols on the ends of the lines

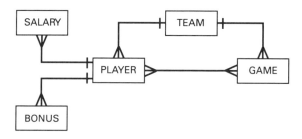

Figure 2.1 Entity-relationship diagram for baseball team information.

connecting the boxes to represent relationships. As shown in Fig. 2.1, we draw a line to represent the "one" side of a relationship and a "crow's foot" symbol to represent the many side of a relationship.

DATABASE RECORDS

In representing the Baseball database using a net-work-structured IDMS/R database, we begin by defining a separate *database record* for each entity. Consider the Team entity and its attributes. We represent the Team attribute using a Team record, and we represent each Team attribute as a *data element* within the Team record, as shown in Fig. 2.2. Data elements are sometimes called *data items,* or *fields.* We name each data element, define its *length,* and define the *type* of data that it will contain.

RECORD TYPES VERSUS RECORD OCCURRENCES

It is important to make a clear distinction between a record *type* and a record *occurrence*. We can think of a record type as a template. It describes the format of all occurrences of a given record type that will be stored in the database. Each occurrence of the Team record type consists of a single set of values for the Team-Name, Team-Phone, and Team-City data elements, as shown in Fig. 2.3.

MANY-WITH-MANY RELATIONSHIPS

IDMS/R does not provide facilities for directly representing many-with-many relationships, and this fact has often been used as a criticism of IDMS/R. However, in the real world, there is generally no need to represent directly many-with-many relationships. For each many-with-many relationship that we identify among a set of entities, we will almost always identify additional attributes that are not associated with either of the two entities alone but are associated with the *intersection* between the two entity types. For example, we saw earlier that there exists a many-with-many relationship between the Player and Game entities: a player plays in many games, and a game has many players. However, suppose we determine that we must store an attribute called Position-Name that identifies the position that a given player plays in a particular game. Position-Name cannot be defined as an attribute of the Player entity because a player may

Team Record

TEAM-NAME PIC X(20)	TEAM-PHONE PIC X(10)	TEAM-CITY PIC X(15)

Figure 2.2 Team record type.

Team Record Type

TEAM-NAME PIC X(20)	TEAM-PHONE PIC X(10)	TEAM-CITY PIC X(15)

Team Record Occurrences

TOUCANS	419 555 6161	TOLEDO

ZEPHYRS	313 555 3326	DETROIT

STARS	217 555 8722	SPRINGFIELD

Figure 2.3   Record type versus record occurrences.

play a different position in each game. Position-Name cannot be defined as an attribute of the Game entity either because there are many positions associated with each game.

To represent the Position-Name attribute correctly, we must first create a Position record type, as shown in Fig. 2.4, in which information about the Position-Name attribute can be stored. Position has a one-with-many relationship with the Player record and also a one-with-many relationship with the Game record. We call the Position record a *junction record* because it represents a *junction,* or *intersection,* between the Player record and the Game record. With it, we can get from games to players, and from players to games, thus eliminating the need to directly represent the many-with-many relationship between Players and Games. The junction record resolves the many-with-many relationship and implements this many-with-many relationship indirectly. In designing network-structured databases, such junction records are added to the initial design to resolve the many-with-many relationships that are identified.

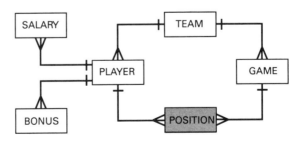

Figure 2.4   The need for a many-with-many relationship can be eliminated through the use of a junction record.

BACHMAN DIAGRAMS

Many IDMS/R installations use a line with an arrow at one end to show each one-with-many relationship instead of using crow's foot notation, as shown in Fig. 2.5. Such a diagram is called a *Bachman diagram,* after Charles Bachman who was instrumental in developing the network database model. The end of the relationship without the arrow always represents the "one" side of the relationship, and the end of the relationship with the arrow always represents the "many" side. Since IDMS/R network-structured databases implement only one-with-many relationships, this type of notation can generally be used without confusion. However, many installations prefer the more explicit approach that crow's foot notation provides. For a detailed discussion of data analysis diagramming techniques, see the author's *Recommended Diagramming Techniques for Analysts and Programmers.*

DEFINING SETS

A one-with-many relationship in an IDMS/R network database is implemented by defining a *set.* A set consists of two or more record types that participate in one-with-many relationships with one another. The record type on the "one" side of the relationship is designated the *owner* of the set; the record type on the "many" side is designated the *member* record type. Each set must be assigned a unique name. Figure 2.6 shows the names of all the sets that we might define for the baseball database. Although any name can be given to a set, a set that consists of only two record types (the most common form of set) is generally given a name that is a concatenation of the two record names. For example, notice that the set that implements the one-with-many relationship between the Team record and the Player is named Team-Player.

Some record types must be an owner or a member in more than one set. For example, the Team record is the owner of both the Team-Player and the Team-Game sets. And the Position junction record is a member in both the Player-Position set and the Game-Position set.

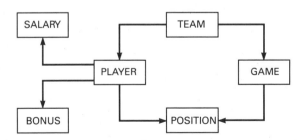

Figure 2.5 A Bachman diagram uses an arrow instead of a crow's foot to indicate the many side of a one-with-many relationship.

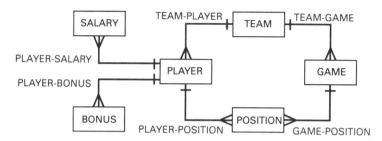

Figure 2.6 Sets defined for the Baseball database.

SET TYPE VERSUS SET OCCURRENCE

As with record types and record occurrences, there is an important distinction between a set type and a set occurrence. Like a record type, a set type can be thought of as a template that describes the general nature of the set. A set occurrence, on the other hand, consists of a specific single occurrence of the owner record type and all occurrences of the member records that are associated with it.

Figure 2.7 shows the way that the Cullinet software documentation typically shows in a diagram a specific occurrence of a set, in this case the Team-Player set. There exists one occurrence of the Team-Player set for each occurrence of the set's owner record type. The arrow shows how the member records are chained together. (Various types of pointer are used to implement set relationships, but these pointers are of no concern to us now.) In a set occurrence diagram, the arrowhead always points to the owner record of the set occurrence. We will be using this type of diagram throughout this book to show occurrences of sets.

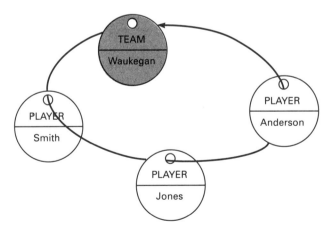

Figure 2.7 A Team-Player set occurrence.

CHOICES IN DEFINING SETS

In some cases we must make choices in how sets are to be used to implement the one-with-many relationships identified in the entity-relationship model. For example, Fig. 2.8 shows two different types of set relationships that could be used to represent the relationships between the Player, Salary, and Bonus record types. At the top of Fig. 2.8, the relationships are represented using two separate sets with the Player record type being the owner of both. Alternatively, we can define Salary and Bonus as members of a multiple-member set, as shown at the bottom of Fig. 2.8. The choice between a multiple-member set and separate set types is generally made based on the processing requirements of the record types that make up the sets. We would use a multiple-member set if we always access both record types together. However, if we access one of the member record types more than the other, then separate sets would typically be more efficient.

THE SCHEMA

The definition of all record types and all set types that make up an IDMS/R network database is called a *schema*. We will see in Chapters 4 and 5 how we can represent a schema visually using a *data structure diagram,* which is an expansion of the entity-relationship diagram used during the initial stages of logical design. When database design has been completed, we then define the schema to IDMS/R using a set of schema data definition language statements. We will examine schema DDL statements in Chapter 6.

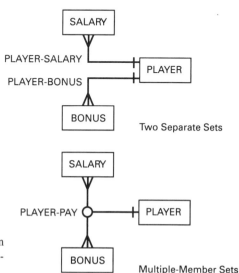

Figure 2.8 Different set combinations can be used to implement groups of one-with-many relationships.

SUBSCHEMAS   In real-world systems, most application programs do not require access to all the record types and all the set types that are defined in the schema. The designer must define one or more *subschemas* that each specify the particular record types, data elements, and set types that each group of application programs needs access to. Subschemas provide a means of simplifying the view of the database for each application program. Subschemas also provide the ability to restrict access to only those record types, data elements, and set types that a particular application program is authorized to access.

Figure 2.9 shows the logical structure of a possible subschema that we might specify for giving an application program access to a particular subset of the data and set relationships defined for the Baseball database. It is important to point out that an application program always accesses the database by referring to a subschema. So even if a program requires access to all the record types, data elements, and set types defined in the schema, the designer must still define a subschema that includes all the elements defined in the schema. As with the schema, we define all subschemas to IDMS/R using a set of subschema DDL statements. Subschema DDL statements are also discussed in Chapter 6.

TYPES OF SET   The set relationships that we defined for the Baseball
RELATIONSHIPS   database are quite simple. However, the capabilities that IDMS/R provide for defining sets allow us to build quite complex database structures. We will next examine more closely the fundamental types of logical data relationships that can exist between owner and member record types in an IDMS/R database. These are *hierarchies* and *network structures*.

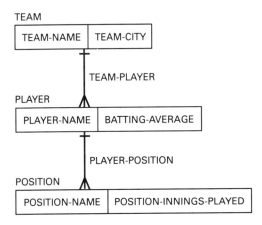

Figure 2.9 The logical structure of a possible subschema that can be derived from the Baseball database schema.

HIERARCHIES   Three forms of hierarchies can be represented with sets:

- Two-level hierarchies
- Multilevel hierarchies
- Hierarchies with multiple set ownership

Two-Level Hierarchies

As we have seen, a single set implements a *two-level hierarchy*. The owner record type is on the first level, and the member record types are on the second level. A one-with-many relationship exists between the owner record type and its member record types. Figure 2.10 shows the relationships that exist between teams and players. One way to handle this one-with-many relationship is as we have done with the Baseball database—by defining a Team-Player set that implements the relationship directly by storing separate Team and Player record types.

The one-with-many relationship that is represented using a two-level hierarchy can alternatively be represented using a single record with groups of one or more repeating data elements. Figure 2.11 shows how we might represent the relationship between Team data and Player data using a single Team-Player record that contains a repeating data element. IDMS/R provides the capability for using either sets or repeating groups to represent a simple hierarchical relationship. However, there are a number of advantages to using sets over repeating groups:

- **Simplified application programming.** Records can be addressed directly, data elements cannot. When we use a set, IDMS/R implements the hierarchical relationship for us. If we use repeating groups, our application program must implement the relationship through program logic. The use of repeating groups normally makes for more complex application program logic.

- **Multiple relationships.** Records can participate in many sets. This allows us to represent combinations of relationships that would be difficult to implement using repeating groups. For example, it would be very difficult to represent all of

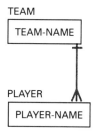

Figure 2.10   The one-with-many relationship between teams and players.

TEAM-PLAYER

| TEAM-NAME | PLAYER-NAME 1 | PLAYER-NAME 2 | | }} | | PLAYER-NAME n |

Figure 2.11   A one-with-many relationship can be represented using a repeating group.

the relationships that exist among the Team, Player, and Game entities by using repeating data elements.

- **Storage utilization.** If we use repeating groups, some record occurrences may be very large. For example, if we use repeating data elements to implement the relationship between the Team and Player entities, a single record occurrence would contain all the data about a given team and the players on that team. A program normally reserves storage for the largest record that it expects to process. This means that we would have to allocate enough storage for all of the data about the largest team. Space in variable storage would be wasted when we processed the records for smaller teams. If we use a set to implement the relationship between the team and player entities, we need to allocate only enough variable storage to contain the data elements for one team and for one player.

- **Normalization.** Perhaps the most compelling reason for avoiding repeating groups is that repeating groups will only appear in data that has not been optimally normalized. It is now well understood that databases that implement logical data models that have not been optimally normalized have many problems associated with them that will have far-reaching ramifications for the installation. Appendix III presents an introduction to the process of designing optimally normalized logical data structures.

Even though there are significant advantages to using sets for representing hierarchical relationships, there are a few cases where the use of repeating groups is appropriate. A good example is where quarterly totals must be maintained. There will always be only four occurrences of the data element in each record. There would probably be little advantage gained in creating a quarterly total record type in which four occurrences are stored. The choice between using a set and using repeating data elements must be evaluated during the later stages of database design, where data that has been optimally normalized during logical database design is sometimes deliberately denormalized for performance reasons.

Multiple Set Relationships

It is quite possible for two record types to participate in multiple one-with-many relationships with one another. For example, in the Baseball database, we might decide that it is advantageous to separate Game record occurrences into two categories: *home games* and *away games*. One way of implementing this is to define two different one-with-many relationships between the Team record type and the Game record type, with each being implemented by a different set type,

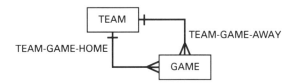

Figure 2.12   Two record types can participate in multiple set types.

as shown in Fig. 2.12. The same two record types, Team and Game, now participate in two different sets. However, a given Game record occurrence will be a member of only one of the two possible set types. For each Team record occurrence, there are two *different* groups of Game record occurrences associated with it.

Figure 2.13 shows an occurrence of each of the two sets. Notice that each occurrence has the same owner occurrence, Chicago, but different member occurrences. One set has the St. Louis, Rockford, and Gary games as members, while the other set has the Peoria and Toledo games as members.

Multilevel Hierarchies

Another form of hierarchy uses multiple levels of sets to define relationships among three or more record types. Remember that a *member* of one set can also

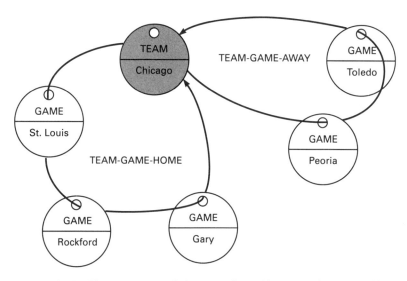

Figure 2.13   The occurrence of the Team-Game-Home set shows that Chicago played St. Louis, Rockford, and Gary in home games; the occurrence of the Team-Game-Away set shows that Chicago played Peoria and Toledo in away games.

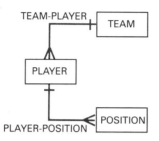

Figure 2.14 The Team, Player, and Position records form a three-level hierarchy.

be the *owner* of another set. This results in a *multilevel hierarchy*. For example, position assignments, which are stored in Position records, are associated with the appropriate players in the Player-Position set. The owner of this set, Player, is in turn a member of the Team-Player set, resulting in the three-level hierarchy, shown in Fig. 2.14.

Hierarchies with Multiple Set Ownership

A third form of hierarchy uses one record type as the owner record in more than one set. In Fig. 2.15, the Team record type is the owner record in both the Team-Player set and the Team-Game set. This allows us to keep track of both the players on a team and the games that a team plays. The common owner record provides the means of movement between the two different member record types.

NETWORK STRUCTURES

As we have already seen in the Baseball database examples, hierarchical structures are not powerful enough to represent many of the relationships that exist in the real world. For example, in the Baseball database we needed to create the Position record, which is owned by both the Player and Game records, as shown in Fig. 2.16. IDMS/R allows us to create network structures freely because any given record type can be a member in any number of different set types. This ability to create network structures gives IDMS/R a significant advantage over database management systems that allow only strictly hierarchical relationships to be represented.

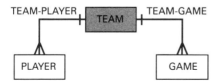

Figure 2.15 A record can be the owner in multiple set relationships.

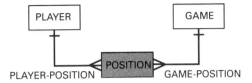

Figure 2.16 In the network-structured database, a member record type can be owned by more than one owner record type.

LOOPS AND CYCLES

Two special types of network structures often occur in the real world that sometimes require special handling by database management systems. These are called *cycles* and *loops* or, more generically, *nested structures*. Nested structures often arise when modeling bill-of-materials structures in the manufacturing environment.

A cycle refers to a situation in which one of a record's descendants is also one of its ancestors. Figure 2.17 shows an example of a cycle in which a plant has many contracts, each of which involves the manufacture of many products. However, some of those products may be subcontracted out to other plants. We can represent this in a data structure diagram by showing a one-with-many relationship between Plant and Product.

A loop is a special case of a cycle in which occurrences of a record type are related to other record occurrences of the same type. Figure 2.18 shows an example of how some of the players in the Baseball database might be related to one another. In this example, some of the players are also coaches who may coach one or more other players. The relationship is shown as many-with-many because a player may have many coaches. For example, one coach may help players with batting and another coach with fielding, and so on.

IDMS/R can handle cycles that involve only one-with-many relationships, but cannot handle loops. A restriction of the set relationship is that a record type cannot be both an owner and a member of the same set. However, the technique we examined earlier of creating junction records can be used to resolve into simpler structures cycles that contain many-with-many relationships and also loops.

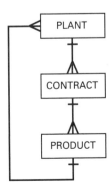

Figure 2.17 A cycle is a data structure in which a record's ancestor is also one of its descendants.

Figure 2.18   A loop is a special case of a cycle in which occurrences of a record type are related to other occurrences of the same record type.

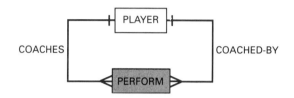

Figure 2.19   A loop can be resolved by using a junction record.

For example, to resolve the loop that results from the foregoing coaching relationship, we look for possible intersection data. One example might be performance data for each player. Performance data cannot be stored in the Player record, because a player may have many coaches, each of whom has to record performance data separately for a given player. Therefore, as shown in Fig. 2.19, we could create a junction record called Perform that allows a coach to record a performance rating for each player assigned to that coach. The Perform junction record is related to the Player record using two sets. Coaches allows us to determine which players are coached by a given coach, and Coached-By lets us find the coaches that are assigned to a given player.

SUMMARY

The issues that involve the logical structure of an IDMS/R database concern the nature of the entities that will be stored in the database and the types of relationship that exist between them. Database records are used to store information about entity attributes; sets are used to implement the relationships between record types. A set consists of two or more record types that participate in one-with-many relationships. The record types that participate in sets are members, owners, or both. Many-with-many relationship can be implemented using sets by defining a network structure that involves a junction record. The junction record contains intersection data that does not belong to either the owner or the member record type. Junction records can also be used to resolve loops.

3 PHYSICAL DATABASE STRUCTURE

In Chapter 2, we examined the way in which an IDMS/R database is logically structured. In this chapter, we proceed to the next level of design where we concern ourselves with how an IDMS/R network-structured database is physically implemented.

DATABASE AREAS An IDMS/R database is divided into one or more *areas*. An area is defined as the major named subdivision of addressable storage in the database. Areas are of two types: *standard* areas, which contain occurrences of the records that make up network-structured databases, and *extent* areas, which are used to contain the tables that make up a relational database. In this chapter, we will concern ourselves only with standard areas, since the physical storage of relational tables in extent areas is handled automatically by IDMS/R. Each standard area can contain occurrences of one or more record types, but all occurrences of a particular record type must be located in the same area.

An area can be further subdivided into *pages,* which constitute the smallest logical units of database storage. A page is the unit of data that is moved between the database and the system buffers that are used by IDMS/R to hold the retrieved records. Figure 3.1 shows the structure of a page from a database area. For simplicity, the illustration shows the records grouped together by record type. They would actually appear on a page in the order in which they were stored.

Each page in a database area contains control information and up to 255 record occurrences. Each record occurrence is assigned a unique numeric identifier, called its *database key (db-key),* whose format is shown in Fig. 3.2. A record's db-key consists of a 32-bit field that typically contains a 23-bit page number and an 8-bit line number. The page number identifies the page in which

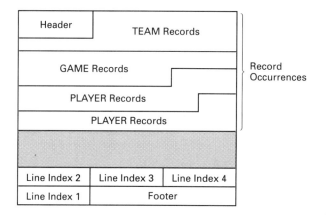

Figure 3.1 A database page contains record occurrences and control information.

the record is stored, and the line number identifies the location of the record within that page. IDMS/R uses database keys to keep track of where in the database record occurrences are physically stored.

MULTIPLE AREAS   As we mentioned earlier, IDMS/R stores all occurrences of a particular record type in the same area. However, occurrences of multiple record types can be stored in the same area if desired. A database could be divided into multiple areas for several reasons:

● **Processing efficiency.** Programs can open areas individually. If we group records into areas appropriately, programs can open only the areas that contain the record types they need. For example, if all the programs need access to the Team, Player, and Game records, but only some of the programs need access to the Salary, Bonus, and Position records, we might define three areas. Figure 3.3 shows how we have grouped together the Team, Player, and Game records in an area named Team-Area, placed the Position records in another area named Position-Area, and grouped the Salary and Bonus records together in Salary-Area. With this arrangement, programs that do not need access to the Position, Salary, or Bonus records can open only Team-Area. Programs that need access

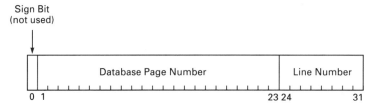

Figure 3.2 A database key value consists of a database page number and a line number.

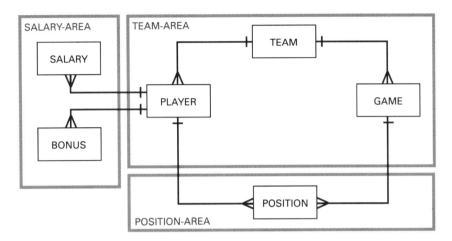

Figure 3.3   The records of the Baseball database are stored in three areas.

to *Position* records can open Position-Area, and programs that need access to Salary and Bonus information can open Salary-Area.

- **Security.** If we need to restrict access to certain record types, we might place them together in an area that is protected using IDMS/R security facilities. For example, we might protect Salary-Area to prevent unauthorized access to salary and bonus information.

- **Search efficiency.** If retrieval of occurrences of a certain record type is accomplished mainly by sequential scans through the database, assignment of the record type to an area enhances execution efficiency.

- **Concurrent updating.** A program can request exclusive use of an area and prevent other programs from accessing it concurrently.

- **Database recovery and backup.** The database can be initialized, restructured, and backed up on an area-by-area basis. Areas assigned to highly volatile record types can be given different treatment from areas that are assigned to record types whose occurrences are changed little.

MAPPING AREAS INTO FILES

Each page corresponds to a physical record that is stored in a file, and all data transfers between the database and the system buffers are accomplished a page at a time. The following rules govern the way in which areas can be mapped into files in direct access storage:

- Many (or all) areas can be mapped into one file if all the areas have the same page size.

- Each area can be mapped into a different file.

- One area can be mapped into several files.

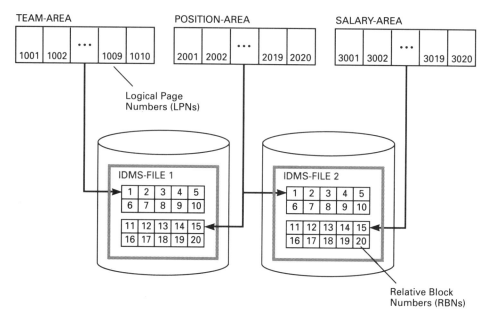

Figure 3.4   The three Baseball database areas can be mapped into two files.

Assume that the three areas of the Baseball database are defined as follows:

Area Name	Lowest Page	Highest Page	Records
Team-Area	1001	1010	Team, Player, Game
Position-Area	2001	2020	Position
Salary-Area	3001	3020	Salary, Bonus

Figure 3.4 shows the database containing the Team-Area, Position-Area, and Salary-Area areas mapped into two 20-block files. IDMS-File1 contains all of Team-Area and the first ten pages of Position-Area. IDMS-File2 contains the last ten pages of Position-Area and the entire Salary-Area.

DATABASE RECORDS
An IDMS/R database consists physically of a collection of *record occurrences*. The record occurrence represents the smallest directly addressable unit of data. A record occurrence consists of a fixed or variable number of characters that are subdivided into units called *data elements*. These data element values follow the formats that were defined in the schema for this record type. In an

Prefix				Data			
Pointer 1	Pointer 2	Pointer 3	•••	Data Element 1	Data Element 2	Data Element 3	•••

Figure 3.5 An IDMS/R database record consists physically of a prefix, which stores pointers, and a data portion, which stores data element occurrences.

application program, we cannot address an individual data element without first retrieving the record occurrence in which it is stored.

The physical records stored in the database consist of more than the data elements used by the application program. IDMS/R also maintains information about the *relationships* that exist between records. These relationships are physically implemented by linking record occurrences together with pointers. Pointers contain the addresses of related record occurrences and are stored with the data elements that make up each record occurrence.

Figure 3.5 shows the format of a record occurrence as it is physically stored in the database. A record occurrence in the database is made up of two parts: a *data* portion and a *prefix* portion. Data element values are stored in the data portion. Pointers to related record occurrences are stored in the prefix portion. Application programs generally work only with the data element values that are stored in the data portion. IDMS/R automatically maintains the pointers in the prefix portion.

As we saw in Chapter 2, a particular application program may use a subschema that allows access to only some of the records and sets defined in the schema. For a particular record, the subschema may define only some of the data elements that are defined for that record in the schema. For example, Fig. 3.6 shows the database as it is defined by the schema and a possible subschema view of that record. When an application program requests the retrieval of a Player record occurrence using a particular subschema, IDMS/R locates the appropriate Player record occurrence in the database. It then constructs for the application program an image of the record based on the mapping that is defined between the subschema the program references and the schema from which the

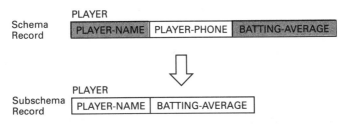

Figure 3.6 IDMS/R derives a subschema record from a schema record when a record occurrence is accessed.

subschema is derived. The application program's view of the Player record is as shown at the bottom of Fig. 3.6, even though the data is stored in the database as shown at the top of Fig. 3.6.

SUMMARY

The physical design of an IDMS/R database involves defining how database records are grouped into areas, which define the major subdivisions of addressable storage. Areas are further divided into pages, which are the units of data involved in physical transfers of data between the database and the system buffers. Pages hold occurrences of database records, the smallest units of addressable data in an IDMS/R network-structured database. A database record contains data elements in a data portion and pointer information in a prefix portion. Pointer information is used to implement sets. A program normally deals only with the data portion of the database record; the prefix is maintained and used by the IDMS/R DBMS.

4 RECORD CHARACTERISTICS

As we noted in Chapter 2, the various records and sets that make up an IDMS/R database must be assigned a number of characteristics that define the way in which records can be accessed and sets are used. In this chapter, we discuss the various characteristics that can be assigned to records; in Chapter 5, we discuss the characteristics that can be assigned to sets.

The characteristics that apply to record types include

- Record name
- Record identifier
- Storage mode
- Record length
- Location mode
- Duplicates option
- Area name

We will next describe each of these characteristics that we can assign to records.

RECORD NAME   Each record must be assigned a 1- to 16-character name that identifies the record type. The name must begin with an alphabetic character. The application program must reference the record's name in requesting that some data manipulation language (DML) function be performed on one or more occurrences of a record type.

RECORD
IDENTIFIER The record identifier is a number (in the range 100 through 9999) that serves as an internal identifier for the record type. Each record type must be assigned a unique record identifier within the installation. A database administrator or system programmer generally assigns record identifiers for each record type that the installation creates. Application programs do not refer to records using their record identifiers.

STORAGE MODE The storage mode indicates whether occurrences of this record type are fixed or variable in length and whether they are stored in compressed format. Codes used to represent a record's storage mode are as follows:

- **F** (fixed length)
- **V** (variable length)
- **C** (compressed)

The *compressed* storage mode can be used in conjunction with the fixed-length or variable-length storage modes. For example, a storage mode of FC indicates that record occurrences are fixed length and compressed. When data compression is used, an IDMS/R module automatically compresses and decompresses the data. Application programs are not aware that compression and decompression is taking place.

RECORD LENGTH The record length, expressed in bytes, is the actual data length for a fixed-length record or the maximum data length for a variable-length record.

LOCATION MODE The location mode defines the way a record is stored in its database area and tells the application programmer the way in which occurrences of this record type must be accessed. The three possible location modes are:

- CALC
- VIA
- DIRECT

CALC Location Mode

With the CALC location mode, a particular data element within the record itself must be declared as the CALC-key. When the application program requests that record occurrences be stored into the database, IDMS/R uses the CALC-key value to calculate the page into which the record should be placed. IDMS/R uses a randomizing routine to distribute records evenly over its area. To retrieve a record later, the application program supplies IDMS/R with a CALC-key value, and IDMS/R uses the randomizing routine to locate the proper page and directly retrieve the record occurrence that has the supplied CALC-key value.

For example, suppose we have assigned the CALC location mode to the Player record type and have declared the Player-Name data element to be the CALC-key. When we add each new Player record to the database, IDMS/R uses the Player-Name value contained in the record we are adding to calculate the specific page within the database to store the record. It then stores the record occurrence on that page. To retrieve the record for a particular player later, the application program moves the Player-Name value for the desired player into a designated application program storage area and executes a DML retrieval function. IDMS/R then uses the randomizing routine to locate the page on which the desired record is stored, searches through the page for the desired Player record occurrence, and builds an image of the required subschema record in an applications program storage area.

The use of the CALC location mode results in record occurrences being distributed relatively evenly over the pages in the area, thus minimizing overflow conditions and leaving space for adding new records. Second, it allows us to retrieve records directly by supplying a CALC-key value. A desired record is typically retrieved with a single access rather than requiring IDMS/R to search through the database for it.

VIA Location Mode

With the VIA location mode, each member record in a set is stored on or near the page that contains the member record's owner. The use of the VIA location mode tends to group together in close physical proximity records that are likely to be accessed together and minimizes the number of disk accesses needed to retrieve all the records that belong to a given set occurrence.

Figure 4.1 shows records stored using the VIA location mode. Each new Position record occurrence is stored as close as possible to its owner Game record occurrence. When an occurrence of the Game record is retrieved, some or all of its member record occurrences will tend to be on the same page. Since IDMS/R transfers data into its buffers one page at a time, only a single physical I/O operation is needed, in many cases, to retrieve an owner record and all of its members.

If the owner and member record types are assigned to different areas, or to

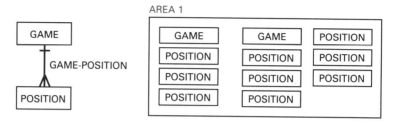

Figure 4.1 When occurrences of a VIA record type are stored in the same area as occurrences of the owner record type, IDMS/R clusters the VIA records as close as possible to their respective owners, storing them on the same page when possible.

different page ranges in the same area, record occurrences are distributed within their associated page range in the same relative position as their owner occurrence is in its assigned page range. Figure 4.2 shows records stored using the VIA location mode when owner and member record types are assigned to different areas.

When the VIA location mode is assigned to a record type, no CALC-key can be defined for that record type. This means that CALC retrievals cannot be requested for record types that are assigned the VIA location mode. In many cases, the owner record type of a set type is assigned the CALC location mode, and the member record type is assigned the VIA location mode. This allows an owner record type to be retrieved directly, after which all the owner's member record occurrences can then be quickly located.

DIRECT Location Mode

The third mode is the DIRECT location mode. When storing records into the database using the DIRECT location mode, the application program explicitly specifies the page into which the program should be stored. Then when retriev-

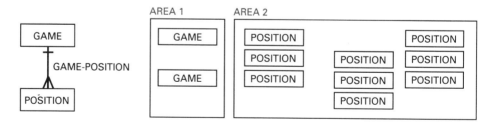

Figure 4.2 When occurrences of a VIA record type are stored in a different area from occurrences of the owner record type, IDMS/R clusters together the VIA records of each owner and stores each cluster at a point that is proportionally as far from the beginning of the area as the owner record is from the beginning of its area.

ing a record, the program must specify the db-key value of the desired record. Since it is often difficult for the program to determine the db-key value of the record it wants, this location mode is less often used than CALC or VIA.

The DIRECT location mode is sometimes used to store records sequentially into the area. To do this, the program stores the first record into the first page of an empty area and then asks IDMS/R to write each new record into the same page as the previous record. IDMS/R then fills up the first page, switches to the next page and fills it, and then fills up each subsequent page as required. Each time IDMS/R writes a record into the database, it returns the db-key value that was assigned to that record. The application program can store these db-key values into a cross-reference table or file that it can later use in any desired way to determine the db-key values of records that it needs to retrieve. Sometimes the program saves only the db-key values of certain record occurrences that it determines will have to be directly retrieved later.

DUPLICATES OPTION

The duplicates option is specified only for records that are stored using the CALC location mode. This option specifies whether records having duplicate CALC-keys are allowed, and if duplicates are allowed, where records having duplicate CALC-key values are to be placed in the area. Codes used to represent the duplicates options are as follows:

- **DN (duplicates not allowed).** With this option, a record occurrence with a duplicate CALC-key value will *not* be accepted. IDMS/R will signal an error if the program attempts to store a record that has the same CALC-key value as an existing record in the database.

- **DF (duplicates first).** With this option, a record occurrence with a duplicate CALC-key value will be accepted. IDMS/R will store the record *before* any record in the database that has a matching CALC-key value. When a CALC retrieval is made using that CALC-key value, the new record will be retrieved *first*.

- **DL (duplicates last).** With this option, a record occurrence with a duplicate CALC-key value will be accepted. IDMS/R will store the record *after* any record in the database that has a matching CALC-key value. When a CALC retrieval is made using that CALC-key value, the new record will be retrieved *last*.

AREA NAME

The area name is the name of the area into which all record occurrences of the record type are to be stored.

DIAGRAMMING RECORD CHARACTERISTICS

Figure 4.3 shows how record characteristics can be added to the entity-relationship diagram we created during the early stages of logical design. Figure 4.4 shows the interpretation of each piece of information in the boxes used to describe records. We will see in Chapter 6 how each of these record characteristics is defined to IDMS/R through the use of a set of schema DDL statements. The information that we are supplying for the Team record is as follows:

- **Team**—The record name.
- **1100**—The unique record identifier assigned to the record type, typically chosen by a database administration staff member.
- **F**—The storage mode, indicating *fixed-length* records.
- **50**—The record length.
- **CALC**—The location mode, indicating records are stored in the database area using the CALC location mode.
- **Team-Name**—The data element name designated as the CALC-key. For a record that is defined with the VIA location mode, this space is used to specify the name of the *set* that is used in locating and storing record occurrences.
- **DN**—The duplicates option, indicating *duplicates not allowed*.
- **Team-Area**—The name of the area in which the Team records are stored.

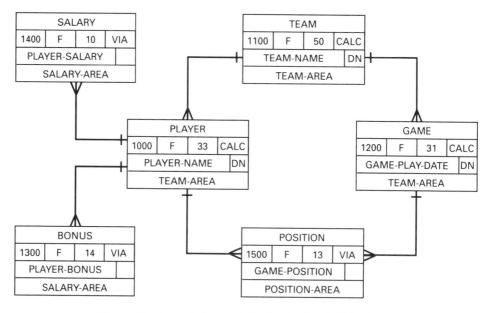

Figure 4.3   Record characteristics for the Baseball database.

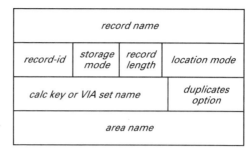

Figure 4.4   Data structure diagram symbology for documenting record characteristics.

SUMMARY

Database records are collections of data element values that are stored in the database. Characteristics that are assigned to record types include a name, location mode, duplicates option, and the name of the database area that is used to store occurrences of the record type. A record's location mode determines how a record is stored in the database and how it can be accessed. The CALC location mode uses a CALC-key to determine the page in which a record is stored. To retrieve the record, the program supplies its CALC-key, and the IDMS/R DBMS locates the page that contains the record. The VIA location mode causes member records of a set to be stored near the owner of the set, thus allowing members of a set to be located quickly. The DIRECT location mode allows a program to state a db-key value explicitly when accessing a record. The duplicates option applies only to records that are stored using the CALC location mode. This option specifies whether records having duplicate CALC-keys are allowed.

5 SET CHARACTERISTICS

In this chapter we examine in detail the characteristics of the sets that are used to implement one-with-many relationships between record types. As discussed in Chapter 2, a *set* consists of an *owner* record type and one or more *member* record types. A *set occurrence* consists of one occurrence of the owner record type and any number of member record occurrences. Records in each occurrence of the set are physically linked together by pointers. Figure 5.1 shows an example of a set occurrence. Notice that the set occurrence begins with an owner record occurrence. The owner record occurrence points to the first occurrence of the member record type, that occurrence points to the next member record occurrence, and so on until the last member record occurrence is encountered. The last member record occurrence then points back to its owner. Accessing members by following the pointers from one record occurrence to the next is called *walking the set*. A set occurrence can also consist only of an owner record occurrence and no member record occurrences, in which case the set occurrence is said to be *empty*. In Fig. 5.2, the Player record for Jones is the owner record of an empty set.

Set relationships are defined according to the following rules:

- Any record type can be a member of any number of sets.
- Any record type can be the owner of any number of sets.
- Any record type can be a member of one set and the owner of another.
- A record need not be part of any set.

SET CHARACTERISTICS   A database administration staff member typically assigns set characteristics to each set when defining the

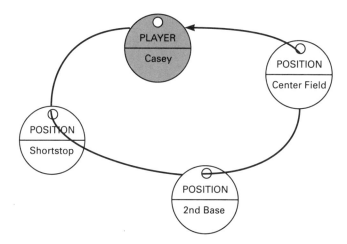

Figure 5.1   A typical occurrence of the Player-Position set.

database to IDMS/R in the schema DDL. These characteristics include:

- Set name
- Linkage options
- Membership options
- Order options

We will discuss the various options available for each characteristic and show the graphical notation that is typically used to describe this information in an IDMS/R schema diagram.

SET NAME   A unique name must be assigned to each set type in the database. The set's name must be referenced whenever an application program accesses records using that set relationship. As discussed in Chapter 2, it is a generally accepted convention to incorporate the names of the member records into the name of the set, although IDMS/R does not require the use of this convention. For example, in the Baseball data-

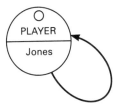

Figure 5.2   An empty set consists of an owner record occurrence that has no member record occurrences chained to it.

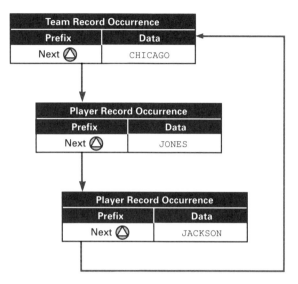

Figure 5.3 NEXT pointers.

base, the set Team-Player implements the one-with-many relationship between the Team record and the Player record.

LINKAGE OPTIONS   The linkage option indicates the types of pointers that are used to implement the set. Pointers control flexibility in accessing records within a set. Codes used to represent the linkage options are as follows:

- **N (NEXT pointers).** With this linkage option, the pointers in the set identify the NEXT record occurrence. Figure 5.3 shows the use of NEXT pointers in implementing a set occurrence. This option allows access to member records only in the forward direction. To access a particular member record occurrence, we must typically begin with the owner record and then walk through all the member records until we access the one we want. When only NEXT pointers are used to implement a set, space is required in the prefix of each record for only one pointer. NEXT pointers must be specified for all sets; all other types of pointers are optional.

- **NP (NEXT and PRIOR pointers).** With this linkage option, a set of PRIOR pointers are used in addition to the set of NEXT pointers, as shown in Fig. 5.4. This linkage option allows us to access member records in both a forward and backward direction. The use of PRIOR pointers also allows us to delete record occurrences physically and reclaim the space they occupy at the time that a member record occurrence is erased. We will discuss record deletion in detail in Chapter 11.

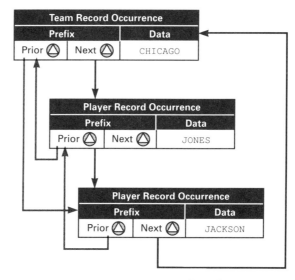

Figure 5.4   NEXT and PRIOR pointers.

- **NO (NEXT and OWNER pointers).** With this linkage option, a set of OWNER pointers are used in addition to the NEXT pointers, as shown in Fig. 5.5. OWNER pointers provide direct access from any member record occurrence to its owner record occurrence.
- **NPO (NEXT, PRIOR, and OWNER pointers).** With this option, the set includes all three pointer options, as shown in Fig. 5.6. This linkage option al-

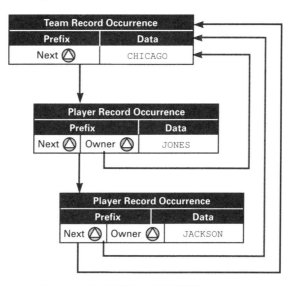

Figure 5.5   NEXT and OWNER pointers.

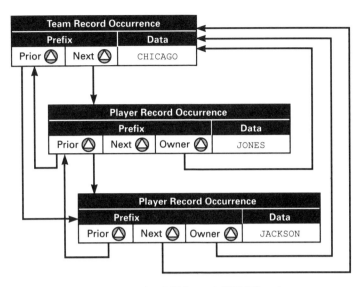

Figure 5.6   NEXT, PRIOR, and OWNER pointers.

lows access to member records in a set occurrence in both the next and prior directions and direct access from a member record to the owner record.

MEMBERSHIP OPTION

The membership option indicates the way a member record occurrence is connected to and disconnected from a set occurrence. It is defined in two parts. The first part is a *disconnect option,* which indicates the way a record is *disconnected from* a set. The second part is a *connect option,* which indicates the way a record is *connected to* a set.

The disconnect option specifies whether a member record can later be disconnected from a set once its membership has been established. Codes used to represent the disconnect options are as follows:

- **M (mandatory).** With this option, the membership of a record occurrence in a set is permanent once it is established. A record occurrence *cannot* be disconnected from a set unless that record is erased from the database, as shown in Fig. 5.7. To disconnect Casey from the Team-Player set, we must erase the Casey record from the database. Erasing the Casey record also causes the record to be disconnected from the set.

- **O (optional).** With this option, a record occurrence *can* be disconnected from a set, as shown in Fig. 5.8. The record occurrence remains in the database and may be accessible in other ways. For example, after disconnecting the Casey record occurrence from one set occurrence, we might then connect it to some other set occurrence, as when we are transferring a player from one team to

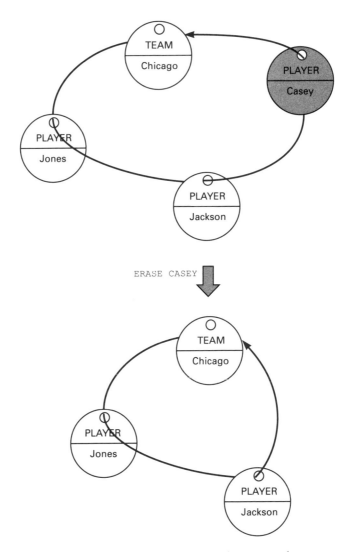

Figure 5.7 With the mandatory disconnect option, a record occurrence can be disconnected from a set only by erasing it.

another. To transfer player Casey from the Chicago team to St. Louis, we disconnect Casey from the set occurrence whose owner record is Chicago and connect it to the set occurrence whose owner record is St. Louis.

The second part of the membership option indicates the type of connect option defined for this set. A connect option specifies whether or not a member record is automatically connected to a set occurrence when it is added to the database. Codes used to represent the connect options are as follows:

- **A (automatic).** With this option, a new member record is *automatically* connected to a set occurrence when it is added to the database. With the automatic connect option, the program needs to indicate in which set the new member is to belong at the time that it adds a new record occurrence.

- **M (manual).** With this option, a new member record is *not* automatically connected to a set occurrence when it is added to the database. The application program must execute an explicit connect function after it adds a new record occurrence to connect the member record to a set occurrence.

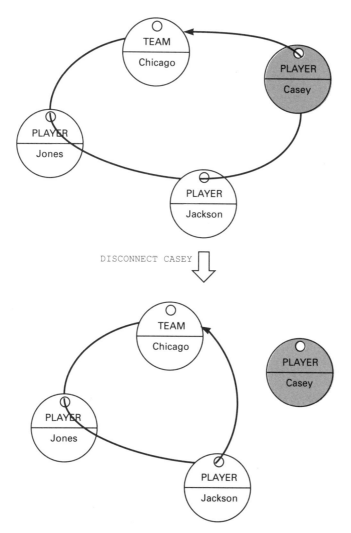

Figure 5.8 With the optional disconnect option, a record occurrence can be disconnected from a set without erasing it. It can then be later connected to some other set.

ORDER OPTION The order option specifies the logical order in which member record occurrences are placed within a set occurrence. The logical order of member record occurrences is independent of the physical placement of the records themselves. The order options are as follows:

- **FIRST.** With the FIRST order option, each new member record occurrence is placed immediately after the owner record (in the next direction). If a database retrieval asks for the *next* member record after an owner record has been retrieved, then the *last* member record stored becomes the *first* member record accessed. The FIRST order option achieves a member order of last in, first out.

- **LAST.** With the LAST order option, each new member record occurrence is placed immediately *before* the owner record (in the prior direction). This option achieves a member order of first in, first out. PRIOR pointers are required (NP or NPO linkage option) to specify the LAST order option.

- **NEXT.** With the NEXT order option, each new member record occurrence is placed immediately after the member record occurrence that was *last accessed* (in the next direction).

- **PRIOR.** With the PRIOR order option, each new member record occurrence is placed immediately *before* the member record occurrence last accessed within the set (in the prior direction). Prior pointers are required in order to specify the PRIOR order option.

- **SORTED.** With this option, a new member record occurrence is placed in *ascending* or *descending sequence,* based on the value of a designated sort-control data element, or *sort key,* contained in each record occurrence. When a record is placed into a set, the DBMS examines the sort key in each member record occurrence to determine the logical position of the new member record in the set.

DUPLICATES OPTION A sorted set order is defined by the keywords ASC (ascending) or DES (descending), followed by the data element name of the sort key. A duplicates option indicates the action to be taken by the DBMS when a duplicate sort-key value occurs. Codes used to represent the duplicates options for sorted sets are as follows:

- **DF (duplicates first).** With the DF duplicates option, a record with a duplicate sort-key value is stored immediately *before* the existing duplicate record in the set. The first duplicate record encountered in the next direction is always the most recently stored duplicate record.

- **DL (duplicates last).** With the DL duplicates option, a record with a duplicate sort-key value is stored immediately *after* the existing duplicate record in the set. The last duplicate record encountered in the next direction is always the most recently stored duplicate record.

- **DN (duplicates not allowed).** With the DN option, a record with a duplicate sort-key *cannot* be stored in the set. If a program attempts to store a record with a duplicate sort-key value, the DBMS returns an error code.

INDEXED SETS   A special type of set is provided by IDMS/R that allows retrieval of records using an index. In a conventional set, member records are chained together by pointers as we saw in Chapter 2. In an indexed set database key values are stored in a specified order in one or more index records. With an index, retrieval of members can sometimes be more efficient because the index can be traversed more quickly than the set of chained member records. However, indexed sets are used mainly to add flexibility to data retrieval. The use of indexes can simplify processing in the following situations:

- **Random retrieval by key value.** Indexes are useful when member records must be stored in sequence by sort-key value and when member records must also be directly retrieved based on some other key value. A partial, or generic, key value can also be used, which is useful in cases where the full key may not be known or where a group of records needs to be retrieved.

- **Sorted retrieval by key value.** Key values within indexed sets are maintained in sorted order. Multiple indexes can be used in situations where more than one sort sequence is desired.

- **Walking long sets.** Whether or not they are sorted, very long sets can be walked more efficiently by using an index if only the key values themselves are required. In such a situation, it is not necessary to access the record occurrences; only the index is accessed to provide the key values.

- **Physical-sequential processing by key value.** Storing records into the database via an index places the record occurrences into the database in order by key value. This allows them to be accessed efficiently later in order by key value.

- **Multiple-key access.** Sometimes we need to access records based on more than one key. We might store the record based on its CALC key and then retrieve it based on another field on which we have placed an index.

To implement an index, IDMS/R builds an index file that contains the database key values of member record occurrences. These db-key values are maintained in the sequence specified for the index. Indexed sets can be implemented by using two database record types or a single database record type and a system record type. Figure 5.9 illustrates the two types of indexed sets:

- In the first type, an indexed set is implemented with two user-defined record types. This type of set can have only one member record type. The Position record is defined with a location mode of VIA, so it is normally accessed by

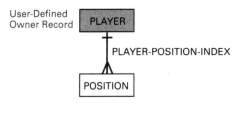

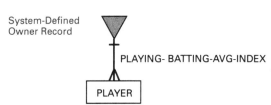

Figure 5.9 The owner of an index set can be either a user-defined record type or a system-defined record type.

walking the Player-Position set. The indexed set Player-Position-Index allows us to retrieve *Position* records based on Position-Name values.

● In the second type of indexed set, an index is placed on a user-defined member record using a system record as the owner. With this index, Player records can be retrieved based on a Batting-Average in addition to the CALC-key Player-Name.

Note that in early versions of the IDMS software, a facility called the *Sequential Processing Facility (SPF)* was used to implement indexing, and some older applications still employ SPF indexes. With current versions of IDMS/R, index processing is integrated into the DBMS, although SPF applications are still supported.

THE DATA STRUCTURE DIAGRAM

Figure 5.10 shows how we can add information about the characteristics of each of the sets to the diagram showing the characteristics of records in the Baseball database. The diagram in Fig. 5.10 is similar to the type of diagram that Cullinet documentation typically uses to show the record and set characteristics of IDMS/R network-structured databases. Note, however, that Cullinet documentation uses arrows to represent one-with-many relationships rather than crow's foot notation. We call this type of diagram a *data structure diagram* to distinguish it from the simpler form of entity-relationship diagram shown in earlier chapters.

The data structure diagram serves as an important piece of documentation in the IDMS/R installation. Application programmers typically use data structure diagrams to develop strategies for accessing and manipulating records and for using the set relationships that are defined.

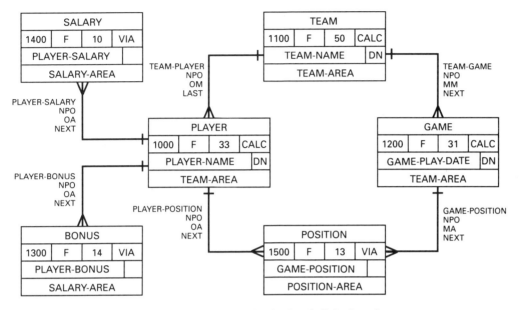

Figure 5.10 A data structure diagram for the Baseball database is an expansion of the entity-relationship diagram and contains complete information about the characteristics of its records and sets.

SET CHARACTERISTICS

The characteristics that we have assigned to each set are specified next to the line indicating that set. The information supplied for the Team-Player set in Fig. 5.10 is as follows:

- **Team-player**—The set name.
- **NPO**—The linkage options, indicating NEXT, PRIOR, and OWNER pointers.
- **OM**—The membership options, indicating the *optional* disconnect option (record occurrences can be disconnected from the set) and the *manual* connect option (new records are not automatically connected to a set occurrence).
- **LAST**—The order option, indicating record occurrences are placed in the set after the last member record and *before* the owner record.

The data structure diagram contains essentially the information that we will need to know later when we create a set of schema data definition language statements to define the schema to IDMS/R. We discuss this process in Chapter 6.

SUMMARY

Sets are used to implement relationships between record types. The characteristics that can be assigned to a set include a name, linkage options, membership options, and order options. Linkage options control the types of pointers that are used in implementing the set. Membership options include a disconnect option, which determines the way in which a member record is disconnected from a set when a member record is deleted, and a connect option, which determines how a member record is connected to a set when a new member record occurrence is added. With the mandatory disconnect option, records cannot be disconnected from a set without first being erased from the database; with the optional disconnect option, a member record can be disconnected without first being erased. With the automatic connect option, a record is automatically connected to the set when the record is added; with the manual connect option, the record is not automatically connected. The order option determines the logical sequence in which member records are placed in sets. The possible options are FIRST, LAST, NEXT, PRIOR, and SORTED. Index sets can be used to enhance the flexibility of database access.

6 DATA DESCRIPTION LANGUAGE

After the database administration staff has completed the logical and physical design of a database and has documented this design in a data structure diagram, the design can then be communicated to IDMS/R in the form of a set of *data description language (DDL)* statements. DDL statements are then processed by the DDL compilers. Data description language is used to define the following:

- Schemas
- Device-media control language (DMCL) modules
- Subschemas

A schema and DMCL module, together, define to IDMS/R the logical and physical structure of the database. A subschema defines a particular view of the data that one or more application programs require.

In this chapter we will look at detailed examples of a schema, a DMCL module, and a subschema defined using data definition language statements. We will also describe how DDL statements are processed by the three DDL compilers.

SCHEMAS

A database administration staff member describes the logical structure of the database to IDMS/R by coding a set of *schema DDL* statements. A set of schema DDL is a computer-readable description of the record and set characteristics that have been documented in the data structure diagram. There is a single schema for a given database. A set of schema DDL statements defines the following:

- Schema name
- Database file names

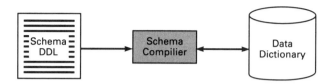

Figure 6.1   The schema DDL is processed by the schema compiler, which
stores the resulting schema definition in the data dictionary.

- Database areas
- Data elements and records
- Sets

The schema DDL is processed by the *schema compiler*. As shown in Fig.
6.1, the schema compiler reads the schema DDL statements and stores a description of the schema in the data dictionary. As we introduced in Chapter 1,
the data dictionary is the central repository for information that IDMS/R maintains about the databases under its control. Part II of this book discusses the role
of the data dictionary in detail. As the schema compiler processes the schema
DDL, it can also copy from the data dictionary descriptions of records that have
been previously defined and stored in the dictionary.

Figure 6.2 shows the schema DDL for the Baseball database. ADD statements are used to define each of the items that comprise the schema.

SCHEMA NAME   The schema DDL begins with an ADD statement to
                         add the schema to the data dictionary:

```
ADD SCHEMA NAME IS SCHBASE VERSION IS 1
    PREPARED BY 'RICK DERER'
    SCHEMA DESCRIPTION IS 'BASEBALL DATABASE'.
```

The ADD SCHEMA statement names the schema and may include additional
pieces of documentation. Here, we have included the name of the person who
prepared the schema and a schema description.

FILE NAMES   Files are defined to the schema using the ADD FILE
                         NAME statement:

```
ADD FILE NAME IS TEAM-FILE
    ASSIGN TO TEAM.
```

This statement names one of the files that will be used to contain the database
and assigns a ddname (MVS) or filename (VSE) to it. In the full example in
Fig. 6.2, we have defined three files for the database.

```
ADD SCHEMA NAME IS SCHBASE   VERSION IS 1
    PREPARED BY 'RICK DERER'
    SCHEMA DESCRIPTION IS 'BASEBALL DATABASE'.

ADD FILE NAME IS TEAM-FILE
    ASSIGN TO TEAM.
ADD FILE NAME IS POSITION-FILE
    ASSIGN TO POSITION.
ADD FILE NAME IS SALARY-FILE
    ASSIGN TO SALARY.

ADD AREA NAME IS TEAM-AREA
    PAGE RANGE IS 702000 FOR 100
    WITHIN FILE TEAM-FILE.
ADD AREA NAME IS POSITION-AREA
    PAGE RANGE IS 601000 FOR 100
    WITHIN FILE POSITION-FILE.
ADD AREA NAME IS SALARY-AREA
    PAGE RANGE IS 903000 FOR 100
    WITHIN FILE SALARY-FILE.

ADD RECORD NAME IS PLAYER-REC   RECORD ID IS 1000
    LOCATION MODE IS CALC USING (PLAYER-NAME)
        DUPLICATES ARE NOT ALLOWED
    WITHIN AREA TEAM-AREA.
02  PLAYER-NAME      PICTURE IS X(20)    USAGE IS DISPLAY.
02  PLAYER-PHONE     PICTURE IS 9(10)    USAGE IS DISPLAY.
02  BATTING-AVERAGE  PICTURE IS 9(3)     USAGE IS DISPLAY.

ADD RECORD NAME IS TEAM-REC    RECORD ID IS 1100
    LOCATION MODE IS CALC USING (TEAM-NAME)
    DUPLICATES ARE NOT ALLOWED
    WITHIN AREA TEAM-AREA.
02  TEAM-NAME       PICTURE IS X(20)    USAGE IS DISPLAY.
02  TEAM-PHONE      PICTURE IS 9(10)    USAGE IS DISPLAY.
02  TEAM-CITY       PICTURE IS X(20)    USAGE IS DISPLAY.

ADD RECORD NAME IS GAME-REC    RECORD ID IS 1200
    LOCATION MODE IS CALC USING (GAME-PLAY-DATE)
    DUPLICATES ARE NOT ALLOWED
    WITHIN AREA TEAM-AREA.
02  GAME-PLAY-DATE  PICTURE IS 9(6)     USAGE IS DISPLAY.
02  HOME-AWAY-IND   PICTURE IS X(1)     USAGE IS DISPLAY.
02  OPPONENT-TEAM   PICTURE IS X(20)    USAGE IS DISPLAY.
02  TEAM-SCORE      PICTURE IS 9(2)     USAGE IS DISPLAY.
02  OPPONENT-SCORE  PICTURE IS 9(2)     USAGE IS DISPLAY.

ADD RECORD NAME IS BONUS-REC   RECORD ID IS 1300
    LOCATION MODE IS VIA PLAYER-BONUS SET
    WITHIN AREA SALARY-AREA.
02  BONUS-DATE      PICTURE IS 9(6)     USAGE IS DISPLAY.
02  BONUS-AMOUNT    PICTURE IS 9(8)     USAGE IS DISPLAY.
```

Figure 6.2 Schema DDL for the Baseball database.

(Continued)

```
ADD RECORD NAME IS SALARY-REC  RECORD ID IS 1400
    LOCATION MODE IS VIA PLAYER-SALARY SET
    WITHIN AREA SALARY-AREA.
02  SALARY-YEAR       PICTURE IS 9(2)      USAGE IS DISPLAY.
02  ANNUAL-SALARY     PICTURE IS 9(8)      USAGE IS DISPLAY.

ADD RECORD NAME IS POSITION-REC  RECORD ID IS 1500
    LOCATION MODE IS VIA GAME-POSITION SET
    WITHIN AREA POSITION-AREA.
02  POSITION-NAME     PICTURE IS X(10)     USAGE IS DISPLAY.
02  POSITION-INNINGS-PLAYED
                      PICTURE IS 9(3)      USAGE IS DISPLAY.

ADD SET NAME IS TEAM-PLAYER
    ORDER IS LAST
    MODE IS CHAIN LINKED TO PRIOR
    OWNER IS TEAM-REC
    MEMBER IS PLAYER-REC  LINKED TO OWNER  OPTIONAL MANUAL.

ADD SET NAME IS TEAM-GAME
    ORDER IS NEXT
    MODE IS CHAIN LINKED TO PRIOR
    OWNER IS TEAM-REC
    MEMBER IS GAME-REC  LINKED TO OWNER  MANDATORY MANUAL.

ADD SET NAME IS PLAYER-POSITION
    ORDER IS NEXT
    MODE IS CHAIN LINKED TO PRIOR
    OWNER IS PLAYER-REC
    MEMBER IS POSITION-REC  LINKED TO OWNER  OPTIONAL AUTOMATIC.

ADD SET NAME IS PLAYER-SALARY
    ORDER IS NEXT
    MODE IS CHAIN LINKED TO PRIOR
    OWNER IS PLAYER-REC
    MEMBER IS SALARY-REC  LINKED TO OWNER  OPTIONAL AUTOMATIC.

ADD SET NAME IS PLAYER-BONUS
    ORDER IS NEXT
    MODE IS CHAIN LINKED TO PRIOR
    OWNER IS PLAYER-REC
    MEMBER IS BONUS-REC  LINKED TO OWNER  OPTIONAL AUTOMATIC.

ADD SET NAME IS GAME-POSITION
    ORDER IS NEXT
    MODE IS CHAIN LINKED TO PRIOR
    OWNER IS GAME-REC
    MEMBER IS POSITION-REC  LINKED TO OWNER  MANDATORY AUTOMATIC.

VALIDATE.
```

Figure 6.2 (Continued)

AREA NAMES

An ADD AREA NAME statement gives a name to each area, specifies its page range, and assigns the area to one or more of the files defined by the ADD FILE statements:

```
ADD AREA NAME IS TEAM-AREA
    PAGE RANGE IS 702000 FOR 100
    WITHIN FILE TEAM-FILE.
```

In this example, TEAM-AREA contains 100 pages ranging from page 702000 through page 702099. Optionally, we can use the SAME AS statement to copy the entire area description from an area in another schema into the new schema:

```
ADD AREA NAME IS TEAM-AREA
    SAME AS AREA DIVISION-AREA OF SCHEMA SCHCOMP
    VERSION IS 1.
```

We can also include an optional CALL statement in an ADD AREA statement to define system- or user-defined procedures, as in the following ADD AREA statement. Such a procedure will automatically be invoked, in various situations, when application programs access the areas in question. The following statement will call the user-defined security checking routine whose load module name is SECURITY whenever a STORE DML statement is executed for a record type whose occurrences are stored in the TEAM-AREA area.

```
ADD AREA NAME IS TEAM-AREA
    PAGE RANGE IS 702000 FOR 100
    WITHIN FILE TEAM-FILE
    CALL SECURITY BEFORE STORE.
```

RECORD NAMES   The schema DDL must contain ADD RECORD statements that define the information included in the record boxes of the data structure diagram in Fig. 5.10. The following ADD RECORD statements define information for the Team record:

```
ADD RECORD NAME IS TEAM-REC    RECORD ID IS 1100
    LOCATION MODE IS CALC USING (TEAM-NAME)
    DUPLICATES ARE NOT ALLOWED
    WITHIN AREA TEAM-AREA.
 02   TEAM-NAME       PICTURE IS X(20)    USAGE IS DISPLAY.
 02   TEAM-PHONE      PICTURE IS 9(10)    USAGE IS DISPLAY.
 02   TEAM-CITY       PICTURE IS X(20)    USAGE IS DISPLAY.
```

The record names as defined in the schema are longer than the names we have been using, for example, TEAM-REC instead of TEAM. For clarity, we will continue to use the shorter names in referring to record names throughout this book. Notice that the ADD RECORD statement also contains COBOL-like data descriptions of each record type. Alternatively, we can use the SHARE STRUCTURE statement to copy the structure of an existing record in the data dictionary or to copy the structure of a record that belongs to another schema. The following example takes the data element description from the schema named SCHCOMP:

```
ADD RECORD NAME IS TEAM-REC    RECORD ID IS 1100
    LOCATION MODE IS CALC USING (TEAM-NAME)
    DUPLICATES ARE NOT ALLOWED
    WITHIN AREA TEAM-AREA.
SHARE STRUCTURE OF RECORD REGION OF SCHEMA SCHCOMP.
```

As with the procedures defined in the AREA DESCRIPTION section, we can also include in an ADD RECORD statement a CALL statement to define system- or user-defined procedures to be performed whenever occurrences of that particular record type are accessed. For example, the following statement causes the system-defined record compression routine, whose load module name is IDMSCOMP, to be executed after each DML STORE statement is executed.

```
ADD RECORD NAME IS TEAM-REC     RECORD ID IS 1100
    LOCATION MODE IS CALC USING (TEAM-NAME)
    DUPLICATES ARE NOT ALLOWED
    WITHIN AREA TEAM-AREA
    CALL IDMSCOMP BEFORE STORE.
```

Invoking the IDMSCOMP routine with STORE DML statements causes the DBMS to compress the information in the Team record before storing it into the database.

SET NAMES

The ADD SET NAME statement defines to IDMS/R all of the information included next to a set arrow in the data structure diagram:

```
ADD SET NAME IS TEAM-PLAYER
    ORDER IS LAST
    MODE IS CHAIN LINKED TO PRIOR
    OWNER IS TEAM-REC
    MEMBER IS PLAYER-REC  LINKED TO OWNER  OPTIONAL MANUAL.
```

As in the ADD AREA statement, we can use the SAME AS clause to copy set descriptions from another schema:

```
ADD SET NAME IS TEAM-GAME
    SAME AS SET DIVISION-SALES OF SCHEMA SCHCOMP VERSION IS 1.
```

DEVICE-MEDIA CONTROL LANGUAGE MODULES

Although some schema DDL statements describe some aspects of the physical structure of the database, most aspects of the database's physical structure, such as disk device assignments and page sizes, are described in a *DMCL module definition*.

The DMCL module completes the mapping of logical areas into physical files. It can use all or a subset of the areas and files that are defined in one or more schemas. The DMCL module also identifies and describes the journal files that are used for recording changes that are made to the database. The journal files are used to implement IDMS/R backup and recovery facilities. (See Chapter 12.) Although any number of DMCL modules can exist for a given database, only one is typically implemented. A set of DMCL DDL statements defines the following:

- DMCL module name
- Schema name associated with this DMCL module
- Sizes of the input/output buffers that IDMS/R will use
- Information about the database areas that this DMCL module will make accessible
- Information about the journal files that will be used for backup and recovery

The DMCL definition is processed by the *DMCL compiler*. Like the schema compiler, the DMCL compiler reads the DMCL source statements and stores a description of the DMCL module in the data dictionary. This is shown in Fig. 6.3. As the DMCL compiler processes the source statements, it must have access to the corresponding schema definition in the data dictionary. For this reason, the schema must be compiled before its associated DMCL module.

The DMCL compiler also produces a set of assembler language source statements. These source statements are processed by the assembler and the linkage editor to form an executable DMCL load module. The linkage editor places this load module into a load module library (core-image library with VSE). The DMCL load module is used by IDMS/R at execution time when an application program accesses the database files described by the DMCL module.

Figure 6.4 shows a complete set of DMCL DDL statements for our Baseball database. Each set of DMCL DDL contains the following four sections:

- DEVICE–MEDIA DESCRIPTION section
- BUFFER section
- AREA section
- JOURNAL section

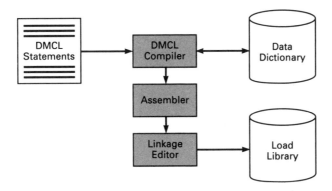

Figure 6.3   DMCL statements are processed by the DMCL compiler and then by the assembler and the linkage editor to create a DMCL load module.

```
DEVICE-MEDIA DESCRIPTION.
DEVICE-MEDIA NAME IS DMCLBASE OF SCHEMA NAME SCHBASE VERSION 1.

DATE.           08/26/88.
INSTALLATION.   MIDWEST BASEBALL LEAGUE
                MIDTOWN, ILLINOIS.

BUFFER SECTION.
    BUFFER NAME IS BASBUFF
        PAGE CONTAINS 4276 CHARACTERS
        BUFFER CONTAINS 5 PAGES.
    JOURNAL BUFFER NAME IS BASJBUFF
        PAGE CONTAINS 3188 CHARACTERS
        BUFFER CONTAINS 3 PAGES.

AREA SECTION.
    COPY TEAM-AREA AREA
        BUFFER IS BASBUFF.
    COPY POSITION-AREA AREA
        BUFFER IS BASBUFF.
    COPY SALARY-AREA AREA
        BUFFER IS BASBUFF.

JOURNAL SECTION.
    JOURNAL BUFFER IS BASJBUFF.
    FILE CONTAINS 3000 BLOCKS.
    FILE NAME IS BASJRNL1
        ASSIGN TO SYSJRNL1.
    FILE NAME IS BASJRNL2
        ASSIGN TO SYSJRNL2.
    ARCHIVAL JOURNAL BLOCK CONTAINS 19068 CHARACTERS.
    FILE NAME IS BASARCH1
        ASSIGN TO ARCHJRNL.
```

Figure 6.4 DMCL statements for the baseball database.

DEVICE–MEDIA DESCRIPTION SECTION

An example of the DEVICE-MEDIA DESCRIPTION section, taken from Fig 6.4, is

```
DEVICE-MEDIA DESCRIPTION.
DEVICE-MEDIA NAME IS DMCLBASE OF SCHEMA NAME SCHBASE VERSION 1.
```

The only mandatory entry in this group of statements is the *name* of the DMCL module. Other entries can associate the DMCL with a schema and provide additional documentation.

BUFFER SECTION

The BUFFER section assigns a page size and defines the buffers that IDMS/R will use to handle database accesses:

```
BUFFER SECTION.
    BUFFER NAME IS BASBUFF
        PAGE CONTAINS 4276 CHARACTERS
        BUFFER CONTAINS 5 PAGES.
```

The size of the buffers that IDMS/R allocates is a function of the page size and the number of pages that must be accommodated at one time in main memory. In the example, the page size is 4276 characters and the buffer accommodates five pages. Thus, the buffer will be 21380 bytes in size. A database administration staff member typically makes page size and buffer size decisions based on performance considerations.

AREA SECTION

Information about each area is copied from the schema into the AREA section of the DMCL definition:

```
AREA SECTION.
    COPY TEAM-AREA AREA
        BUFFER IS BASBUFF.
    COPY POSITION-AREA AREA
        BUFFER IS BASBUFF.
    COPY SALARY-AREA AREA
        BUFFER IS BASBUFF.
```

This section also assigns each area to one of the buffers that was defined in the BUFFER section.

JOURNAL SECTION

The JOURNAL section describes the disk files to be used for journaling:

```
JOURNAL SECTION.
    JOURNAL BUFFER IS BASJBUFF.
    FILE CONTAINS 3000 BLOCKS.
    FILE NAME IS BASJRNL1
        ASSIGN TO SYSJRNL1.
    FILE NAME IS BASJRNL2
        ASSIGN TO SYSJRNL2.
    ARCHIVAL JOURNAL BLOCK CONTAINS 19068 CHARACTERS.
    FILE NAME IS BASARCH1
        ASSIGN TO ARCHJRNL.
```

Journal files are used by IDMS/R to keep records of database activity. This section is required unless a tape journal has been defined in the schema DDL.

We will next examine the DDL statements that are used to define subschemas.

SUBSCHEMAS

The views that individual application programs have of the database are defined in *subschemas* and described to IDMS/R with sets of *subschema DDL* statements. Any number of subschemas can be defined for a given database. Typically, there is one subschema for a group of related application programs. A set of subschema DDL statements identifies the following:

- Subschema name
- Associated schema and DMCL module
- Database areas to be accessible by this subschema
- Records to be included in this subschema
- Sets to be included in this subschema

The subschema definition is processed by the *subschema compiler*. The subschema compiler reads the subschema source statements and stores a description of the subschema in the data dictionary. It also stores an executable load module in an area of the data dictionary called the *load area*. This is shown in Fig. 6.5. IDMS/R uses this load module whenever an application program that uses this subschema is executing. Like the DMCL compiler, the subschema compiler must have access to the corresponding schema definition in the data dictionary, so the schema must be compiled before any of its associated subschemas can be compiled. After compiling the subschema, the data dictionary has all the required information about the logical and physical structures of the database. It also contains the subschema load module required by IDMS/R for database access and program communication.

Figure 6.6 shows a complete set of DDL statements for a possible subschema that might be used in conjunction with the Baseball database. Each set of subschema DDL contains the following sections:

- Names of subschema, schema, and DMCL module
- Names of areas
- Names of records and data elements
- Names of sets

We will next take a closer look at this information.

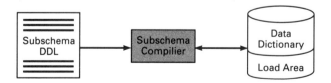

Figure 6.5   The subschema DDL is processed by the subschema compiler, which stores a subschema definition and a load module in the data dictionary.

```
ADD SUBSCHEMA NAME SUBBASE   OF SCHEMA NAME SCHBASE   VERSION 1
    DMCL NAME DMCLBASE   OF SCHEMA NAME SCHBASE   VERSION 1
    COMMENTS
        'LIMITED VIEW OF SCHBASE FOR GENERAL REPORTING'.

ADD AREA NAME TEAM-AREA.
ADD AREA NAME POSITION-AREA.

ADD RECORD NAME TEAM-REC
    ELEMENTS ARE ALL.
ADD RECORD NAME PLAYER-REC
    ELEMENTS ARE PLAYER-NAME BATTING-AVERAGE.
ADD RECORD NAME POSITION-REC
    ELEMENTS ARE ALL.

ADD SET NAME TEAM-PLAYER.
ADD SET NAME PLAYER-POSITION.

GENERATE.
```

Figure 6.6   Subschema DDL statements for a baseball database subschema.

SUBSCHEMA NAME, SCHEMA, AND DMCL MODULE

The first ADD statement names the subschema and identifies the schema and DMCL module with which the subschema is associated:

```
ADD SUBSCHEMA NAME SUBBASE   OF SCHEMA NAME SCHBASE   VERSION 1
    DMCL NAME DMCLBASE   OF SCHEMA NAME SCHBASE   VERSION 1
    COMMENTS
        'LIMITED VIEW OF SCHBASE FOR GENERAL REPORTING'.
```

AREAS

The next two ADD statements identify the areas that are to be made accessible to this subschema:

```
ADD AREA NAME TEAM-AREA.
ADD AREA NAME POSITION-AREA.
```

In this example, two of the three database areas are accessible to programs that use this subschema.

RECORDS AND DATA ELEMENTS

The next three ADD statements identify the records and data elements that are accessible to programs using this subschema:

```
ADD RECORD NAME TEAM-REC
    ELEMENTS ARE ALL.
ADD RECORD NAME PLAYER-REC
    ELEMENTS ARE PLAYER-NAME BATTING-AVERAGE.
ADD RECORD NAME POSITION-REC
    ELEMENTS ARE ALL.
```

In this example, all the data elements from the Team and Position records will be accessible, but only selected data elements from the Player records will be available to programs that use this subschema. None of the data elements in the Game, Salary, or Bonus records will be accessible using this subschema.

SETS

The last two ADD statements identify the sets that are accessible to programs using this subschema:

```
ADD SET NAME TEAM-PLAYER.
ADD SET NAME PLAYER-POSITION.
```

In this example, programs using this subschema will be able to access the Team-Player and Player-Position sets.

SUMMARY

Data description language statements describe the logical and physical structures of the database to IDMS/R by defining schemas, device–media control language modules, and subschemas. A set of schema DDL statements defines the structure of a database. The schema compiler processes the schema DDL and stores into the data dictionary a description of the database it defines. Schema DDL statements describe database areas, database file names, data elements, records, and sets. A set of DMCL statements, processed by the DMCL compiler, maps database areas to physical files in direct access storage. DMCL statements specify buffer sizes and define journal files to be used in implementing backup and recovery procedures. A set of subschema DDL statements defines a subschema that describes a view of the database that is used by one or more application programs. The subschema DDL is processed by the subschema compiler and describes the structure of the subschema. The subschema also identifies the schema and DMCL module from which the subschema view is derived. The subschema defines the database areas, records, and sets to which a program using the subschema has access.

PART **II** **THE INTEGRATED
DATA DICTIONARY**

7 IDD ENTITIES AND COMPONENTS

The *integrated data dictionary (IDD)* maintains a central repository of information about the IDMS/R databases employed by the installation. IDD is designed to be a storehouse of information about the entire information systems environment. It documents information about the various formats, meanings, usages, and contexts that apply to the data used by the installation and about the storage media on which it is maintained. IDD also maintains information about the users of data, application systems, and the programs that implement those systems, including even the source code for programs. Information about the communication network environment can also be stored in the data dictionary.

It is important to remember that the dictionary holds *data about the data,* not the data itself. We sometimes use the term *meta-data* to mean data about data. Meta-data is, of course, data, but meta-data is a different kind of data than the data we store in a typical production database. For example, IDD can provide us with information about the Player-Name data element, telling us, perhaps, that it is 20 characters in length, contains alphanumeric characters, and is currently a data element in the Player record. To learn the names of our players, however, we must go to the Baseball database itself; the data dictionary cannot help us.

As its name implies, the data dictionary is *integrated* with virtually every other software component that works in conjunction with IDMS/R. This is shown in Fig. 7.1 for a number of Cullinet software subsystems. This high degree of integration means that the data dictionary has day-to-day significance not only to the database administrator, but also to systems analysts, systems designers, application programmers, operations personnel, auditors, and end users.

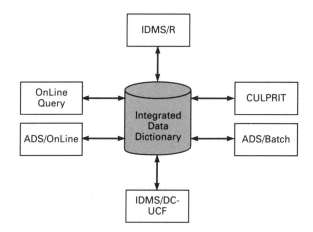

Figure 7.1   The integrated data dictionary.

COMPONENTS OF IDD

The integrated data dictionary is composed of four functional components:

- **The dictionary database.** At the heart of IDD is the *dictionary database*. It is implemented in the form of an IDMS/R network-structured database that contains the dictionary entity occurrences we will be examining in this chapter. It is the repository of the installation's meta-data.

- **The DDDL compiler.** The *data dictionary definition language (DDDL) compiler* processes statements written in the data dictionary definition language. DDDL statements are used to communicate with IDD, in either batch or online mode. DDDL statements can be used to display, update, add, and delete information in the dictionary database.

- **Batch load programs.** The *dictionary loader* and the *COBOL and PL/I syntax converters* are batch programs that provide various means of loading information into the dictionary database. For example, the syntax converters extract record and element descriptions from COBOL and PL/I programs and create DDDL statements for processing by the DDDL compiler.

- **The DML processor.** The *data manipulation language (DML)* consists of statements that can be issued by application programs to access IDMS/R databases. The DML processor stores program activity statistics in the dictionary and copies information from the dictionary into a source program before compilation. It also expands IDMS/R DML statements into standard CALL statements prior to compilation and provides diagnostic messages to assist the programmer.

- **The data dictionary reporter.** The *data dictionary reporter (DDR)*, based on Cullinet's CULPRIT report generator, creates various reports, both standard and user generated, about information stored in the dictionary database.

DICTIONARY ENTITIES

When we discuss Player-Name from the Baseball database we are referring to a specific example of one of the *entity types* about which information is stored in the dictionary database. In this case the entity is the *element* entity type. For each entity type, IDD maintains specific kinds of information. For example, a data element description provides a clear explanation of what the element represents and includes a COBOL-like PICTURE clause that describes the characteristics of the data element. Figure 7.2 contains an entity-relationship diagram that shows the main types of dictionary entities that IDD maintains and some of the more important relationships that exist between them. The dictionary entities are related in the same way as records in an application database. Although loops and many-with-many relationships are shown in the diagram, the dictionary database uses junction records and conventional IDMS/R sets to represent the relationships shown in the chart.

We next describe the main entities that IDD maintains in the dictionary database and provide more information about the ways in which they are related.

The *System* Entity

Occurrences of the System entity type store information about application systems and subsystems, both manual and automated. Figure 7.3 shows how a system entity occurrence for the baseball player management system, along with one

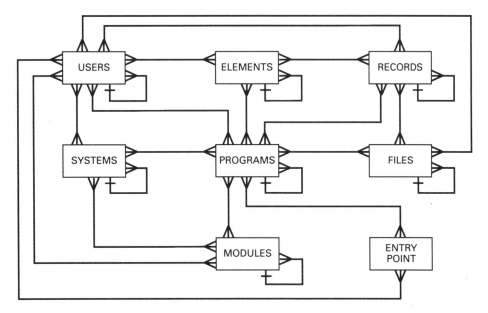

Figure 7.2 Major dictionary database entity types and their relationships.

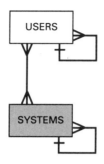

```
ADD SYSTEM 'BASEBALL PLAYER MANAGEMENT'
        USER IS 101
        USER IS RFD RESPONSIBLE
        DEFINITION 'THIS SYSTEM MAINTAINS INFORMATION ON TEAMS,'
     -             'PLAYERS, AND GAMES IN MIDWEST BASEBALL LEAGUE.'.

ADD SUBSYSTEM 'PLAYER STATISTICS'
        WITHIN SYSTEM 'BASEBALL PLAYER MANAGEMENT'
        USER IS 101
        USER IS RFD RESPONSIBLE
        DEFINITION 'THIS SUBSYSTEM TRACKS AND PRODUCES'
     -             'STATISTICS REPORTS ON ALL GAMES PLAYED'
     -             'IN MIDWEST BASEBALL LEAGUE.'.
```

Figure 7.3   Adding System entity occurrences.

of its subsystems, might be added to the dictionary database. The ADD statement is an example of a DDDL statement. The DDDL syntax is similar to the DDL syntax used in defining schemas and subschemas. The ADD statement shown in Fig. 7.3 adds a new System entity occurrence to the dictionary database. We will further discuss the data dictionary definition language in Chapter 8.

The *User* Entity

User entity occurrences store information about people. A user may be an individual, such as a programmer or a clerk, or an entire organization, such as the Payroll Department or the Manufacturing Division. Figure 7.4 shows examples of ADD statements for User entity occurrences. Notice that the occurrences are related. One occurrence is for the Baseball Statistics Department, another is for user SOF, a user in that department, and a third is for a user JNH who reports to SOF.

The *File* Entity

A file consists of any collection of named records. File entity occurrences can be used to document conventional files stored on magnetic media, paper files stored in a filing cabinet, or even a collection of index cards stored in a desk drawer. As shown in Fig. 7.5, files can be related to their users and to other

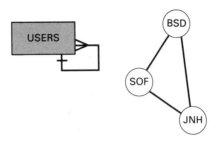

```
ADD USER BSD
    FULL NAME 'BASEBALL STATISTICS DEPT.'.

ADD USER SOF
    FULL NAME 'SCOTT O. FITZGERALD'
    WITHIN USER BSD.

ADD USER JNH
    FULL NAME 'JOHN NATHANIAL HUMPHREY'
    WITHIN USER SOF
    WITHIN USER BSD.
```

Figure 7.4 Adding related User entity occurrences.

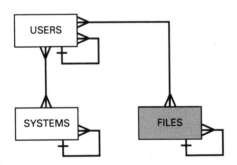

```
ADD FILE GAME-STAT-TRANSACTIONS
    FILE DESCRIPTION 'GAME STATISTICS INPUT TRANSACTIONS'
    USER 101
    USER RFD RESPONSIBLE
    RELATED FILE IS EDITED-GAME-STAT-TRANSACTIONS
    LABELS ARE OMITTED
    BLOCK SIZE IS 8000
    RECORD SIZE IS 80
    RECORDING MODE IS F
    DEFINITION 'FILE OF UNEDITED GAME STATISTICS TRANSACTIONS'.
```

Figure 7.5 Adding a File entity occurrence.

files. The descriptors used for files are similar in appearance to the file descriptions found in a COBOL program.

The *Element* Entity

Occurrences of the Element entity type store information about data elements, or fields, which constitute the smallest meaningful units of data that are maintained by the organization. Although elements are stored in groups called records, information about each data element is maintained in a separate entity occurrence. A single Element occurrence can be included in many Record occurrences. Figure 7.6 shows first how Element occurrences for City-Name,

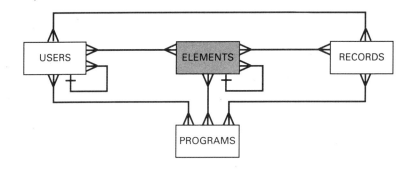

```
ADD ELEMENT CITY-NAME
    ELEMENT DESCRIPTION 'TEAM CITY NAME'
    USER 101
    USER RFD RESPONSIBLE
    PICTURE X(20)
    USAGE DISPLAY.

ADD ELEMENT STATE-NAME
    ELEMENT DESCRIPTION 'TEAM STATE NAME'
    USER 101
    USER RFD RESPONSIBLE
    PICTURE X(10)
    USAGE DISPLAY.

ADD ELEMENT ZIP-CODE
    ELEMENT DESCRIPTION 'TEAM ZIP CODE'
    USER 101
    USER RFD RESPONSIBLE
    PICTURE 9(9)
    USAGE DISPLAY.

ADD ELEMENT TEAM-ADDRESS
    ELEMENT DESCRIPTION 'TEAM CITY, STATE, AND ZIP CODE'
    USER 101
    USER RFD RESPONSIBLE
    SUBORDINATE ELEMENTS ARE
        CITY-NAME
        STATE-NAME
        ZIP-CODE.
```

Figure 7.6   Adding Element entity occurrences.

State-Name, and Zip-Code are added to the dictionary and then referenced again as subordinate elements when adding an element occurrence for Team-Address.

The *Record* Entity

As we learned in Chapter 2, the smallest unit of data that IDMS/R can address is the *record*. Occurrences of the Record entity type store information about records. The Record entity can also document reports and transactions. The example in Fig. 7.7 shows a typical record definition. Notice that the record is related to its users, the files in which it resides, and the elements that it contains.

The *Module* Entity

Module entity occurrences contain actual source module statements coded in a particular programming language. Programmers can copy these from the dictionary into their programs by using the appropriate DML processor. Organizations often use Module entities to standardize routines that are shared by several programs. Examples of these include date routines, error routines, and routines to perform common calculations. Figure 7.8 shows how a module entity can be added to the dictionary database.

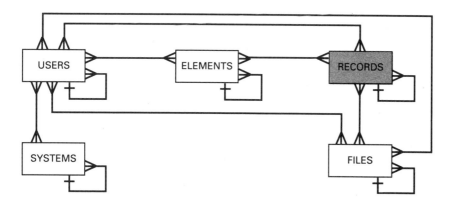

```
ADD RECORD TEAM-TRANSACTIONS
     USER 101
     USER RFD RESPONSIBLE
     WITHIN FILE STAT-TRANSACTIONS
     WITHIN FILE EDITED-STAT-TRANSACTIONS
     LANGUAGE COBOL
     RECORD ELEMENT IS TRANS-CODE
     RECORD ELEMENT IS TEAM-NAME
     RECORD ELEMENT IS TEAM-CITY
     RECORD ELEMENT IS TEAM-PHONE.
```

Figure 7.7   Adding a Record entity occurrence.

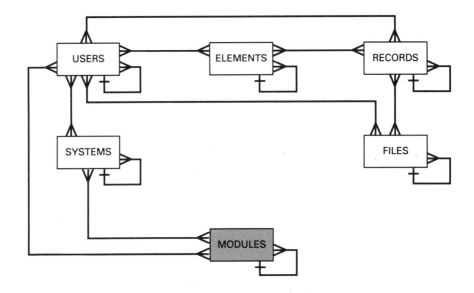

```
ADD MODULE 9999-DATE-MODULE
    USER 101
    WITHIN SYSTEM 'BASEBALL PLAYER MANAGEMENT'
    DEFINITION 'THIS MODULE IS USED TO FORMAT'
-              'CALLS TO DATE CONVERSION ROUTINE.'
    MODULE SOURCE FOLLOWS
9999-DATE-MODULE.
        MOVE WS-DATE-AREA TO DATE-CALL-AREA.
        CALL 'DATECON' USING DATE-CALL.
        IF SUCCESSFUL-CALL
            NEXT SENTENCE
        ELSE
            CALL '9999-ERROR-MODULE' USING DATE-CALL-AREA.
MSEND.
```

Figure 7.8 Adding a Module entity occurrence.

The *Program* Entity

Entire application programs, as well as manual processes, can be documented with occurrences of the Program entity type. Figure 7.9 shows a typical Program entity occurrence description. Programs are related to all of the other basic entity types, as follows:

- The Users of the program
- The Systems to which the program belongs
- The Files used by the program
- The Records used by the program
- The Elements in those records

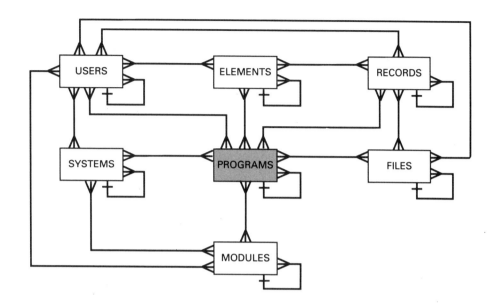

```
ADD PROGRAM STATEDIT
    PROGRAM DESCRIPTION 'GAME STATISTICS EDIT'
    ENTRY POINT NAME IS EDIT004
    USER IS 101
    USER IS RFD RESPONSIBLE
    RECORD COPIED IS TEAM-TRANSACTION
    INPUT FILE IS GAME-STAT-TRANSACTIONS
        EXTERNAL NAME IS STATIN01
    OUTPUT FILE IS EDITED-GAME-STAT-TRANSACTIONS
        EXTERNAL NAME IS STATOT01
    LANGUAGE COBOL
    ESTIMATED LINES 2000
    COMMENTS 'THIS PROGRAM EDITS THE GAME STATISTICS'
             'TRANSACTIONS AND PRODUCES FILE OF VALID'
             'TRANSACTIONS WHICH ARE INPUT TO STATUPDT.'.
```

Figure 7.9 Adding a Program entity occurrence.

- The Modules used by the program
- Other Programs that the program calls

Program entity occurrences do not store actual source code. Program entity occurrences can, however, name Module entity occurrences that do store the source code that makes up the program.

The *Entry Point* Entity

Many program modules contain multiple entry points, each of which defines a point at which processing can begin. These are documented with occurrences of

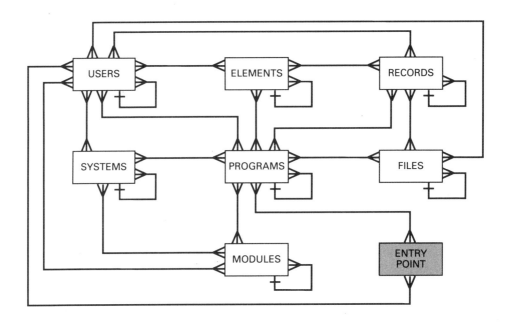

```
ADD ENTRY POINT EDIT004
    USER IS 101
    USER IS RFD RESPONSIBLE
    DEFINITION 'ENTRY POINT TO BEGIN EDITING ADDS.'.
```

Figure 7.10   Adding an Entry Point entity occurrence.

the *entry point* entity type. Figure 7.10 shows how a typical Entry Point entity occurrence can be added to the dictionary database.

OTHER ENTITY TYPES

There are a number of additional dictionary entity types that IDD maintains that are beyond the scope of this book. In addition, the individual installation can create any number of user-defined entity types that can be used to tailor the data dictionary to the specific needs of the organization. See the Cullinet IDD documentation for a complete list of dictionary database entity types.

SUMMARY

The dictionary database maintains a number of different entity types, including information about systems, users, files, data elements, records, modules, and entry points. The

DDDL compiler allows staff members to communicate with IDD in both batch and online mode to create, update, and document information about dictionary entities. The batch load programs and syntax converters can be used to process existing application programs and create DDDL statements that can be used to add entity occurrences to the dictionary database. The DML processor accepts program source code, generates diagnostics, and translates IDMS/R statements into standard syntax. The data dictionary reporter creates various reports about information stored in the dictionary database.

8 DATA DICTIONARY DEFINITION LANGUAGE

The *data dictionary definition language (DDDL)* compiler is the dictionary component with which the technical staff member most often interacts. Although it is called a compiler by Cullinet, it is not a compiler in the usual sense. It does not translate source code to object code, but serves rather as an editor. The DDDL compiler can be executed as a batch program or in online mode. When processing a large number of entries, such as when developing a new system, it may be easier and more efficient to process DDDL statements in batch mode. Online mode is normally preferred for a small number of additions or changes. The DDDL compiler's full-screen editing capability makes it easy to correct typing errors and provides immediate feedback on all processing. The compiler's text editor stores in a work file the DDDL statements that the user enters. The user can then display or modify the statements in the work file before submitting them for compilation. The text editor can also be used to modify information retrieved from the data dictionary for display at the workstation.

When processing DDDL statements, the DDDL compiler checks each statement for proper syntax and then verifies that any prerequisite entity occurrences have already been defined in the dictionary. The DDDL compiler then creates, updates, or deletes entity occurrences, as specified.

DDDL VERBS

There are five DDDL verbs that we can use to manipulate entity occurrences in the data dictionary. These verbs are

- **ADD.** We use ADD to add a new entity occurrence to the dictionary database. We showed examples of ADD statements in Chapter 7.

- **MODIFY.** We use MODIFY to change an existing entity description. We can add, change, or delete any descriptor that is maintained for the particular entity occurrence being modified.
- **DELETE.** We use DELETE to remove an entity occurrence from the dictionary database.
- **DISPLAY.** We use DISPLAY to show all or portions of an entity occurrence description. In online mode the information is displayed on the workstation screen.
- **PUNCH.** We use the PUNCH verb in batch mode to copy entity information from the dictionary database to a conventional file. In online mode, PUNCH performs the same function as DISPLAY.

DDDL STATEMENT FORMAT

All DDDL statements conform to the format shown in Fig. 8.1. The verb name is followed by the type of entity being manipulated and the name of the entity occurrence. The keywords "NAME IS" are always optional. The name of the entity is followed by one or more optional clauses. These usually consist of a keyword followed by a user-specified value. The Cullinet IDD documentation contains detailed descriptions of all the optional clauses that can be included for each DDDL statement for each type of dictionary entity. Each statement must end with a period. Other coding conventions include the following:

- A comment line is indicated by coding "*+" in positions 1 and 2.
- At least one blank is required between words.
- Most keywords can be abbreviated by eliminating letters at the end. As few as three characters can be coded as long as the keyword remains unique.
- Commas, colons, and semicolons are treated as blanks.
- Embedded blanks are designated by surrounding them with quotation marks.

Syntax:

```
⎡ ADD    ⎤
⎢ MODIFY ⎥
⎨ DELETE  ⎬ entity-type-name   NAME   IS   entity-occurrence-name
⎢ DISPLAY ⎥
⎣ PUNCH  ⎦

          optional clauses
```

Example:

```
ADD USER NAME IS AMD
    FULL NAME IS 'ARTHUR M. DAVIDSON'
    PASSWORD IS DOCTOR.
```

Figure 8.1   DDDL statement format.

AN ONLINE SESSION

The first step in using the DDDL compiler in online mode is to sign on to the communication network to which the user's workstation is attached. Various software subsystems on the host processor can be used to perform communication services. In this chapter we are assuming that the installation uses Cullinet Software's IDMS-DC communication subsystem, which displays a message something like this:

```
V8   ENTER NEXT TASK CODE:
     _
```

This message asks us to enter the name of the next program to run. We then enter the name of the DDDL compiler, which is "IDD" in many installations, and IDD displays its opening screen. Depending on installation conventions, we may now be required to enter a SIGNON statement such as the one shown in Fig. 8.2 to identify ourselves to IDD or to sign onto an alternate dictionary. After signing on, we can begin entering DDDL statements. (Keep in mind as you read this chapter that screen formats may vary somewhat depending on the operating environment, the software release, and any installation customization that has been done.)

```
                IDD 10.0 ONLINE          PAGE 1 LINE 1           EMPTY
   SIGNON USER AMD PASSWORD DOCTOR.



```

Figure 8.2 Sample SIGNON statement.

THE IDD TEXT EDITOR

When we use the DDDL compiler, we do not interact with the compiler directly. Instead, we use a text editor to build a work file, which is sent to the DDDL compiler upon request. The process of using the text editor is shown in Fig. 8.3. The work file is divided into pages that contain as many lines as can be displayed on the screen at any one time. The text editor provides a number of commands that we can use to manipulate the contents of the work file. We issue a text editor command by directly entering the command at the beginning of the first line of the display or by pressing the program function (PF) key that is assigned to the command. Box 8.1 briefly describes the most commonly used text editor commands and lists the default PF key assignment for those that have default key assignments. Note that individual installations can change these PF key assignments.

DDDL COMPILER OPERATING PROCEDURE

To invoke the DDDL compiler, we begin by entering one or more DDDL statements beginning on the second line of the screen. We can use all the normal workstation editing keys to edit the statements as we enter them. After we are satisfied with the statement or statements that we have entered, we press the ENTER key. This causes the text editor to update the

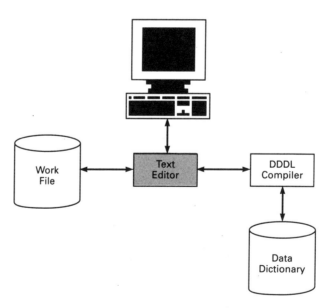

Figure 8.3 The IDD text editor.

BOX 8.1 DDDL compiler text editor commands

- **UPDATE (PF6 and ENTER).** The UPDATE command invokes the DDDL compiler. When UPDATE is issued, the text editor first updates the work file to reflect changes made to the screen. The text editor then invokes the compiler, which processes the DDDL statements contained in the work file, updating the dictionary database.

- **APPLY (PF5).** The APPLY command instructs the text editor to apply to the work file any changes entered on the screen, but does not invoke the DDDL compiler.

- **ENTER (no key).** The ENTER command is used to change the function of pressing the ENTER key. Issuing the command ENTER=APPLY changes the function of ENTER key so it has the same affect as issuing the APPLY command. Issuing the ENTER=UPDATE command changes it back so it has the same affect as issuing the UPDATE command.

- **ESCAPE (no key).** Allows the operator to specify the character to be used to denote line commands. The '%' character is the default.

- **INSERT (PF4).** Inserts a blank line in the display. After typing INSERT on the top line, the cursor is moved to the line where a blank is desired. Pressing enter creates the blank line.

- **SWAP (PF9).** Restores the contents of the work file that existed at the beginning of the session, thus nullifying any changes made during the current session.

- **PRINT (PF12).** Prints the contents of the work file (IDMS-DC only).

- **RESHOW (PA2).** Redisplays the previous screen.

- **CLEAR (CLEAR).** Erases the current contents of the work file and clears the workstation screen.

- **(ERASE EOF).** Erases the line on which the cursor is positioned.

- **REPEAT (no key).** Makes a duplicate of the line on which the cursor is positioned.

- **SWITCH (no key).** Switch causes the IDD session to be suspended with control passing to the Transfer Control Facility briefly introduced in Appendix I.

- **HELP (no key).** Displays a description of all text editor commands and their associated PF key assignments.

- **FIND (no key).** Locates the specified character string in the work file.

(Continued)

BOX 8.1 *(Continued)*

- **END (no key).** Ends the session and returns control to the communication subsystem.
- **SUSPEND (no key).** Temporarily interrupts the session and returns control to the communication system. The session can later be restarted with the contents of the work file restored to its contents at the time that the session was suspended.
- **DISPLAY (no key).** The text editor DISPLAY command, which is different from the DDDL DISPLAY statement, controls which portion of the work file is currently displayed on the screen. We can scroll backward or forward any specified number of lines or pages. The following are examples of DISPLAY commands:

DISPLAY PAGE NEXT	Scroll forward 1 page in the work file.
DISPLAY PAGE PRIOR	Scroll backward 1 page in the work file.
DISPLAY PAGE FIRST	Scroll to the first page in the work file.
DISPLAY PAGE LAST	Scroll to the last page in the work file.
DISPLAY PAGE *	Redisplays the current page.
DISPLAY PAGE *+3	Scrolls forward 3 pages in the work file.
DISPLAY PAGE *-1	Scrolls backward 1 page in the work file.
DISPLAY PAGE 7	Scrolls to page 7 in the work file.
DISPLAY LINE NEXT	Scrolls forward 1 line in the work file.
DISPLAY LINE PRIOR	Scroll backward 1 line in the work file.
DISPLAY LINE FIRST	Scroll to the first line in the work file.
DISPLAY LINE LAST	Scroll to the last line in the work file.
DISPLAY LINE *	Redisplays the current line.
DISPLAY LINE *+10	Scrolls forward 10 lines in the work file.
DISPLAY LINE *-15	Scrolls backward 15 lines in the work file.
DISPLAY LINE 65	Scrolls to line 65 in the work file.

work file based on the contents of the display screen and to send the contents of the work file to the DDDL compiler. If the compiler detects any errors, it returns a screen that flags the parts of the statement that were in error and displays appropriate error messages immediately following each incorrect line. Figure 8.4 shows the screen that the DDDL compiler displays after processing the work

```
                        IDD 10.0 ONLINE           1 ERROR              1/7
ADD SYSTEM NAME IS 'BASEBALL MANAGEMENT SYSTEM'
    UESR IS RFD RESPONSIBLE
*+  E UNKNOWN KEYWORD                                            WORD 1
*+  E UNKNOWN KEYWORD                                            WORD 2
*+  E UNKNOWN KEYWORD                                            WORD 3
*+  E UNKNOWN KEYWORD                                            WORD 4
    USER IS 101
*+  W END OF FILE ENCOUNTERED BEFORE END OF SENTENCE PERIOD ASSUMED   WORD 1
```

Figure 8.4   IDD screen format.

file contents. Notice that it contains error messages. The compiler, instead of finding the keyword 'USER' as the operator intended, found 'UESR'. Finding an "unknown keyword" causes the compiler to search through the statement for a keyword. After failing to find one, it rejects the entire statement. The final message warns that the compiler searched through the work file for a period to complete the statement formally but did not find one. After viewing the error message, we can correct the indicated errors and press ENTER again to have the DDDL compiler reprocess the corrected statement. In this case we would replace 'UESR' with 'USER' and enter the missing period. Since each error message is formatted as a comment, the DDDL compiler ignores the error messages, and they can be left on the screen if desired.

We next begin a discussion of the various DDDL statements that we can enter using the DDDL compiler.

ADDING AN ENTITY   The DDDL ADD statement is used to add a new entity occurrence to the dictionary. We can add a new program called PLAYUPDT by entering the following ADD statement:

```
ADD PROGRAM NAME IS PLAYUPDT.
```

```
                        IDD 10.0 ONLINE              NO ERRORS                    1/7
ADD PROGRAM NAME IS PLAYUPDT
    PROGRAM DESCRIPTION ' PLAYER UPDATE'
    USER IS 101
    USER IS RFD RESPONSIBLE
    INPUT FILE IS IN-PLAYER-TRANSACTIONS
        EXTERNAL NAME IS PLAYIN01
    OUTPUT FILE IS OUT-PLAYER-TRANSACTIONS
        EXTERNAL NAME IS PLAYOT01
    ESTIMATED LINES 2000
    COMMENTS 'THIS PROGRAM EDITS THE PLAYER UPDATE'
    -         'TRANSACTIONS AND UPDATES PLAYER MASTER.'
```

Figure 8.5 Adding a Program entity.

Although this is sufficient to add PLAYUPDT to the dictionary, if we have optional clauses that we would like to enter, we can add them all at once. The alternative is to first ADD the entity and then use the MODIFY command to add the optional clauses later. Figure 8.5 shows the former approach. We have entered all the clauses at one time, and we press ENTER to have the DDDL compiler process the completed statement.

DISPLAYING AN ENTITY   The DDDL DISPLAY statement can be used to display information about existing entity occurrences. For example, we can display the information we previously added for our program named PLAYUPDT by entering the following DISPLAY statement:

```
DISPLAY PROGRAM PLAYUPDT.
```

IDD responds to this command by displaying the requested information in the form of valid DDDL clauses, as shown in Fig. 8.6. Notice that IDD has included an ADD verb at the beginning of the display. In this example, we are assuming that the session default is set to AS COMMENTS, which directs IDD to display requested information in the form of comments. Note that each line in

```
                        IDD 10.0 ONLINE          NO ERRORS                1/7
DISPLAY  PROGRAM PLAYUPDT.
 *+  ADD
 *+  PROGRAM NAME IS PLAYUPDT VERSION IS 1
 *+     PROGRAM DESCRIPTION ' PLAYER UPDATE'
 *+     USER IS 101
 *+     USER IS RFD RESPONSIBLE
 *+     INPUT FILE IS IN-PLAYER-TRANSACTIONS
 *+          EXTERNAL NAME IS PLAYIN01
 *+     OUTPUT FILE IS OUT-PLAYER-TRANSACTIONS
 *+          EXTERNAL NAME IS PLAYOT01
 *+     ESTIMATED LINES 2000
 *+     COMMENTS 'THIS PROGRAM EDITS THE PLAYER UPDATE'
 *+     -        'TRANSACTIONS AND UPDATES THE PLAYER MASTER.'
 *+          .
```

Figure 8.6   Displaying a Program entity occurrence.

the display in Fig. 8.6 begins with the characters "*+," causing each line to be treated as a comment if we later submit this statement for processing by the DDDL compiler. If the session default is set to AS SYNTAX, IDD omits the *+ from the beginning of each line. Whether displayed dictionary information is displayed AS COMMENTS or AS SYNTAX can be controlled through the use of the SET OPTIONS command. For information on using the SET OPTIONS command, refer to the Cullinet IDD documentation. We can also specify explicitly how we want the dictionary information displayed by adding an AS clause to the DISPLAY statement, as in the following example:

```
DISPLAY PROGRAM PLAYUPDT AS SYNTAX.
```

MODIFYING DISPLAYED INFORMATION   Since IDD displays entity information in the form of valid DDDL clauses, we can use the text editor to modify the information on the screen and then resubmit it as input to the DDDL compiler. Suppose that we wish to modify the PLAYUPDT program entity occurrence from the previous example. The screen shown in Fig. 8.7 shows that we have made the following modifications:

```
                       IDD 10.0 ONLINE          NO ERRORS                1/7
          MODIFY
          PROGRAM NAME IS PLAYUPDT VERSION IS 1
     *+      PROGRAM DESCRIPTION ' PLAYER UPDATE'
     *+      USER IS RFD RESPONSIBLE
     *+      INPUT FILE IS UB-PLAYER-TRANSACTIONS
     *+          EXTERNAL NAME IS PLAYIN01
     *+      OUTPUT FILE IS OUT-PLAYER-TRANSACTIONS
     *+          EXTERNAL NAME IS PLAYOT01
             LANGUAGE IS COBOL
             ESTIMATED LINES 5000
     *+      COMMENTS 'THIS PROGRAM EDITS THE PLAYER UPDATE'
     *+      -        'TRANSACTIONS AND UPDATES PLAYER MASTER.'
     *+         .
```

Figure 8.7   Modifying a Program entity occurrence.

1. We deleted the line containing the statement 'USER IS 101'.

2. We changed the verb ADD to MODIFY.

3. We typed over the "*+" with spaces for those lines that contain clauses we wish to have processed.

4. We changed the value specified in the ESTIMATED LINES clause from 2000 to 5000.

5. We inserted the statement 'LANGUAGE IS COBOL' in the middle of our entry.

When we invoke the compiler by pressing the ENTER key, the compiler ignores all the lines that still begin with "*+." The result is equivalent to entering the following statement:

```
MODIFY
    PROGRAM NAME IS PLAYUPDT VERSION IS 1
    LANGUAGE IS COBOL
    ESTIMATED LINES 5000.
```

DELETING AN ENTITY

Just as we can add an entity occurrence, we can delete an entity occurrence by using the DELETE statement:

```
DELETE PROGRAM NAME IS PLAYUPDT.
```

ENDING AN IDD SESSION

The standard method of ending an IDD session is to execute a SIGNOFF DDDL statement. We type SIGNOFF on the second line and submit it to the compiler like any other DDDL statement. This ends the session and returns control to the communication subsystem. In response to a SIGNOFF statement, the DDDL compiler also displays a transaction summary for the session. Figure 8.8 shows an example. The text editor END command can also be used to terminate the session. (See Box 8.1.) However, with END, no transaction summary or messages are displayed. The text editor SUSPEND command lets us suspend a session and return control to the communication subsystem. This allows us to execute some other function without losing the results of the previous IDD session. We can then later return to IDD and pick up where we left off. IDD saves the contents of our work file for us. Because SUSPEND and END are text editor commands, they must be entered in the command area of the top line. Neither has an associated workstation key.

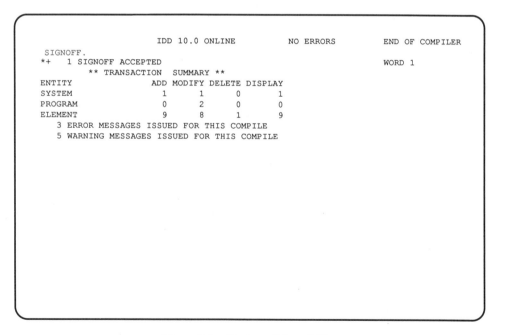

```
                    IDD 10.0 ONLINE          NO ERRORS        END OF COMPILER
  SIGNOFF.
  *+   1 SIGNOFF ACCEPTED                                     WORD 1
            ** TRANSACTION  SUMMARY **
  ENTITY              ADD MODIFY DELETE DISPLAY
  SYSTEM               1     1     0       1
  PROGRAM              0     2     0       0
  ELEMENT              9     8     1       9
    3 ERROR MESSAGES ISSUED FOR THIS COMPILE
    5 WARNING MESSAGES ISSUED FOR THIS COMPILE
```

Figure 8.8 Signing off from IDD.

SUMMARY

The data dictionary definition language allows the user to manipulate entity occurrences in the IDD dictionary using five verbs. The ADD verb adds a new entity occurrence to the dictionary database. The MODIFY verb changes an existing entity description.

The DELETE verb removes an entity occurrence from the dictionary database. The DISPLAY verb shows all or portions of an entity occurrence description. The PUNCH verb is used in batch mode to copy entity information from the dictionary database to a conventional file. In online mode, the DDDL compiler supports a text editor that the user employs to build a work file of DDDL statements. There are three commands that can be used for terminating an online DDDL compiler session. SIGNOFF returns control to the communication subsystem and displays a transaction summary for the session. END omits the summary. SUSPEND saves the work file, allowing the user to return later to the suspended online session.

PART III PROGRAMMING WITH NETWORK-STRUCTURED DATABASES

9 DATA MANIPULATION LANGUAGE

IDMS/R performs many of the functions that traditional application programs perform in manipulating data files and provides powerful facilities for increasing application programmer productivity. One such facility is the IDMS/R *data manipulation language (DML)*. DML provides a number of verbs that can be embedded in source programs to perform a variety of functions, including accessing the database. This chapter briefly describes the major DML statements that can be used in application programs. Next, it contrasts the steps that are involved in preparing a conventional application program for execution with the steps involved in executing an IDMS/R application program. Finally, we present an example of a complete IDMS/R application program written in COBOL.

IDMS/R OPERATING ENVIRONMENT

A conventional application program generally begins by issuing one or more OPEN statements. OPEN statements prepare files for processing and establish linkages between the application program and the operating system data management routines. The program then makes requests for file accesses by issuing READ, WRITE, GET, or PUT statements. These statements result in calls to the operating system data management routines that handle the requests.

In an IDMS/R application program, there are no file description statements or OPEN and CLOSE statements for the database. The reason for this is that the application program does not interface directly with the operating system data management routines that handle data transfer operations. Instead, the application program issues DML statements that direct IDMS/R to access the database.

THE RUN UNIT

Before we begin examining DML statements, we must define the term *run unit*. The run unit represents an important IDMS/R concept that we reference throughout this book. A run unit is the portion of the program's processing during which it has access to one or more database areas and can request IDMS/R services. The program may perform some processing before it begins an IDMS/R run unit, and it may perform processing after the run unit is completed. Also, the program may begin and end more than one run unit in the same program execution.

DATA MANIPULATION LANGUAGE

The IDMS/R data manipulation language provides a number of statements that enable the programmer to access an IDMS/R database and to perform a number of support functions. Box 9.1 provides a brief description of each DML statement. As shown in Box 9.1, DML statements can be divided into five categories:

- **Control statements.** Control statements are used to initiate and terminate a run unit. Control statements can also be used to begin restart and recovery processing, to prevent the concurrent retrieval or update of records, and to check for conditions of sets (e.g., is the set empty).

- **Retrieval statements.** Retrieval statements are used to locate data in the database and, optionally, to make it available to the program.

- **Modification statements.** Modification statements are used to update the database.

- **Save statements.** Save statements are special-purpose statements that are used to pass database-key values, storage address information, and statistics from IDMS/R to the program.

- **Compiler-directive statements.** Compiler-directive statements control the compilation of the program. For example, a compiler-directive statement is used to identify the subschema that the program should use.

PREPARING A PROGRAM FOR EXECUTION

Figure 9.1 illustrates the steps required to prepare an application program for execution. An IDMS/R application program has DML statements embedded in the source code to request database accesses and other support functions. Before the source program is compiled, the program is first read by a DML processor. DML processors are available for a number of commonly used programming languages. The DML processor validates the DML statements and creates a translated version of the source program in which DML statements have been replaced by appropriate calls to IDMS/R. Output from the DML processor is a new source program, which serves as the input to the host programming language compiler. In addition, the DML processor can

BOX 9.1   DML statements

Control Statements

- **BIND.** One form of the BIND statement is used to begin a run unit. A second form is used to identify the record types that the program will access.

- **READY.** The READY statement is used to begin a run unit and to indicate the type of processing that will be performed.

- **FINISH.** The FINISH statement is used to end a run unit by releasing database resources and terminating database processing.

- **COMMIT.** The COMMIT statement is used to write checkpoint records to the journal file and to release record locks.

- **KEEP.** The KEEP statement is used to prevent a record occurrence from being updated and/or accessed by another run unit.

- **ROLLBACK.** The ROLLBACK statement is used to reverse any changes to the database that the run unit made.

- **IF.** The IF statement is used to test a set occurrence for the presence of member record occurrences or to determine whether a record is a member of a set.

Database Retrieval Statements

- **FIND.** The FIND statement is used to locate a record occurrence in the database.

- **GET.** The GET statement is used to make available to the program a record that was located by a previous FIND statement.

- **OBTAIN.** The OBTAIN statement performs the functions of a FIND followed by a GET.

Database Modification Statements

- **STORE.** The STORE statement is used to add a new record occurrence to the database.

- **MODIFY.** The MODIFY statement is used to change data element values in an existing record occurrence.

- **CONNECT.** The CONNECT statement is used to link a record occurrence into a set.

(Continued)

BOX 9.1 *(Continued)*

- **DISCONNECT.** The DISCONNECT statement is used to remove a member record occurrence from a set.
- **ERASE.** The ERASE statement is used to delete from the database a record occurrence and, under some conditions, to also delete its member records.

Save Statements

- **ACCEPT.** The ACCEPT statement is used to move database-key and storage-address information to specified storage locations.
- **RETURN.** The RETURN statement is used to retrieve a database-key or symbolic-key value for an indexed record without actually retrieving the record.

Compiler-Directive Statements

- **IDMS-CONTROL section.** The IDMS-CONTROL section establishes the environment in which the program will execute.
- **PROTOCOL.** The PROTOCOL statement specifies the operating mode to be used by the DML compiler: BATCH, IDMS-DC, or DC-BATCH. The DEBUG option causes the DML compiler to associate sequence numbers with source statements.
- **IDMS-RECORDS.** The IDMS-RECORDS statement determines whether data description code for database records is automatically inserted into the DATA DIVISION when the program is processed by the DML processor.
- **COPY IDMS FILE.** The COPY IDMS FILE statement is used to copy non-IDMS file descriptions from the data dictionary into the program. The COPY IDMS FILE statement can also be used to bring subschema information into the WORKING-STORAGE section or LINKAGE SECTION of the program.
- **SCHEMA SECTION.** The SCHEMA SECTION statement names the subschema and schema the program references and determines which record descriptions are to be copied into the program from the data dictionary.
- **COPY IDMS SUBSCHEMA-BINDS.** This statement generates appropriate BIND statements that the program executes.
- **COPY IDMS MODULE.** This statement copies module source code from the data dictionary into the program.

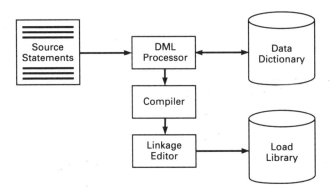

Figure 9.1   IDMS/R application program preparation.

optionally generate a source statement listing containing error diagnostics. The source program that the DML processor generates differs from the input source file in the following ways:

- Additional source code, such as database record descriptions, has been copied into the program from the data dictionary.
- IDMS/R DML statements have been changed to comment entries in accordance with the syntax of the host programming language.
- DML requests that involve the transfer of control to IDMS/R have generated appropriate CALL statements.

     After the translated source program has been compiled, the resulting object module is processed by the linkage editor to create an executable load module. If the program consists of multiple-source modules, a number of object modules can be combined by the linkage editor to create a composite load module, as with conventional programs. The linkage editor also includes a copy of a routine called the *IDMS Interface Module* in the finished load module. Requests that the program makes for IDMS/R services result in calls to the IDMS Interface Module.

THE DML PROCESSOR AND THE DATA DICTIONARY

The DML processor must have access to the data dictionary as it processes the source program. The programmer can use COPY or INCLUDE statements to merge in predefined program modules, record descriptions, and file definitions. The DML processor automatically includes record description entries defined by the subschema the program is using. In addition, the DML processor automatically updates the data dictionary. For example, the DML processor stores into the dictionary information about the types of DML statements that the program executes against database records.

ADDITIONAL DML PROCESSOR FUNCTIONS

In addition to allowing the programmer to issue database requests, the DML processor performs the following functions:

- Supplies all necessary code to generate an IDMS/R control block that is needed for program communication.
- Supplies necessary code for the description of nondatabase files and records that are defined in the data dictionary.
- Ensures that all DML statements issued by the program are consistent with the logical structure of the database, the program's subschema view, and the privacy restrictions defined in the subschema.
- Maintains compile-time statistics used to monitor database activities for a given application program.
- Allows programs to be compiled for execution in conjunction with various communication subsystems, without source code changes for DML statements.

VIRTUAL STORAGE LAYOUT

Figure 9.2 shows the layout of virtual storage when an IDMS/R program executes. IDMS/R is generally contained in its own area of virtual storage (e.g., a partition in a VSE system or an address space in an MVS system). The IDMS/R area of virtual storage contains the IDMS/R database management system and the system buffers. The system buffers are the storage locations that IDMS/R uses in transferring database pages to and from direct access storage. The IDMS/R area also contains the subschema tables for the IDMS/R application programs currently in execution. Subschema tables are loaded when an application program requests database access.

The area of virtual storage occupied by the IDMS/R application program contains variable storage, the IDMS/R interface module, and executable code. Variable storage contains the data areas to be modified by the program during execution. In addition to other storage areas used by the program, variable storage contains a control block called the *IDMS Communications Block*. IDMS/R stores into the IDMS Communications Block information about the results of each request for an IDMS/R service.

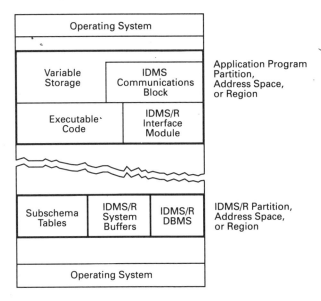

Figure 9.2 Virtual storage layout.

DML STATEMENT EXECUTION

We next examine the steps that are involved in the execution of a typical DML statement, in this case for a retrieval.

1. **Call the IDMS/R Interface Module.** The CALL statement generated by the DML processor passes control to the IDMS/R Interface Module and provides it with information that will be needed to perform the requested database access. This information includes the type of database service desired and record, set, and area names.

2. **Transfer control to IDMS/R.** The IDMS/R interface module transfers control to the IDMS/R DBMS, which performs the requested service. Since access to the database is controlled by the subschema tables, the DBMS reads the tables to determine record, set, and area definitions, currencies, and access restrictions.

3. **Retrieve database record and build subschema record.** The required database record is retrieved, if required, and an image of the requested subschema record is built in variable storage. It is not always necessary for the DBMS to read the database to satisfy a retrieval request. For example, the required record may already be in a system buffer due to a previous retrieval. If the desired record is not already in a buffer, the DBMS uses operating system data management facilities to read the required database page from direct access storage.

4. **Update currencies.** The DBMS updates run-unit, record type, set type, and area currencies, as required. This is done by moving the database key and other control data from the system buffers to the subschema tables.

5. Store status information. The DBMS moves status information to appropriate locations within the IDMS Communications Block. This information describes the results of the requested DML function.

6. Return to the program. After updating the Communication Block, control is passed first from the DBMS to the IDMS/R Interface Module and then to the application program at the statement following the DML statement just executed.

7. Test status information. The application program should contain code to check the results of each requested service. Error checking can be made automatic by using the AUTOSTATUS protocol to generate the statements to examine the status fields.

SAMPLE IDMS/R APPLICATION PROGRAM

We will conclude this chapter by examining a complete, although simple, IDMS/R application program. The program that we examine here is a COBOL program that reads an input file containing player names and produces a listing of the position assignments for each of those players. Figure 9.3 shows a sample of the output report that the sample program produces. Figure 9.4 shows the occurrences of the Team, Player, and Position database records that are accessed in this execution of the program. Figure 9.5 shows the complete program listing.

ID DIVISION

The ID division of the program is similar to that of a conventional COBOL program:

```
ID DIVISION.
PROGRAM-ID.   BASELIST.
```

We have assigned the name BASELIST to the program. Generally, this is the same name as the name of the load module that is referenced in the EXEC statement when the program is run.

```
POSITIONS PLAYED BY PLAYER:   JONES          ON TEAM   : CHICAGO SPARROWS

         POSITION PLAYED:  SHORTSTOP     INNINGS PLAYED:  9
         POSITION PLAYED:  RIGHT FIELD   INNINGS PLAYED:  3

POSITIONS PLAYED BY PLAYER:   JOHNSON        ON TEAM   : CHICAGO SPARROWS

         POSITION PLAYED:  1ST BASE      INNINGS PLAYED:  4
         POSITION PLAYED:  2ND BASE      INNINGS PLAYED:  4
         POSITION PLAYED:  3RD BASE      INNINGS PLAYED:  9
```

Figure 9.3 Sample program output.

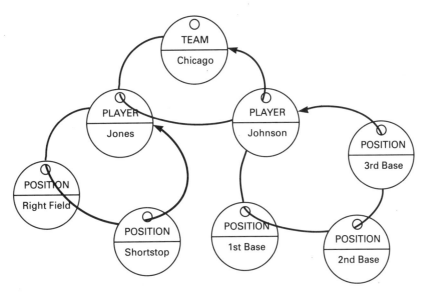

Figure 9.4   Record occurrences.

ENVIRONMENT DIVISION

Notice that the INPUT-OUTPUT section contains references to the input file and the report file, but not to the Baseball database:

```
INPUT-OUTPUT SECTION.
FILE-CONTROL.
    SELECT REPORT-FILE ASSIGN TO S-SYSPRINT.
    SELECT INPUT-FILE  ASSIGN TO S-SYSIN.
```

In addition to the normal INPUT-OUTPUT section, the ENVIRONMENT division contains a new section called the IDMS-CONTROL section:

```
IDMS-CONTROL SECTION.
PROTOCOL.
    MODE IS BATCH DEBUG
    IDMS-RECORDS WITHIN WORKING-STORAGE SECTION.
```

The PROTOCOL statement is a compiler-directive statement that specifies the manner in which the DML processor will generate CALL statements. In this example, BATCH indicates that the program will run in the batch rather than the online mode. DEBUG indicates that the DML processor will supply additional code in the resulting source program that will be helpful in program debugging. The IDMS-RECORDS clause indicates that data descriptions for the records and data elements defined in the subschema used by this program will be copied automatically from the data dictionary and placed at the end of the WORKING-STORAGE section.

```
ID DIVISION.
PROGRAM-ID.   BASELIST.

ENVIRONMENT DIVISION.
IDMS-CONTROL SECTION.
PROTOCOL.
    MODE IS BATCH DEBUG
    IDMS-RECORDS WITHIN WORKING-STORAGE SECTION.

CONFIGURATION SECTION.
SOURCE-COMPUTER.   IBM-370.
OBJECT-COMPUTER.   IBM-370.

INPUT-OUTPUT SECTION.
FILE-CONTROL.
    SELECT REPORT-FILE ASSIGN TO S-SYSPRINT.
    SELECT INPUT-FILE  ASSIGN TO S-SYSIN.

DATA DIVISION.
SCHEMA SECTION.
DB  SUBBASE  WITHIN SCHBASE.

FILE SECTION.

FD  REPORT-FILE
    LABEL RECORDS ARE STANDARD
    BLOCK  CONTAINS   0 RECORDS
    RECORD CONTAINS 133 CHARACTERS.
01  REPORT-REC              PIC X(133).

FD  INPUT-FILE
    LABEL RECORDS ARE STANDARD
    BLOCK  CONTAINS  0 CHARACTERS
    RECORD CONTAINS 80 CHARACTERS.
01  INPUT-RECORD.
    05  INPUT-PLAYER-NAME  PIC X(20).
    05  FILLER             PIC X(60).

WORKING-STORAGE SECTION.

01  EOF-SWITCH             PIC X        VALUE 'N'.
    88  END-OF-FILE                     VALUE 'Y'.

01  PLAYER-LINE.
    05  FILLER            PIC X(01).
    05  FILLER            PIC X(28)
                          VALUE 'POSITIONS PLAYED BY PLAYER:
    05  RPT-PLAYER-NAME   PIC X(20).
    05  FILLER            PIC X(12)    VALUE 'ON TEAM
    05  RPT-TEAM-NAME     PIC X(20).
01  POSITION-LINE.
    05  FILLER            PIC X(01).
    05  FILLER            PIC X(20)
                          VALUE 'POSITION PLAYED:
    05  RPT-POSITION-NAME  PIC X(20).
    05  FILLER            PIC X(18)
                          VALUE 'INNINGS PLAYED:
    05  RPT-INNINGS-PLAYED PIC ZZ9.
```

Figure 9.5 IDMS/R Baseball Player Report program.

```
PROCEDURE DIVISION.

BEGIN-PROGRAM.

        OPEN   OUTPUT   REPORT-FILE
               INPUT    INPUT-FILE.

        COPY IDMS SUBSCHEMA-BINDS.

        READY USAGE-MODE IS RETRIEVAL.
        PERFORM IDMS-STATUS.

        READ INPUT-FILE
             AT END MOVE 'Y' TO EOF-SWITCH.

        PERFORM MAINLINE-ROUTINE
             THRU MAINLINE-EXIT
             UNTIL END-OF-FILE.

        FINISH.
        PERFORM IDMS-STATUS.

        CLOSE REPORT-FILE
              INPUT-FILE.

        STOP RUN.

******************************************************************
*  MAINLINE ROUTINE
*     READ PLAYER NAME FROM INPUT
*     OBTAIN PLAYER RECORD FROM DATABASE
******************************************************************
 MAINLINE-ROUTINE.

        MOVE INPUT-PLAYER-NAME TO PLAYER-NAME.

        OBTAIN CALC PLAYER-REC.

        IF DB-REC-NOT-FOUND
             MOVE '* NO PLAYER RECORD *' TO RPT-TEAM-NAME
             PERFORM WRITE-PLAYER-LINE-ROUTINE
        ELSE
             PERFORM IDMS-STATUS
             PERFORM OBTAIN-TEAM-RECORD-ROUTINE
             PERFORM WRITE-PLAYER-LINE-ROUTINE
             PERFORM OBTAIN-POSITION-RECORD-ROUTINE
                 UNTIL DB-END-OF-SET.

        READ INPUT-FILE
             AT END MOVE 'Y' TO EOF-SWITCH.

 MAINLINE-EXIT.
        EXIT.
```

Figure 9.5   (Continued)

(Continued)

```
******************************************************************
* WRITE PLAYER LINE ON REPORT
*    MOVE INFO FROM PLAYER DATABASE RECORD TO PRINT LINE
*    WRITE PRINT LINE
******************************************************************
 WRITE-PLAYER-LINE-ROUTINE.

     MOVE PLAYER-NAME TO RPT-PLAYER-NAME.
     MOVE TEAM-NAME   TO RPT-TEAM-NAME.
     WRITE REPORT-REC  FROM PLAYER-LINE
          AFTER ADVANCING 2 LINES.

******************************************************************
* OBTAIN TEAM RECORD
*    READ OWNER OF TEAM-PLAYER SET
*
******************************************************************
 OBTAIN-TEAM-RECORD-ROUTINE.

     OBTAIN OWNER WITHIN TEAM-PLAYER.
     IF DB-REC-NOT-FOUND
          MOVE '*******************' TO RPT-TEAM-NAME
     ELSE
          PERFORM IDMS-STATUS
          MOVE TEAM-NAME TO RPT-TEAM-NAME.

******************************************************************
* OBTAIN POSITION RECORD
*    READ ALL POSITION RECORDS WITHIN PLAYER-POSITION SET
*        FOR EACH POSITION RECORD FOUND, WRITE LINE ON REPORT
******************************************************************
 OBTAIN-POSITION-RECORD-ROUTINE.

     OBTAIN NEXT POSITION-REC WITHIN PLAYER-POSITION.

     IF NOT DB-END-OF-SET
          PERFORM IDMS-STATUS
          MOVE POSITION-NAME            TO RPT-POSITION-NAME
          MOVE POSITION-INNINGS-PLAYED TO RPT-INNINGS-PLAYED
          WRITE REPORT-REC  FROM POSITION-LINE
               AFTER ADVANCING 1 LINE.

 IDMS-ABORT SECTION.
 IDMS-ABORT-EXIT.
     EXIT.

 COPY IDMS IDMS-STATUS.
```

Figure 9.5   (Continued)

DATA DIVISION

In the sample program, the DATA division begins with a SCHEMA section, which indicates that the subschema used by the program is named SUBBASE, which is derived from the schema named SCHBASE:

```
DATA DIVISION.
SCHEMA SECTION.
DB  SUBBASE  WITHIN SCHBASE.
```

The remaining DATA division sections are similar to those of a conventional COBOL program. The FILE section describes the input file and the report output file. The WORKING-STORAGE section describes any required data areas in variable storage.

In this program, the only data descriptions in the WORKING-STORAGE section that we have coded are the entries that define EOF-SWITCH and the report line definitions. All the remaining data descriptions that define the IDMS Communications Block and the Team, Player, and Position records have been inserted by the DML processor.

PROCEDURE DIVISION

As in a conventional application program, the PROCEDURE division defines the processing that the program performs. The main difference between the PROCEDURE division of an IDMS/R application program and that of a conventional COBOL program is the inclusion of DML statements that request IDMS/R services. The sample program begins by opening the input file and the report file.

BIND STATEMENTS

Following the OPEN statements is a COPY statement that copies in the BIND statements that will be required for database access:

```
COPY IDMS SUBSCHEMA-BINDS.
```

With this sample program, the BIND statements that will be generated include a BIND RUN-UNIT statement and a BIND statement for each of the records defined in the program's subschema:

```
BIND RUN-UNIT.
BIND TEAM.
BIND PLAYER.
BIND POSITION.
```

The first BIND statement establishes addressability for the IDMS Communications Block and causes IDMS/R to load the subschema identified in the SCHEMA section. The following three BIND statements establish addressability for the WORKING-STORAGE areas that will be used to contain record occurrences.

READY STATEMENT

The READY statement performs an equivalent function as an OPEN statement for a conventional file:

```
READY USAGE-MODE IS RETRIEVAL.
```

This form of the READY statement gives the program access to all the areas defined by the SUBBASE subschema and begins a run unit. The USAGE-MODE clause indicates that the program will retrieve data only and will not be allowed to execute database modification DML statements. The READY statement can optionally name one or more areas that the program wishes to access. This option is useful when the program does not require access to all the areas defined by the subschema and schema.

Additional usage mode options are available for controlling the way in which areas are allowed to be concurrently accessed by two or more areas. The subschema that the program uses generally specifies USAGE-MODE options for each of the areas that the program accesses. If the program omits the READY statements or does not specify usage mode options, the READY options specified in the subschema are used. Usage mode options are discussed in detail in Chapter 13.

STATUS CHECKING The statement immediately following the READY statement performs a paragraph named IDMS-STATUS:

```
READY USAGE-MODE IS RETRIEVAL.
PERFORM IDMS-STATUS.
```

The IDMS-STATUS routine is brought into the program as a result of a COPY IDMS statement that is coded toward the end of the source listing:

```
COPY IDMS IDMS-STATUS.
```

The program performs the IDMS-STATUS paragraph after each DML statement is executed to determine if the requested operation executed successfully. IDMS/R returns, in the ERROR-STATUS field of the IDMS Communications Block, a status code that describes the results of the requested operation. Box 9.2 describes the fields that are contained in the IDMS Communications Block.

If IDMS/R completes a requested DML operation successfully, it returns an error-status code of zero. If IDMS/R detects an error condition, it returns a nonzero error-status code. The data elements that define the layout of the IDMS Communications Block specify a number of status code values. These represent the status code values most often returned by IDMS/R. A status code value of "0000" is labeled DB-STATUS-OK, and indicates a successful DML operation. An end-of-set condition is indicated by "0307". When a retrieval fails because a record is not found, a value of "0326" is returned. Many other status code values are possible; consult the Cullinet documentation for a complete list.

The IDMS-STATUS paragraph performs error-status code checking and abnormally terminates the program if a nonzero error-status code is found. For the READY statement, anything other than a zero status code is unaccept-

BOX 9.2   The IDMS Communications Block

- **PROGRAM NAME.** An 8-byte alphanumeric field that contains the name of the program being executed, as defined in the IDENTIFICA-TION division. This field is initialized by IDMS/R if the program contains a COPY IDMS/R SUBSCHEMA-BINDS statement in the PROCE-DURE division. Otherwise, it must be initialized by the program.

- **ERROR STATUS.** A 4-byte field that contains a value indicating the outcome of the last DML statement the program executed. The ERROR-STATUS field must be initialized to a value of 1400. This field is updated by IDMS/R immediately before control is returned to the program.

- **DB-KEY.** A 4-byte (full-word binary) field that contains the database-key value of the last record accessed successfully by the run unit. For example, after a successful FIND, the DB-KEY field contains the database-key value of the located record. The DB-KEY field is not updated if the call to IDMS/R results in an error condition.

- **RECORD NAME.** A 16-byte alphanumeric field that contains the name of the record most recently accessed successfully by the program. It is left justified and padded with spaces on the right.

- **AREA NAME.** A 16-byte alphanumeric field that contains the name of the area most recently accessed successfully by the program. It is left justified and padded with spaces on the right.

- **ERROR SET NAME.** A 16-byte alphanumeric field that contains the name of the set last involved in an operation that produced an error condition.

- **ERROR RECORD NAME.** A 16-byte alphanumeric field that contains the name of the record last involved in an operation that produced an error condition.

- **ERROR AREA NAME.** A 16-byte alphanumeric field that contains the name of the area last involved in an operation that produced an error condition.

- **IDBMSCOM AREA.** A 100-byte field that is used internally by IDMS/R for specification of runtime function information.

- **DIRECT DB-KEY.** A 4-byte (full-word binary) field that contains a user-suggested database-key value or a null database-key value of -1. This field is used for storing a record with a location mode of DIRECT. It must be initialized by the program and is not updated by IDMS/R.

able. So the IDMS-STATUS routine will abnormally terminate the program if IDMS/R returns anything but a zero error-status code.

THE AUTOSTATUS OPTION   The PROTOCOL statement can request an option called AUTOSTATUS that causes all DML statements to perform the IDMS-STATUS paragraph automatically, thus eliminating the need to code a PERFORM statement specifically after each DML statement. However, many programs perform their own error-status code checking before executing the IDMS-STATUS paragraph, and so do not use the AUTOSTATUS option. Some installations require the use of AUTOSTATUS, since it guarantees status checking after each IDMS statement. The programmer can include an ON clause after individual statements to trap certain error-status code values. The ON clause is checked before control is passed to the IDMS-STATUS paragraph.

DATABASE ACCESS   After executing the READY statement, the program executes an initial READ for the input file and then executes the main paragraph of the program, once for each record on the input file. The program moves the player name from the input record to the field in working storage that contains the player name in the description of the Player record. The program then issues a DML statement to read the appropriate Player database record:

```
OBTAIN CALC PLAYER-REC.
```

If IDMS/R cannot locate a Player record having the requested player name, the program moves an error message to the print line in working storage and writes a line on the report. If the Player record is found, the program attempts to find the owner Team record:

```
OBTAIN OWNER WITHIN TEAM-PLAYER.
```

If IDMS/R finds the owner record, it moves the team name value from that record to the report; if the owner record cannot be found, it moves asterisks to the report. The program then repeatedly performs a routine to locate all the Position records for the player. The routine uses this statement:

```
OBTAIN NEXT POSITION-REC WITHIN PLAYER-POSITION.
```

For each Position record, the program prints a line on the report showing the name of the position played and the date. After reading the last Position record, which results in an end-of-set condition, the program reads a record from the input file to get the next player name.

THE FINISH STATEMENT

After end-of-file is detected on the input file, the program ends the run unit by executing a FINISH statement. The FINISH statement releases the database areas from the program's control. Finally, the program ends by closing the input and output files and executing a STOP RUN statement.

SUMMARY

A run unit is defined as that portion of an IDMS/R program's execution that has access to the database and can request IDMS/R services. An IDMS/R application program issues data manipulation language statements to specify the IDMS/R services that it requires. DML statements fall into five categories: control, retrieval, modification, save, and compiler directive. Prior to executing an IDMS/R program, the source code must be validated and translated by a DML processor. The program is then processed by a language compiler and the linkage editor in the same manner as a conventional program. The program then normally executes in a partition or address space reserved for IDMS/R, which contains the database management system, system buffers, and subschema tables. The execution of a DML statement involves the following steps: the program calls the IDMS/R interface module, control is transferred to IDMS/R, records are located and the subschema record is built in variable storage, currencies are updated in the subschema tables, status information is stored in the IDMS Communications Block, control is passed back to the program, and the program checks the status information to determine the results of the request.

10 DML RETRIEVAL FUNCTIONS

Strategies that the application programmer must adopt when writing IDMS/R programs are somewhat different from the strategies used in traditional file programs. In this chapter, we show how to code the specific DML statements that are used to retrieve information from an IDMS/R database.

Before we can begin writing an IDMS/R application program, there are a number of things that we must know about the database that we will be accessing. Among these are the names and characteristics of all the data elements, records, sets, and areas that are defined in the subschema. As we have already discussed, these characteristics are specified when the schema, subschema, and DMCL module are defined. The subschema also defines any restrictions that the programmer must be aware of with respect to the types of DML statements that the program is allowed to issue.

BASEBALL DATABASE RECORD OCCURRENCES

Before examining the DML statements we will be using to retrieve records, let us look at some sample record occurrences from the Baseball database. Figure 10.1 repeats the structure diagram for the Baseball database, and Fig. 10.2 shows the record occurrences that we are assuming it contains for the purposes of many of our examples.

We have one Team record that owns two Player record occurrences and two Game record occurrences. The Player record for Smith owns three Position records, and the Player record for Jones owns two. Each Game record also owns a different set of Position record occurrences. Record occurrences are stored in two areas, Team-Area and Position-Area.

Smith currently owns three Position records. Two of these Position occurrences are also owned by the Game record for June 4. They indicate that Smith played first base and second base during the June 4 game. Smith's other Posi-

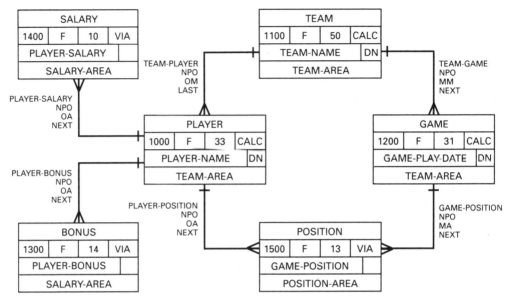

Figure 10.1 Baseball database data structure diagram.

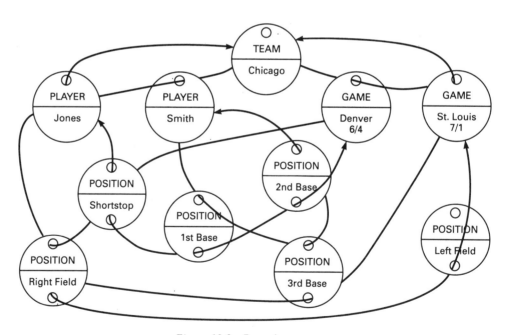

Figure 10.2 Record occurrences.

tion record is owned by the Game record for July 1. So Smith played third base in the July 1 game. Looking at the other Player record, we see that Jones has played two different positions, shortstop and right field. He played shortstop in the June 4 game and right field in the July 1 game against St. Louis. We can also see that one Position occurrence, Left Field, is owned by the July 1 record, but it has no owner in the Player-Position set. Since the membership options for the Player-Position set are optional and automatic, the Left Field Position record must have been manually disconnected.

PLAN FOR EXECUTION

Once we understand the characteristics of our database, we can develop a plan of attack for accessing the database. In many cases, we will be able to access the database using a number of different search strategies to perform the required processing. Often, one of these search strategies may be more advantageous than the others in terms of processing efficiency. In general, a program should use the processing strategies that require the fewest number of database accesses.

CHOOSING A RETRIEVAL TECHNIQUE

To choose the appropriate search strategy for accessing a network-structured database, we must know all the various ways in which we can access the data. In general, a program can access data in the following ways:

- By performing a CALC retrieval
- By walking sets
- By sweeping areas
- By performing a direct database-key retrieval
- By using an index
- By specifying record selection criteria for a logical record

Our choice of a retrieval technique depends upon judgments involving the problem to be solved, processing efficiency, and available input information. In this chapter, we will discuss the first five methods for accessing the database. We discuss retrieval techniques for logical records in Chapter 18. To simplify our discussion, we will look only at the DML statements and any associated programming required to handle each type of retrieval. We begin with CALC retrievals.

RETRIEVAL BY CALC-KEY VALUE

To perform a CALC retrieval, the record type we are retrieving must have a CALC-key defined for it, and we must know the CALC-key value of the record occurrence we are retrieving. In the Baseball database, we can perform CALC retrievals for Team, Player, and Game records. We cannot perform a CALC retrieval for Position records. The following CALC retrieval, taken from the retrieval program example in Chapter 9, retrieves a particular Player record occurrence:

```
MOVE INPUT-PLAYER-NAME TO PLAYER-NAME.
OBTAIN CALC PLAYER-REC.
```

In the example, we moved the CALC-key value contained in the Input-Player-Name element into the field that defines the CALC key of the Player record. The Player-Name data element is part of the description of the Player record that was copied into the WORKING-STORAGE section by the DML processor. We then issue an OBTAIN CALC statement for the Player record. IDMS/R then uses the CALC-key value we supply to locate the appropriate page in the database, retrieves the desired Player record occurrence, and constructs a subschema record in variable storage.

OBTAIN VERSUS FIND AND GET

As we introduced in Chapter 9, an OBTAIN statement performs the same function as a FIND followed by a GET. The find function causes IDMS/R to locate the appropriate record in the database and place it in the system buffers. If we like, we can later follow a successful FIND with a GET. GET causes IDMS/R to move the appropriate data element values from the system buffers into our program's variable storage. We need not, however, follow a FIND with a GET. In some cases, we only wish to locate a record, but do not need actually to retrieve it. For example, we may only need to verify that a particular record occurrence exists, or we may need to establish a starting point for some subsequent retrieval sequence. Following are the separate FIND and GET statements that we could use to perform the same retrieval as the previous OBTAIN CALC statement:

```
MOVE INPUT-PLAYER-NAME TO PLAYER-NAME.
FIND CALC PLAYER-REC.
GET.
```

We can also code a record name on the GET:

```
MOVE INPUT-PLAYER-NAME TO PLAYER-NAME.
FIND CALC PLAYER-REC.
GET PLAYER-REC.
```

Including a record name in a GET statement causes IDMS/R to verify that the record that was located by the previous FIND was, in fact, a Player record. If the record types do not match, IDMS/R returns an error code.

The remaining retrieval examples in this chapter are coded in the form of OBTAIN statements. Keep in mind that each form of OBTAIN retrieval that we show can alternatively be coded in the form of a FIND statement if we only want to locate the record and do not need to examine its data element values.

DUPLICATE CALC-KEY VALUES

In some cases, we will have to perform CALC retrievals for record types that allow duplicate CALC-key values. If we assume that the Player record type allows duplicates, we would retrieve the first record occurrence that has a particular CALC-key value by performing an OBTAIN CALC retrieval. We could then determine if there is another record with the same CALC-key value by executing an OBTAIN DUPLICATE statement:

```
MOVE INPUT-PLAYER-NAME TO PLAYER-NAME.
OBTAIN CALC PLAYER-REC.
OBTAIN DUPLICATE PLAYER-REC.
```

If the database contains another record occurrence with the same CALC-key value, IDMS/R retrieves it. If none exists, or if a previous OBTAIN DUPLICATE statement retrieved the last one, IDMS/R returns an error code.

CURRENCY

The next type of retrieval call that we discuss depends on some position having already been established in the database. To help keep track of where we are in the database, IDMS/R maintains pointers to a number of different record occurrences as each run unit executes. We use the term *currency* to refer to these pointers. IDMS/R maintains four types of currency:

- **Current of run unit.** This is the most recent record occurrence accessed by the program.

- **Current of record type.** This is the most recent occurrence of a particular record type accessed by the program. IDMS/R maintains a separate currency for each record type defined in the subschema.

- **Current of set type.** This is the most recent record occurrence of a particular set type accessed by the program. IDMS/R maintains a separate currency for each set type defined in the subschema.

- **Current of area.** This is the most recent record occurrence in a particular area accessed by the program. IDMS/R maintains a separate currency for each area to which the program has access.

```
RUN UNIT

TEAM-REC          RECORD TYPE
PLAYER-REC        RECORD TYPE
GAME-REC          RECORD TYPE
POSITION-REC      RECORD TYPE


TEAM-PLAYER       SET TYPE
TEAM-GAME         SET TYPE
PLAYER-POSITION   SET TYPE
GAME-POSITION     SET TYPE


TEAM-AREA         AREA
POSITION-AREA     AREA
```

Figure 10.3   Baseball database currencies.

For the Baseball database, IDMS/R maintains separate pointers to as many as 11 record occurrences, depending on the program's subschema view, as shown in Fig. 10.3. At a given point in time, many of these positions may point to the same record occurrence.

ESTABLISHING CURRENCIES

At the beginning of a run unit, all currencies start out as null. If we then retrieve a particular Player record occurrence, perhaps by executing an OBTAIN statement specifying a CALC retrieval, IDMS/R establishes 5 of the 11 possible currencies. This is shown in Fig. 10.4. IDMS/R establishes as current of run unit the Player record that we retrieved. This same record also becomes current of the Player record type. Since the Player record type belongs to two sets, the retrieved Player record becomes current of each of these two sets. The retrieved Player record also becomes current of the Team-Area area. The other currencies remain null until some future database access sets them.

RETRIEVING MEMBER RECORDS

In many application situations, it is necessary to retrieve a particular owner record occurrence and then to retrieve one or more of that owner's member record occurrences. We choose the set occurrence that we wish to access by executing a retrieval statement (either an OBTAIN or a GET) for a particular occurrence of the set's owner record type; a CALC-type retrieval is often useful for this purpose. Once we have established the set's owner record occurrence as current of its record type and also current of its set type, the most straightforward option we have is to retrieve the first member record occurrence in the set:

```
OBTAIN FIRST WITHIN PLAYER-POSITION.
```

```
RUN UNIT                                       -

TEAM-REC          RECORD TYPE         -
PLAYER-REC        RECORD TYPE         -
GAME-REC          RECORD TYPE         -
POSITION-REC      RECORD TYPE         -


TEAM-PLAYER       SET TYPE            -
TEAM-GAME         SET TYPE            -
PLAYER-POSITION   SET TYPE            -
GAME-POSITION     SET TYPE            -


TEAM-AREA         AREA                -
POSITION-AREA     AREA                -
```

Before

```
RUN UNIT                                  WILLIAMS

TEAM-REC          RECORD TYPE         -
PLAYER-REC        RECORD TYPE         WILLIAMS
GAME-REC          RECORD TYPE         -
POSITION-REC      RECORD TYPE         -


TEAM-PLAYER       SET TYPE            WILLIAMS
TEAM-GAME         SET TYPE            -
PLAYER-POSITION   SET TYPE            WILLIAMS
GAME-POSITION     SET TYPE            -


TEAM-AREA         AREA                WILLIAMS
POSITION-AREA     AREA                -
```

After

Figure 10.4 Establishing currencies.

After executing the first statement above, IDMS/R retrieves the first Position record in the Player-Position set, which then becomes current of the Player-Position set. The original Player record remains current of its record type.

If a member's set is defined with prior pointers, we can retrieve the last member record occurrence of a set in a similar manner:

```
OBTAIN LAST WITHIN PLAYER-POSITION.
```

Another useful type of member record retrieval sequence is to retrieve each of an owner record's members in sequence. This is referred to as *walking the set*. The following retrieval statement can be repeatedly executed to retrieve all of an owner record's members.

```
OBTAIN NEXT WITHIN PLAYER-POSITION.
```

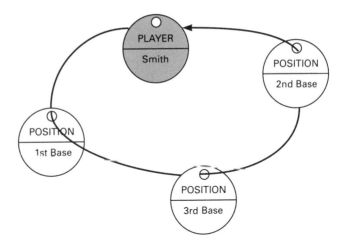

Figure 10.5   The Position record occurrences for Smith.

The particular record occurrence that this statement retrieves depends on which record occurrence in the set is established as current of the Player-Position set; it always retrieves the record that follows the record occurrence that is current of the Player-Position set in the *next* direction. For example, if the Player record for Smith in Fig. 10.5 is current of set type, as it is immediately after retrieving the Smith record, OBTAIN NEXT retrieves the first member record, the one for 1st Base. If we issue the OBTAIN NEXT a second time, IDMS/R retrieves the 3rd Base occurrence, and so on until the Smith record is again retrieved and the sequence begins again. IDMS/R sets an end of set condition code that the program can test to avoid walking the set a second time.

When we issue DML statements for walking a set, we can, if we like, qualify each retrieval with a record name. This is coded as follows:

```
OBTAIN FIRST POSITION-REC WITHIN PLAYER-POSITION.
OBTAIN NEXT POSITION-REC WITHIN PLAYER-POSITION.
OBTAIN LAST POSITION-REC WITHIN PLAYER-POSITION.
```

The foregoing statements cause IDMS/R to retrieve only Position records, no matter where in the set currency is established. Including a qualifying record name is particularly useful when walking sets that have more than one member record type. Specifying a record name limits retrieval to only one of the record types; IDMS/R bypasses member records of other types.

WALKING A SET IN THE PRIOR DIRECTION   If a set has been defined as having PRIOR pointers, we can walk the set in the *prior* direction by repeatedly executing a statement of the following type:

```
OBTAIN PRIOR WITHIN PLAYER-POSITION.
```

OBTAIN PRIOR works in the same manner as OBTAIN NEXT, except in the reverse direction. OBTAIN PRIOR statements cannot be issued for a member record type if the member's set does not include PRIOR pointers. As in the previous examples, we can also include a qualifying record name in an OBTAIN PRIOR statement.

RETRIEVING THE OWNER RECORD

We can use the following DML statement to retrieve the owner of a set occurrence:

```
OBTAIN OWNER WITHIN PLAYER-POSITION.
```

If currency is established anywhere in the set occurrence shown in Fig. 10.5, OBTAIN OWNER will cause IDMS/R to retrieve the Player record for Smith.

An OBTAIN OWNER retrieval can be issued whether or not the set is defined as having OWNER pointers. If owner pointers do not exist, IDMS/R walks the set, if necessary, to locate the owner record. If the set is defined as having OWNER pointers, IDMS/R can get directly to the owner from any member in the set occurrence.

RETRIEVING A PARTICULAR MEMBER

We can retrieve a particular member of a set by a number that specifies the relative sequence in the set of the desired member. There are two methods available for doing this. If we want to retrieve the third record in the Player-Position set, we could execute the following statement:

```
OBTAIN 3 WITHIN PLAYER-POSITION.
```

We can alternatively store into a data element a value that indicates the relative sequence of the desired member and reference that data element in the OBTAIN statement:

```
01  SEQ-FIELD  PIC S9(5) COMP.
      .
    MOVE SEQUENCE-VALUE TO SEQ-FIELD.
    OBTAIN SEQ-FIELD WITHIN PLAYER-POSITION.
```

RETRIEVING CURRENT RECORDS

There are times when it is useful to retrieve records based directly on record and set currency. For example, the following statement directs IDMS/R to retrieve the record occurrence that is current of the Player record type:

```
OBTAIN CURRENT PLAYER-REC.
```

The following statement directs IDMS/R to retrieve the record occurrence that is current of the Team-Player set type:

```
OBTAIN CURRENT WITHIN TEAM-PLAYER.
```

Depending on the currencies that are established, the foregoing statement might retrieve either a Team record or a Player record.

RETRIEVAL BY SWEEPING AREAS

In performing an area sweep, IDMS/R scans through all the records in an area in physical sequence. The order in which records are retrieved will generally have little relationship to the logical sequence of records. Area sweeps are useful when we want to retrieve all the records in an area without regard to the order in which we get them, for example, when we are simply gathering statistics about the database.

Our next two OBTAIN examples can be used for performing an area sweep in the forward direction. The following OBTAIN statement causes IDMS/R to retrieve the first record in the Team-Area area:

```
OBTAIN FIRST WITHIN TEAM-AREA.
```

IDMS/R will simply retrieve the record having the lowest database-key value in the area. In the following example, IDMS/R uses currency within the area to determine which record to retrieve. It uses area currency to retrieve the record having the next highest database-key value.

```
OBTAIN NEXT WITHIN TEAM-AREA.
```

At times it may be desirable to perform an area sweep in the reverse direction. The following statements demonstrate one method of accomplishing this:

```
OBTAIN LAST WITHIN TEAM-AREA.
        .
        .
OBTAIN PRIOR WITHIN TEAM-AREA.
```

Pointers are not used in performing an area sweep, so prior pointers are not necessary for executing OBTAIN PRIOR WITHIN AREA statements.

As with the DML statements for walking sets, we can qualify an area sweep with a record name. IDMS/R will retrieve occurrences only of the named record type when scanning through the area. This is coded as follows:

```
OBTAIN LAST PLAYER-REC WITHIN TEAM-AREA.
        .
        .
OBTAIN PRIOR PLAYER-REC WITHIN TEAM-AREA.
```

We can also retrieve a particular record in an area by using techniques that are similar to retrieving particular records in a set. The following example retrieves the tenth record in physical sequence in the Team-Area area:

```
OBTAIN 10 WITHIN TEAM-AREA.
```

In the next example, we store a value in a data element to indicate the physical sequence within the area of the desired record:

```
01    SEQ-FIELD                PIC S9(5) COMP.
  .
  .
  MOVE SEQ-VALUE TO SEQ-FIELD.
  OBTAIN SEQ-FIELD WITHIN TEAM-AREA.
```

Following is the DML statement that we can use to retrieve directly the record that is current of the Team-Area area:

```
OBTAIN CURRENT WITHIN TEAM-AREA.
```

RETRIEVAL BY SORT-KEY VALUE

If we are retrieving member records and the set type was defined with the order option of SORTED, we can base retrievals on sort-key values. Suppose the Player-Position set type were defined as SORTED on Position-Name values instead of NEXT. The Position records for Smith would then be stored as shown in Fig. 10.6, with the Position record occurrences chained together in alphabetic order by Position-Name value. With a sorted set, we can retrieve a particular member of a set occurrence based on a sort-key value, as in this example:

```
MOVE INPUT-POSITION-NAME TO POSITION-NAME.
OBTAIN POSITION-REC WITHIN PLAYER-POSITION USING POSITION-NAME.
```

In this example, we move a Position-Name value to the data element in the Position record description that defines the sort key and issue an OBTAIN statement that references the sort-key data element. Note that although the retrieval appears similar to a CALC retrieval, the search for a record is limited to the current set occurrence; IDMS/R does not search other set occurrences for a member having the specified sort-key value.

In the previous example, IDMS/R begins searching member records from the first member record in the set, regardless of which record is current of set type. In some application situations, especially with long sets, it is desirable to request that IDMS/R begin the search from the member record that is current of set type rather than beginning the search with the first member record. The following example accomplishes this:

```
MOVE INPUT-POSITION-NAME TO POSITION-NAME.
OBTAIN POSITION-REC WITHIN PLAYER-POSITION CURRENT
    USING POSITION-NAME.
```

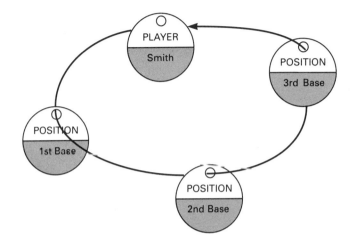

Figure 10.6   In a sorted set, the record occurrences are arranged in alphabetic sequence by sort-key value.

RETRIEVAL BY DATABASE-KEY VALUE

If we know the database-key value of a record, we can direct IDMS/R to retrieve it directly. This technique is useful when we determine that we are going to have to retrieve a particular record again at a later time. After each database access, IDMS/R stores in a field in the IDMS Communications Block the database-key value of the record accessed. After a retrieval, we can store this database-key value in a variable-storage area for later use. An example of this type of retrieval is shown in Fig. 10.7. In the example, after retrieving a particular Player record, we move its database-key value to a field in variable storage named SAVE-DBKEY. Later, we use the value stored in SAVE-DBKEY to again retrieve the same Player record.

One word of warning is in order here. It is generally not desirable to attempt to maintain sets of database-key values for long periods of time, perhaps in an external file or database. This is because database-key values may change when the database is reorganized. After a database reorganization, the database-key values that we stored will not point to the expected records.

RETRIEVAL USING AN INDEX

By using index sets, we can perform three types of retrieval that are difficult or impossible without the use of an index:

- Sequential retrieval in symbolic-key sequence
- Generic-key retrieval
- Random retrieval based on the value of a symbolic key other than a CALC-key

```
01   SAVE-DBKEY                    PIC S9(8) USAGE COMP SYNC.
          .
          .
          .
01   SUBSCHEMA-CTRL.
          .
          .
          .
     03    DBKEY                   PIC S9(8) USAGE COMP SYNC.
             .
             .
             .
01   PLAYER-REC.
     02    PLAYER-NAME             PIC X(30).
     02    PLAYER-PHONE            PIC 9(10).
     02    BATTING-AVERAGE         PIC 9(3).
             .
             .
             .
     MOVE INPUT-PLAYER-NAME   TO PLAYER-NAME.

     OBTAIN CALC PLAYER-REC.
          .
          .
          .
     MOVE DBKEY TO SAVE-DBKEY.
          .
          .
          .
     OBTAIN DB-KEY IS SAVE-DBKEY.
```

Figure 10.7   Retrieval by database-key value.

Indexing *Position* Records

Figure 10.8 shows an index set named IX-Position-Name that indexes Position records based on Position-Name data element values. Figure 10.9 shows some of the entries in this index. Each entry contains a Position-Name data element value and the database-key value of its corresponding Position record. Suppose we wanted to retrieve all the Position records for a particular position. We might

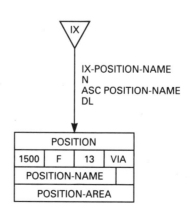

Figure 10.8   Position-Name index.

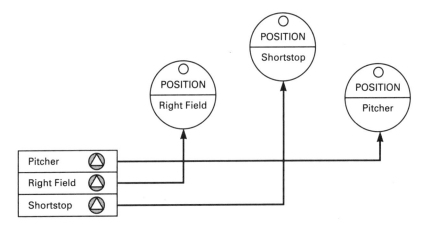

Figure 10.9 Index entries.

want to do this to gather statistics on innings played for each position. Position records are stored with the VIA location mode, so there is no CALC key available. Without the index set, we would have to perform an area sweep and examine every Position record in the database. Using the index set, we can get directly to those Position records that have the desired Position-Name data element value.

Random Retrieval

To use the index to find the first record having a particular Position-Name value, we can do a random retrieval in a similar manner to the method we used for retrieving a member record having a particular sort-key value. We name the desired record type, specify the name of the index set, and supply a data element value for the indexed data element:

```
OBTAIN POSITION-REC WITHIN IX-POSITION-NAME USING POSITION-NAME.
```

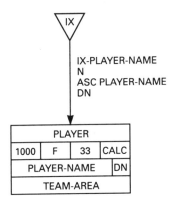

Figure 10.10 Player-Name index.

```
01  PLAYER-NAME-WORK.
    05  FIRST-INITIAL          PIC X.
    05  FILLER                 PIC X(29).
        .
        .
        .

    MOVE LOW-VALUES       TO PLAYER-NAME-WORK.
    MOVE INPUT-LETTER     TO FIRST-INITIAL.
    MOVE PLAYER-NAME-WORK TO PLAYER-NAME.

    OBTAIN PLAYER-REC WITHIN IX-PLAYER-NAME
        USING PLAYER-NAME.
        .
        .
        .

    OBTAIN NEXT PLAYER-REC WITHIN IX-PLAYER-NAME.
```

Figure 10.11   Generic-key retrieval.

Sequential Retrieval

There may be many Position records all having the same Position-Name value. Once the program locates the first one through random retrieval, it could issue a series of sequential retrievals to locate additional records having that same name:

```
    OBTAIN NEXT POSITION-REC WITHIN IX-POSITION-NAME.
```

The program has to test the name field after each sequential retrieval to determine when it has reached the last record with the specified Position-Name data element value.

Generic-Key Retrieval

To perform a generic-key retrieval using the index, we supply IDMS/R with a partial key value. For example, suppose we are using the IX-Player-Name index shown in Fig. 10.10 and we wanted to retrieve sequentially all the Player records whose Player-Name value begin with the letter "L." Figure 10.11 shows the partial code for this type of retrieval. Notice that the data element in which we store the generic key must be padded to the right with low values. If our subsequent sequential retrievals will move through the index in the opposite direction, from high key values to low, we would pad to the right with high values.

SUMMARY

An application program's subschema defines the records that the program can access and specifies the types of retrieval that can be performed for each record type. A program can perform CALC retrievals for records that are defined as having the CALC location mode. In performing CALC retrievals, the program specifies the CALC key value of the desired record. Currency values that are maintained by IDMS/R determine how database retrieval is handled for many retrieval techniques. Records that are members in one or more sets can be retrieved by walking a set in either the forward or backward direction. Any type of record can be retrieved by sweeping an area or by specifying its db-key value. Member records of sorted sets can be retrieved by specifying their sort-key values. By using index sets, records can be retrieved sequentially in symbolic-key sequence or directly by specifying a symbolic-key value. Index sets also support generic-key retrieval.

11 DML DATA MANIPULATION FUNCTIONS

This chapter concerns the DML statements that are available for manipulating the data in IDMS/R network-structured databases, including statements for adding new records, modifying existing ones, erasing records from the database, disconnecting record occurrences from sets, and connecting them to new set occurrences.

READY STATEMENTS FOR UPDATING

In Chapter 9, we saw an example of a READY statement for a retrieval program. In order to update the records in the database, we must code parameters in the READY statement that inform IDMS/R that we intend to update the database, as in the following example:

```
READY USAGE MODE IS UPDATE.
```

A READY statement for update can also specify additional usage mode options that control the way in which database areas can be concurrently accessed by two or more run units. The subschema for an update program may also specify the appropriate default usage mode options for updating. If the appropriate usage mode is specified in the subschema, READY statements can be omitted from the update program. Usage mode options for updating are discussed in detail in Chapter 13.

THE MODIFY FUNCTION

Once we have readied one or more areas with one of the UPDATE usage mode options, we can use the MODIFY statement to replace the data element values in a record occurrence with new data element values. In modifying a record occurrence we generally perform the following steps:

1. Execute an OBTAIN for the desired record. This establishes run-unit currency on the record we are going to change and also places a copy of the record in variable storage.
2. Make changes to the record by storing new data element values in variable storage.
3. Execute the MODIFY function, naming the record type that we are modifying.

   IDMS/R then replaces the data element values in the database with the new data element values in variable storage.

   There are two requirements for successful execution of the MODIFY statement:

1. We must execute a READY statement with one of the UPDATE usage mode options for the area that contains the record we are modifying.
2. We must issue an OBTAIN for the record we are updating before we execute the MODIFY statement.

A MODIFY EXAMPLE

Figure 11.1 shows an example of a program that issues a MODIFY statement. Notice the Input-Player Name data element contains the CALC-key value of the Player record that we are modifying. The Input-Batting-Average data element contains the new value to replace the current value of the Batting-Average data element in the Player record. The program example performs the following functions:

- Moves the value in Input-Player-Name to Player-Name in variable storage.
- Performs a CALC retrieval of the Player record, using the CALC-key value moved from the Input-Player-Name data element to the Player-Name data element.
- Modifies the value of the Batting-Average data element in variable storage.
- Executes a MODIFY statement to replace the data element values in the database record with the values now contained in variable storage.

THE STORE STATEMENT

The STORE statement is used to add a new record occurrence to the database. Adding a new record to the database is a simple three-step process:

1. Construct the new record occurrence in the record's area in variable storage.
2. Establish currency within appropriate occurrences of the set types in which the new

```
01   INPUT-RECORD.
     02   INPUT-PLAYER-NAME          PIC X(30).
     02   INPUT-BATTING-AVERAGE      PIC 9(3).
     .
     .
     .

01   PLAYER-REC.
     02   PLAYER-NAME                PIC X(30).
     02   PLAYER-PHONE               PIC 9(10).
     02   BATTING-AVERAGE            PIC 9(3).
     .
     .
     .

RETRIEVE-ROUTINE.

     MOVE INPUT-PLAYER-NAME TO PLAYER-NAME.

     OBTAIN CALC PLAYER-REC.

     IF DB-STATUS-OK
         PERFORM REPLACE-ROUTINE
     ELSE
         IF DB-REC-NOT-FOUND
             PERFORM RECORD-NOT-FOUND-ROUTINE
         ELSE
             PERFORM IDMS-STATUS.
         .
         .
         .

REPLACE-ROUTINE.

     MOVE INPUT-BATTING-AVERAGE TO BATTING-AVERAGE.

     MODIFY PLAYER-REC.
     PERFORM IDMS-STATUS.
```

Figure 11.1 Example of MODIFY.

record participates as an automatic member. We can use FIND for this purpose, since we do not need the records to be moved to variable storage.

3. Execute the store function, specifying the name of the record type we are adding.

The syntax for the store function is simple; the only required parameter is the name of the record type. The following STORE statement adds a new occurrence of the Player record type:

```
STORE PLAYER-REC.
```

However, IDMS/R must know more than the information we supply in the STORE statement to add the new record occurrence correctly, including the following:

- The location in the database in which the new record occurrence should be written.

- Whether the new record should be made a member of any sets and, if so, to which set occurrences it should be connected.
- Where in the set occurrences the new record should be inserted.

IDMS/R uses record currencies and the attributes assigned to records and sets to obtain this information.

Determining Where to Write the New Record

IDMS/R finds an appropriate location for a new record by examining the location mode defined for the record type being added. If the location mode is CALC, IDMS/R converts the CALC-key value to a database-key value and then stores the new record as close as possible to the calculated page. If the location mode is VIA, IDMS/R finds an optimum location for the new record based on the location of the owner record occurrence in the VIA set type. If the location mode is DIRECT, the program must have previously stored an appropriate database-key value in the IDMS Communications Block. IDMS/R uses this value in finding a place for the record.

Connecting the Record to Sets

IDMS/R next determines the set occurrences in which the new record should be a member and where in each set to insert the record. As shown in Fig. 11.2, the Position record participates in two set types. For this example, suppose it is an automatic member of the Player-Position set and a manual member of the Game-Position set. Before issuing a STORE, the program must establish currency within all the sets in which the new record is an automatic member. Be-

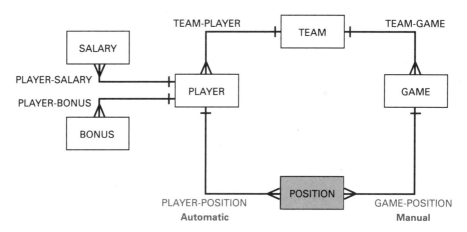

Figure 11.2   Baseball database sets.

fore storing a Position record, we can establish currency within the Player-Position set by accessing the appropriate Player record.

IDMS/R connects the new record to an occurrence of each set for which it is an automatic member; it does not automatically connect it to any sets in which it is a manual member. For sets in which the record is a manual member, the program can locate the appropriate set occurrences and issue CONNECT statements for the record once the record has been stored. We will discuss the CONNECT statement later in this chapter.

Before connecting records to sets, IDMS/R examines the order option for the set. Since the Player-Position set is ordered NEXT, each new Position record occurrence is placed in the set immediately after the record occurrence that is current of the Player-Position set.

To summarize, the STORE statement performs the following functions:

- Acquires space and a database key for a new record occurrence.

- Transfers data element values from variable storage to the database.

- Connects the new record occurrence to all sets in which it participates as an automatic member.

A STORE Example

The program example in Fig. 11.3 shows the use of the STORE function to store a new occurrence of the Position record. We are assuming that the Position record is an automatic member of the Player-Position set and a manual member of the Game-Position set. The input record contains the CALC-key value of the Player owner record with which the new Position record is to be associated. It also contains the data element values that make up the new Position record occurrence. The program performs the following functions:

- Moves the value in Input-Player-Name to Player-Name in variable storage.

- Establishes currency on the appropriate Player-Position set occurrence by performing an OBTAIN CALC for the Player record occurrence, using the CALC-key value moved from the Input-Player-Name data element to the Player-Name data element.

- Stores data element values in the area of variable storage that defines the Position record.

- Executes a STORE statement that names the Position record type.

The new Position record will be automatically connected to the current occurrence of the Player-Position set. The new Position record will not be automatically connected to an occurrence of the Game-Position set. We will have to later use a CONNECT statement to connect the Position record to an appropriate occurrence of the Game-Position set.

```
01  INPUT-RECORD.
    02   INPUT-PLAYER-NAME       PIC X(30).
    02   INPUT-POSITION-NAME     PIC X(10).
    02   INPUT-POSITION-DATE     PIC 9(6).
    .
    .
    .

01  POSITION-REC.
    02   POSITION-NAME           PIC X(10).
    02   POSITION-DATE           PIC 9(6).
    .
    .
    .

STORE-ROUTINE.

    MOVE INPUT-PLAYER-NAME TO PLAYER-NAME.

    OBTAIN CALC PLAYER-REC.

    IF DB-REC-NOT-FOUND
        PERFORM NO-PLAYER-RTN
    ELSE
        PERFORM IDMS-STATUS

        MOVE INPUT-POSITION-NAME TO POSITION-NAME
        MOVE INPUT-POSITION-DATE TO POSITION-DATE

        STORE POSITION-REC
        PERFORM IDMS-STATUS.
        .
        .
        .

NO-PLAYER-RTN.

    MOVE '** NO PLAYER RECORD ** ' TO PRINT-LINE.
    PERFORM WRITE-PLAYER-LINE-RTN.
    GO TO MAINLINE-RTN.
```

Figure 11.3 STORE example.

THE ERASE STATEMENT

The modify and store functions are fairly straightforward; they each operate on a single record occurrence. When we use the erase function, however, the ERASE often affects not only the record that is the object of the ERASE statement but also, in some cases, members of sets owned by that record. The ERASE function gives us a variety of options. If we choose, we can tell IDMS/R to erase a record only if it is not the owner of any nonempty sets. Or we can specify one of three options for erasing owners of nonempty sets. The following four ERASE options are available:

- ERASE
- ERASE PERMANENT MEMBERS
- ERASE SELECTIVE MEMBERS
- ERASE ALL MEMBERS

The ERASE statement with no member option is straightforward. We begin by retrieving the record we want to erase, making it current of run unit. We then issue an ERASE, naming the record type. IDMS/R first disconnects the record from any sets in which it participates as a member. then removes the record occurrence from the database. If the record we are erasing is the owner of any sets, the record will be erased only if those sets are empty. If we try to erase an owner record of a nonempty set, IDMS/R returns an error status code value.

An ERASE Example

In the program example in Fig. 11.4, the Input-Player-Name data element contains the CALC-key value of the Player record to be erased from the database. The program performs the following functions:

- Moves the value of Input-Player-Name to the Player-Name data element in variable storage.
- Issues a CALC retrieval of a Player record, using the CALC-key value moved from Input-Player-Name to Player-Name.
- Executes an ERASE statement for the Player to remove the record from the database.

```
01   INPUT-RECORD.
     02   INPUT-PLAYER-NAME        PIC X(30).
     02   INPUT-POSITION-NAME      PIC X(10).
     02   INPUT-POSITION-DATE      PIC 9(6).
     .
     .
     .
ERASE-ROUTINE.

     MOVE INPUT-PLAYER-NAME TO PLAYER-NAME.

     OBTAIN CALC PLAYER-REC.

     IF DB-STATUS-OK

          ERASE PLAYER-REC
          PERFORM IDMS-STATUS
     ELSE
          IF DB-REC-NOT-FOUND
               PERFORM NO-PLAYER-RTN
          ELSE
               PERFORM IDMS-STATUS
     .
     .
     .
NO-PLAYER-RTN.

     MOVE '** NO PLAYER RECORD ** ' TO PRINT-LINE.
     PERFORM WRITE-PLAYER-LINE-RTN.
     GO TO MAINLINE-RTN.
```

Figure 11.4   ERASE example.

Notice that, in this case, we did not specify a member option in the ERASE. This means that the Player record occurrence will only be erased if it is the owner of an empty set occurrence. We must use one of the other three ERASE options if we want to erase an owner of one or more nonempty sets.

The ERASE ALL Option

Using ERASE ALL first causes the object record to be removed from the database. Then all its members, both mandatory and optional, will be removed, whether or not they are members in other set occurrences. If we execute an ERASE ALL for a Team record, IDMS/R also removes all its member Player records, along with all their members. In this case all the Game records associated with those Player records are removed as well.

The ERASE PERMANENT Option

With the other two ERASE options, the members that are automatically erased depend on whether the members participate in other sets and what the set disconnect options are. Suppose the Baseball database has the disconnect options shown in Fig. 11.5, and we again execute an ERASE PERMANENT for a Team record.

When we use ERASE PERMANENT, IDMS/R erases the record that is the object of the ERASE. It also erases all mandatory members in all sets owned by the object record. It does not erase optional members; it disconnects them instead. If an erased member is the owner of any sets, it is treated as if an ERASE PERMANENT were issued for it. Its mandatory members will be erased, and its optional members disconnected. This process continues until all members have been processed. So in our example, the Team record would be

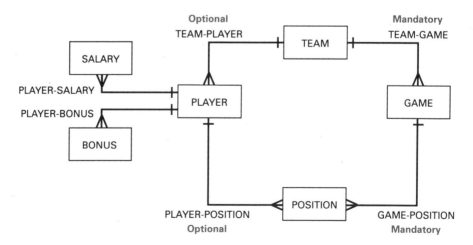

Figure 11.5 Possible disconnect options.

erased and all the Game and Position records removed; the Player records would be disconnected but not erased.

With the membership options that we used in this example and an ERASE PERMANENT, we can disband a team and cancel all its games without releasing all the players from the league.

The ERASE SELECTIVE Option

In some ways, ERASE SELECTIVE works in a similar manner to ERASE PERMANENT. An ERASE SELECTIVE always erases the record that is the object of the ERASE, and it always erases mandatory members in all sets owned by the object record. It also erases optional members if they do not participate in any other sets. If the erased member is the owner of any sets, it is treated as if an ERASE SELECTIVE were issued for it. Its mandatory members will be erased, and its optional members will be erased if they do not participate in any other sets.

To see how members are selectively erased, suppose we change our membership options to make the Position record an optional member in both the Player-Position and Game-Position sets. The top half of Fig. 11.6 shows some of the record occurrences stored in the database before we erase the Game record for July 1. With ERASE SELECTIVE, the Game record would be removed from the database. IDMS/R would then also erase all Position occurrences that were not members in any other set occurrences.

One of the Position records, Left Field, is not a member of any other set occurrence, so it is removed. The two other Position records, Right Field and Third Base, are members of Player-Position set occurrences, so they are only disconnected from the Game-Position set occurrence. The bottom half of Fig. 11.6 shows the database record occurrences and after the Game record is erased.

CHOOSING THE ERASE OPTION　　We must carefully choose the erase option that a program uses. To avoid inadvertent erasing, many installations limit the use of ERASE to only the simple form with no member option specified. Programs that perform the ERASE function must then erase records from the bottom up, explicitly erasing member occurrences in a set before the owner record itself can be erased. This makes for more complex update programs, but there is less possibility that needed records will be erased accidentally.

THE CONNECT AND DISCONNECT FUNCTIONS　　The CONNECT function can be used in conjunction with STORE for records that must be manually connected to sets. The DISCONNECT and CONNECT functions are also often used together to move a

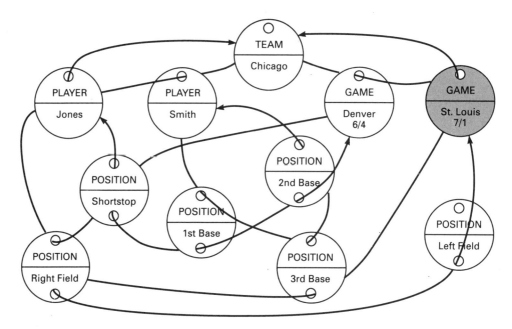

Database records before issuing an ERASE statement for a Game record

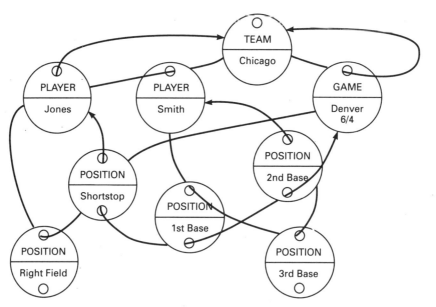

Database records after issuing an ERASE SELECTIVE statement for a Game record

Figure 11.6 Removing a Game record using an ERASE SELECTIVE statement.

record occurrence from one set occurrence to another. DISCONNECT removes the record occurrence that is current of run unit from the named set; CONNECT connects the record that is current of run unit to the named set.

A CONNECT EXAMPLE

The CONNECT statement names both a record type and a set type. The CONNECT function causes the record that is current of the named record type to be connected to the set occurrence that is current of the named set type. Figure 11.7 shows the program code for a CONNECT example in which we add a

```
01   INPUT-RECORD.
     02   INPUT-TEAM-NAME         PIC X(20).
     02   INPUT-PLAYER-NAME       PIC X(30).
     02   INPUT-PLAYER-PHONE      PIC 9(10).
     02   INPUT-BATTING-AVERAGE   PIC 9(10).
     .
     .
     .

01   TEAM-REC.
     02   TEAM-NAME               PIC X(20).
     02   TEAM-PHONE              PIC 9(10).
     02   TEAM-CITY               PIC X(20).
01   PLAYER-REC.
     02   PLAYER-NAME             PIC X(30).
     02   PLAYER-PHONE            PIC 9(10).
     02   BATTING-AVERAGE         PIC 9(3).
     .
     .
     .

CONNECT-ROUTINE.

     MOVE INPUT-TEAM-NAME TO TEAM-NAME.

     OBTAIN CALC TEAM-REC.

     IF DB-STATUS-OK
         PERFORM STORE-ROUTINE
     ELSE
         IF DB-REC-NOT-FOUND
             PERFORM RECORD-NOT-FOUND-ROUTINE
         ELSE
             PERFORM IDMS-STATUS.
     .
     .
     .

STORE-ROUTINE.

     MOVE INPUT-PLAYER-NAME      TO PLAYER-NAME.
     MOVE INPUT-PLAYER-PHONE     TO PLAYER-PHONE.
     MOVE INPUT-BATTING-AVERAGE  TO BATTING-AVERAGE.

     STORE PLAYER-REC.
     PERFORM IDMS-STATUS.

     CONNECT PLAYER-REC TO TEAM-PLAYER.
     PERFORM IDMS-STATUS.
```

Figure 11.7 CONNECT example.

Player record and then connect it to an occurrence of the Team-Player set, thus adding the player to the team. In this example, the Input-Team-Name data element contains the CALC-key value of the Team owner record with which the new Player record is to be associated. We are assuming that the Player record is a manual member of the Team-Player set. The program performs the following functions:

- Moves the value in Input-Team-Name to the Team-Name data element in variable storage.

- Performs a CALC retrieval of a Team record, using the CALC-key value moved from the Input-Team-Name data element to the Team-Name data element. (A FIND could be used here instead of an OBTAIN.)

- Moves data element values for the new Player record into the appropriate areas of variable storage.

- Issues a STORE function to create a new Player record occurrence.

- Issues a CONNECT function to connect the new Player record to the current Team-Player set occurrence.

A DISCONNECT EXAMPLE

Figure 11.8 shows the use of the DISCONNECT statement. The DISCONNECT statement cancels the membership of a record in a set occurrence in which it currently participates as a member. The record that is the object of a DISCONNECT function must be defined as an *optional* member of that set; otherwise, IDMS/R returns an error status code. Notice that the Input-Team-Name and Input-Player-Name data elements contain CALC-key values. The program disconnects the indicated Player record from the occurrence of the Team-Player set in which it is now a member. It then reconnects that Player record to a new Team-Player set occurrence, indicated by the Team-Name value in the input record. The program performs the following functions:

- Moves the value in Input-Player-Name to the Player-Name data element in variable storage.

- Issues a CALC retrieval of the Player record, using the CALC-key value moved from Input-Player-Name to Player-Name.

- Disconnects the retrieved Player record from the Team-Player set occurrence in which it is currently a member.

- Moves the value in Input-Team-Name to the Team-Name data element in variable storage.

- Issues a CALC retrieval of the owner of the Team-Player set occurrence, using the CALC-key value moved from Input-Team-Name to Team-Name.

- Connects the Player record to the current Team-Player set occurrence.

```
01    INPUT-RECORD.
      02    INPUT-TEAM-NAME         PIC X(20).
      02    INPUT-PLAYER-NAME       PIC X(30).
      .
      .
      .

01    TEAM-REC.
      02    TEAM-NAME               PIC X(20).
      02    TEAM-PHONE              PIC 9(10).
      02    TEAM-CITY               PIC X(20).
01    PLAYER-REC.
      02    PLAYER-NAME             PIC X(30).
      02    PLAYER-PHONE            PIC 9(10).
      02    BATTING-AVERAGE         PIC 9(3).
      .
      .
      .

RETRIEVE-ROUTINE.

      MOVE INPUT-PLAYER-NAME TO PLAYER-NAME.

      OBTAIN CALC PLAYER-REC.

      IF DB-STATUS-OK
          PERFORM DISCONNECT-ROUTINE.
      .
      .
      .

DISCONNECT-ROUTINE.

      DISCONNECT PLAYER-REC FROM TEAM-PLAYER.
      PERFORM IDMS-STATUS.

      MOVE INPUT-TEAM-NAME TO TEAM-NAME.

      OBTAIN CALC TEAM-REC.

      IF DB-STATUS-OK
          PERFORM RECONNECT-ROUTINE.
          .
          .
          .

RECONNECT-ROUTINE.

      CONNECT PLAYER-REC TO TEAM-PLAYER.
      PERFORM IDMS-STATUS.
```

Figure 11.8 DISCONNECT example.

Note that in the previous example, after we have issued a DISCONNECT for a record occurrence, the disconnected record is still in the database. It can still be accessed by using appropriate retrieval techniques.

TESTING FOR SET MEMBERSHIP

There are times when we would like to determine if record occurrences are members of a particular set occurrence. The program example in Fig. 11.9 walks

```
OBTAIN FIRST POSITION-REC WITHIN GAME-POSITION.
PERFORM IDMS-STATUS.
PERFORM GET-POSITION-ROUTINE
    UNTIL DB-END-OF-SET.
    .
    .
    .
GET-POSITION-ROUTINE.

IF NOT PLAYER-POSITION MEMBER
    PERFORM PRINT-POSITION-ROUTINE.

OBTAIN NEXT POSITION-REC WITHIN GAME-POSITION.
```

Figure 11.9 Testing for set membership.

```
OBTAIN FIRST GAME-REC WITHIN TEAM-GAME.

PERFORM IDMS-STATUS.
PERFORM GET-GAME-ROUTINE
    UNTIL DB-END-OF-SET.
    .
    .
    .
GET-GAME-ROUTINE.

IF GAME-POSITION EMPTY
    ERASE GAME-REC.

OBTAIN NEXT GAME WITHIN TEAM-GAME.
```

Figure 11.10 Testing for an empty set.

an occurrence of the Game-Position set and lists the contents of the Position record occurrences that are not members of any occurrence of the Player-Position set. This allows us to determine which positions have not yet been assigned to players.

TESTING FOR AN EMPTY SET   It is also often useful to know which sets are *empty,* that is, do not have any members. The program example in Fig. 11.10 walks an occurrence of the Team-Game set and erases all Game record occurrences that do not have any Position member records associated with them.

SUMMARY   DML statements are available for adding, deleting, and modifying database records and for changing the set relationships in which records participate. Prior to issuing DML statements that modify database records, the program must ready the database area using an appropriate UPDATE usage mode option. To modify an existing record, the program performs an OBTAIN to establish currency on the record and move a copy of it to variable storage. After changing the desired values in storage, the program issues a MODIFY to replace data element values in the database. To add a new record to the database, the program constructs a new occurrence of the record in variable storage, establishes appropriate currencies, and executes a STORE to add the record to the database. To ERASE a record, the program must establish it as current of run unit, typically by performing an OBTAIN. It then issues an ERASE for the record. There are four ERASE variations. ERASE with no member option disconnects the record from sets and then removes it from the database only if there are no members in any sets it owns. ERASE ALL removes all members of all sets owned by the erase record. ERASE PERMANENT erases all mandatory members in sets owned by the record; optional members are only disconnected from the set occurrence owned by the record being erased. ERASE SELECTIVE, in addition to erasing mandatory members in all sets owned by the erased record, erases optional members not participating in any other set. CONNECT is used to connect a record manually to a set occurrence. DISCONNECT disconnects a record from a set occurrence.

12 RECOVERY AND RESTART

In this chapter, we discuss the facilities that IDMS/R provides for recovering from problem situations and for restarting after failures occur. These facilities include procedures that IDMS/R automatically invokes when certain types of failures occur and also services that application programs use to handle restart and recovery. We begin this chapter by discussing the two operating environments in which an IDMS/R run unit can execute. We will then see how these operating environments affect recovery and restart considerations.

IDMS/R OPERATING ENVIRONMENTS

It is possible to run an IDMS/R application program in two operating environments: *local mode* or *central version*. All online applications that use IDMS/DC or some other telecommunications monitor to control access to remote terminals must run under central version. An application program that operates in batch mode can be run either under the control of central version or in local mode.

The mode in which a particular application program is run is generally chosen by the systems programming or database administration group and is not of concern to the application developer. However, the mode in which the application executes determines the restart and recovery facilities that are available to it.

Central Version

In most situations, the preferred method of running an IDMS/R application is under the control of IDMS/R central version. With central version, a single copy of the IDMS/R DBMS controls the operation of a particular set of IDMS/R application program run units. With central version, a single DMCL module defines all database areas that will be accessed by all the run units that will execute under a particular IDMS/R central version. Multiple copies of IDMS/R central version can execute in the same computing system with each copy normally accessing a different set of database areas; no two central versions are allowed to update the same database area. All the run units that will execute under the control of a particular central version are chosen so that they all access the same group of database areas. Central version implements facilities for recovering from system failures and for automatically restarting aborted run units.

Local Mode

A batch program that operates in local mode has its own copy of the IDMS/R DBMS loaded into its partition, region, or address space. A local mode run unit operates independently of any other IDMS/R run units that may be operating in the system at the same time. In general, an application runs faster when run in local mode, but IDMS/R provides no automatic restart and recovery facilities for local mode applications. Batch retrieval programs are good candidates for running in local mode, since they do not ordinarily require automatic restart and recovery facilities.

JOURNAL FILES   IDMS/R maintains a set of journal files that can be used to recover from failures and to restart aborted run units. An IDMS/R application can choose to write the journal files to direct access data sets, to tape files, or to ignore completely the journaling facility. IDMS/R provides automatic restart and recovery facilities only for run units that operate under the control of central version, and then only when the run unit writes the journal files to direct access data sets. Applications, either central version or local mode, that write tape journal files can use the journal files to restart manually an aborted run unit. Applications that bypass the journaling facilities are responsible for their own restart processing.

When a run unit begins by issuing the BIND RUN-UNIT statement, IDMS/R writes a *begin* checkpoint record on a journal file. A *checkpoint record* contains information about the current status of the run unit. As a run unit executes, it may update records in the database. As IDMS/R processes each update request, it writes to the journal file a before image and an after image of the updated record. When the application ends the run unit by executing a FINISH statement, IDMS/R writes out an *end* checkpoint record. At the conclusion of the run unit, the journal file contains a *begin* checkpoint, before and after images of all updated records, and an *end* checkpoint.

RECOVERY/RESTART   There are many types of situations that may require recovery and restart processing. A program may cause an error that causes the run unit to be abnormally terminated. IDMS/R may also encounter situations that require it to terminate abnormally one or more run units. For example, IDMS/R may terminate a run unit after a wait time limit has been exceeded to prevent deadlocks from occurring. If a run unit is abnormally terminated after it has updated one or more database records, IDMS/R works backward in the journal file until it reaches the *begin* checkpoint record and uses the information in the before record images to reverse the effect of the database updates already made by the aborted run unit. The run unit can then be restarted from the beginning.

INTERMEDIATE CHECKPOINTS

All run units that terminate normally create at least two checkpoint records on the journal file, a *begin* checkpoint when the READY statement is executed and an *end* checkpoint when the FINISH statement is executed. The before and after record images that are recorded between these two checkpoints constitute a record of all the updating the run unit performed. The processing that a unit performs between checkpoints is called a *recovery unit*. In the simplest case, the entire run unit constitutes a single recovery unit. Many online applications operate in this manner. A separate run unit may be started to process each incoming transaction. In such a case, no more than a few database updates are processed during the execution of each run unit, and each run unit constitutes a single recovery unit.

In some situations, a single online run unit may process many transactions and perform many database updates. Batch applications are even more likely to make a great many updates during the execution of a single run unit. In such situations, it is often necessary to divide a run unit into multiple recovery units to reduce the time that it takes to recover from a run unit failure. To create intermediate checkpoints, the run unit periodically issues a COMMIT statement to make permanent all database updates that the run unit has already made:

```
COMMIT.
```

There is another form of the COMMIT statement that is used in some cases:

```
COMMIT ALL.
```

Whether the run unit issues a COMMIT or a COMMIT ALL depends on how the run unit would like to treat the locks that IDMS/R places on records. The COMMIT statement causes IDMS/R to release all locks except for those that are placed on current records; COMMIT ALL releases all record locks. Record locking facilities are discussed in Chapter 13.

Both forms of the COMMIT statement cause IDMS/R to write a *commit* checkpoint on the journal file. If the run unit is later abnormally terminated after it has issued a COMMIT statement, IDMS/R again works backward in the journal file and uses the information in the before record images to reverse the effect of changes that the run unit made. This time, however, IDMS/R stops at the *commit* checkpoint rather than proceeding all the way back to the *begin* checkpoint that was written when the run unit began. Now, when the run unit is restarted, it can be restarted from the point at which it wrote the most recent *commit* checkpoint.

Many different techniques can be used for determining how often a COMMIT statement should be executed. One simple technique is simply to count the number of updates the run unit processes. Every one hundred updates or so, the run unit might issue a COMMIT statement, causing IDMS/R to write an intermediate checkpoint to the journal file.

RECOVERING FROM FAILURES

If the run unit is operating under the control of central version and is writing the journal files to direct access data sets, IDMS/R handles all the processing that is necessary to roll back database changes and to restart run units that it aborts. No special application programming is necessary to invoke the automatic recovery and restart facilities in the central version environment with journal files written to direct access data sets.

In the local mode environment and in the central version environment with tape journal files, IDMS/R provides utility programs to handle manual restarting of aborted applications. The Cullinet documentation can be consulted to see how manual restarting can be handled. Applications that cannot use the central version automatic recovery and restart facilities and that would like to restart from *commit* checkpoints must provide appropriate application logic to handle restart processing.

For example, suppose a batch application is reading transactions from a sequential transaction file and processing database updates based on the data read from the transaction file. The application issues a COMMIT statement to write a *commit* checkpoint every few hundred updates. Suppose the application now fails. A utility program can be run that backs out the changes that the program made up to the previous commit checkpoint that the aborted run unit wrote to the journal file. To restart the run unit, the run unit must contain application logic that will reposition the transaction file at the appropriate point so the run unit will reapply the changes that were backed out. It may also need to reestablish the appropriate positions within the database to resume processing at the appropriate point in the database.

Run units that must be capable of restarting from a checkpoint often write a special restart record in the database at the time that it issues each COMMIT statement. The restart record contains all the information that the run unit needs to reestablish all positions and reinitialize itself to be able to restart properly from the checkpoint.

THE ROLLBACK VERB

In some cases, a program may itself determine during program processing that it needs to back out the changes that it has made to the database since it wrote the most recent checkpoint record. In the central version environment with journal files written to direct access data sets, the program can request that IDMS/R do this automatically by simply abnormally terminating the run unit. If we would like to back out the changes but not abend the run unit, we can issue a ROLLBACK statement. We have two options when we issue the ROLLBACK.

The simplest form is the unqualified form of the statement:

```
ROLLBACK.
```

This form of the ROLLBACK statement causes IDMS/R to write a checkpoint record to the journal file, nullify all currencies, automatically restore the database using the before images from the journal, and terminate the run unit. After issuing the unqualified ROLLBACK, to access the database again, we must re-issue the BIND/READY sequence.

The following is a second form of the ROLLBACK statement that a program can issue:

```
ROLLBACK CONTINUE.
```

If we issue this statement, IDMS/R restores the database but does not terminate the run unit. We may now access the database immediately without reissuing the BIND/READY sequence.

SUMMARY

Maintaining database integrity requires facilities for recovering from problem situations and for restarting after failures occur. IDMS/R addresses this need by providing recovery/restart facilities. A key feature of recovery/restart is journaling. Journaling uses a tape or disk file to capture before and after images of records as they are being updated. Checkpoints are written to the journal to mark the beginning and end of a recovery unit. If a run unit abnormally terminates, IDMS/R uses the journal file to back out changes made since the last checkpoint. The COMMIT statement is used to write checkpoints as frequently as desired. ROLLBACK allows a program to back out database changes without abnormally terminating the run unit.

13 LOCKING FACILITIES

IDMS/R provides locking facilities for controlling access to areas and to individual records when two or more run units require access to the same database areas. IDMS/R provides three levels of locks. *Area locks* are used to protect the database areas that are under the control of a particular central version or a local mode run unit, *area usage modes* control how the database areas under the control of a single central version can be accessed, and *record locks* prevent individual record occurrences from being updated concurrently by more than one run unit. We begin this chapter with a discussion of area locks.

AREA LOCKS   IDMS/R uses area locks to prevent areas from being updated by more than one IDMS/R central version or by more than one application running in local mode. When a particular IDMS/R central version or an application running in local mode begins executing, IDMS/R examines each area that will be accessed to see if any area locks have been placed on them.

If an area lock is already set on an area that is required by a local mode application, that local mode application abends; if no locks are set on the required areas, those areas are locked by the local mode application, and no other local mode application or IDMS/R central version will be given access to those areas. An area lock that is placed on an area by a local mode application is released when that local mode application executes its FINISH statement.

If an area lock is already set on an area that is required by an IDMS/R central version, the execution of that central version continues, but no run unit executing under the control of that central version will be given access to the already locked area. The area is said to be *varied offline* to that central version. Run units that attempt to access an area that is varied offline are abnormally terminated. All areas that are required by a particular central version and are not already locked when central version execution begins are locked by that central version. All run units that execute under the control of that central version can then access those areas. No other local mode application or central version will be given access to locked areas. An area that is locked by a particular central version is released only when the central version is shut down or when the area is varied offline.

AREA USAGE MODES   All the run units that operate under the control of a particular IDMS/R central version can access the same set of database areas. In the central version environment, IDMS/R provides a set of usage mode options to control the way in which database areas are accessed by the run units executing under the control of the central version. The six possible usage modes for a database area are as follows:

- Retrieval
- Protected retrieval
- Exclusive retricval
- Update
- Protected update
- Exclusive update

The subschema can specify a default usage mode for each database area that the run unit accesses. A run unit that does not explicitly execute READY statements for the areas that it accesses will use the default usage modes specified in the subschema. Alternatively, the run unit can specify an explicit usage mode by issuing a READY statement for each area that it accesses, as in the following example:

```
READY TEAM-AREA USAGE-MODE IS RETRIEVAL.
READY PLAYER-AREA USAGE-MODE IS PROTECTED UPDATE.
```

Note, however, that if a run unit issues a READY statement for one area, it must issue a READY statement for each of the other areas it needs to access. Also, the default usage mode specified in the subschema may prohibit an area from being readied in certain usage modes. The following is a brief description of each of the six usage mode options:

- **Usage mode is RETRIEVAL.** With the RETRIEVAL or SHARED RETRIEVAL usage modes, we are requesting retrieval access to the area, and we are specifying that other run units executing under the control of our central version will also be allowed to retrieve or update records in the same area.

- **Usage mode is PROTECTED RETRIEVAL.** With the PROTECTED RE-TRIEVAL usage mode, we are requesting retrieval access to the area, and we are specifying that no other run unit should *update* the records in the same area for the duration of our run unit. However, other run units executing under the control of our central version can retrieve the records in the area as long as they did not specify a usage mode of EXCLUSIVE for the same area. If another run unit is already updating the records in the area, our run unit will wait until that run unit finishes.

- **Usage mode is EXCLUSIVE RETRIEVAL.** With the EXCLUSIVE RE-TRIEVAL usage mode, we are requesting retrieval access, and we are specifying that no other run unit be allowed to retrieve or update records in the area while our run unit executes. If other run units are already accessing the area, our run unit will wait until all other run units finish with the area. There are few cases where concurrent retrieval of the records in an area will cause problems, so this usage mode is not often used.

- **Usage mode is UPDATE.** With the UPDATE usage mode option, also called shared update mode, we are requesting update access to the area, and we are specifying that other run units also be allowed to retrieve or update records in the area as long as they do not specify the PROTECTED or EXCLUSIVE options in their READY statements.

- **Usage mode is PROTECTED UPDATE.** With the PROTECTED UPDATE usage mode option, we are requesting update access to the area, and we are specifying that no other run unit should be able to update records while our run unit executes. Other run units may also be allowed to *retrieve* records in the same area or areas as long as they do not specify the PROTECTED or EXCLU-SIVE usage mode options. If another run unit is already updating the records in the area, or if other run units are accessing the area with the PROTECTED RE-TRIEVAL or EXCLUSIVE RETRIEVAL usage mode, our run unit will wait until all other run units finish with the area.

- **Usage mode is EXCLUSIVE UPDATE.** With the EXCLUSIVE UPDATE us-age mode option, we are requesting update access to the area, and we are spec-ifying that no other run unit should either retrieve or update records in the area while our run unit executes. This essentially gives the run unit exclusive use of the area.

RECORD LOCKS

Usage mode options that give a run unit controlled access to database areas provide effective control over updating problems when two or more run units are allowed to access the same set of areas. However, for run units that remain in execution for long pe-riods of time, preventing other run units from accessing the same areas can cause systemwide performance problems. When we use usage mode options that allow more than one run unit to access the same area while updating is taking place, IDMS/R sets *implicit record locks* to prevent the same record from being concurrently updated by two or more run units. We can also include options in

DML statements to set explicit record locks. Implicit record locks are only maintained for run units operating under central version. Central version always maintains record locks for run units executing in shared update mode. When central version is generated, an option can be specified to set implicit record locks on run units operating in shared retrieval and protected update usage modes. Record locks are never maintained for run units operating in local mode. In local mode, concurrent updates are prevented by setting locks on entire areas.

IMPLICIT RECORD LOCKS

There are two types of implicit record locks: *implicit shared record locks* and *implicit exclusive record locks*. Implicit shared and exclusive record locks work in a similar manner to the PROTECTED and EXCLUSIVE area usage modes, except that they protect individual record occurrences rather than entire areas. An implicit *shared* record lock is used to guarantee that only one run unit at a time will be allowed to *update* a specific record occurrence; any number of run units will be allowed to *retrieve* a record protected by a shared record lock. An implicit *exclusive* record lock is used to guarantee that no other run unit can either update or retrieve the record while the exclusive lock is in effect.

Implicit locks are placed on records as they are made current of run unit, record type, set type, and area. An implicit *shared* lock is placed on a record when it is retrieved, and an implicit *exclusive* lock is placed on a record when it is accessed via one of the DML update functions. In this way, IDMS/R guarantees that only one run unit at a time will be allowed to access a record that is being updated, but that any number of run units will be allowed to retrieve a given record.

Implicit shared locks remain in effect until currency changes; implicit exclusive locks remain in effect until the run unit ends or until the run unit executes a COMMIT statement. (See Chapter 12.)

In many cases, implicit locks are sufficient to maintain database integrity and to ensure that application systems operate correctly; in other cases, they are not. An example will illustrate how implicit locks operate.

IMPLICIT LOCK EXAMPLE

In this example, the local managers for two different teams, the Rockford Rookies and the Zanesville Zephyrs, are trying to update some information on Louie Spitz. He happened to play for both teams this year, having been traded in midseason. Figure 13.1 illustrates the following sequence of events that occur when both managers, using different terminals, decide to update Spitz's Player record at the same time:

1. Run unit 1 retrieves the Player record for Spitz. IDMS/R places an implicit shared lock on the Spitz record.

Run Unit 1   Run Unit 2

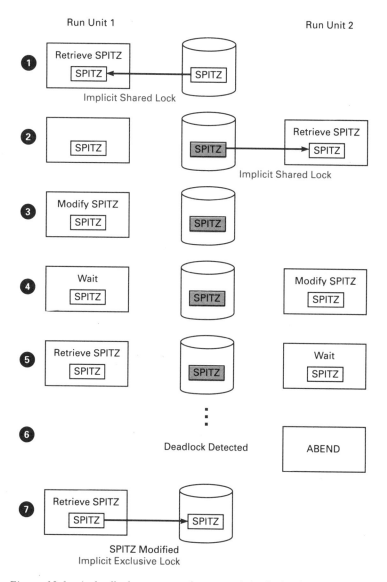

Figure 13.1 A deadlock can occur because of the locks that IDMS/R sets when two run units retrieve and attempt to modify the same record occurrence.

153

2. Run unit 2 retrieves the Player record for Spitz. Since a shared lock does not prevent other run units from accessing a record, IDMS/R gives the record to run unit 2. IDMS/R places another shared record lock on the Spitz record on behalf of run unit 2.

3. Run unit 1 issues a MODIFY function to change the home address for Spitz to Rockford. Since run unit 2 has placed a shared lock on the record, run unit 1 is not allowed to update the record. Run unit 1 waits.

4. Run unit 2 issues a MODIFY function to change the home address for Spitz to Zanesville. Since run unit 1 has also locked the record, run unit 2 also waits.

5. Since each run unit is now waiting for a record that the other run unit locked, a deadlock has occurred.

6. Sensing a deadlock, IDMS/R automatically abends run unit 2 to recover.

7. The lock set by run unit 2 is now removed, the MODIFY issued by run unit 1 is allowed to complete, and IDMS/R sets an implicit exclusive lock on the record until run unit 1 ends.

In the preceding example, IDMS/R automatically maintained the integrity of the database and prevented both managers from updating Spitz's address at the same time. In our application, this approach works adequately. However, in a high-volume application such as an airline reservation system, abnormally terminating a run unit would be an inefficient method of handling a common reservation system problem: contention for the same seat. Explicit locks provide a better way of handling the same situation.

SETTING EXPLICIT RECORD LOCKS

The most common method that is used to set an explicit record lock is to code the KEEP clause in the DML statement that we are using to retrieve the record. Following are two examples of CALC retrievals during which locks are set on the retrieved Player record. The first example sets a shared lock:

```
OBTAIN KEEP CALC PLAYER-REC.
```

The next example sets an exclusive lock:

```
OBTAIN KEEP EXCLUSIVE CALC PLAYER-REC.
```

In either case, the lock remains set until we either end the run unit by executing the FINISH statement or we execute a COMMIT statement.

THE KEEP STATEMENT

As an alternative to coding the KEEP clause in the OBTAIN statement, we can issue a separate KEEP statement to set a lock on a record *after* retrieving it. Following are examples of the eight forms of the KEEP statement that we can code:

- KEEP CURRENT. Sets an explicit shared lock on the record that is current of run unit.
- KEEP EXCLUSIVE CURRENT. Sets an explicit exclusive lock on the record that is current of run unit.
- KEEP CURRENT PLAYER-REC. Sets an explicit shared lock on the record that is current of the Player record type.
- KEEP EXCLUSIVE CURRENT PLAYER-REC. Sets an explicit exclusive lock on the record that is current of the Player record type.
- KEEP CURRENT WITHIN PLAYER-TEAM. Sets an explicit shared lock on the record that is current of the Player-Team set type.
- KEEP EXCLUSIVE CURRENT WITHIN PLAYER-TEAM. Sets an explicit exclusive lock on the record that is current of the Player-Team set type.
- KEEP CURRENT WITHIN PLAYER-AREA. Sets an explicit shared lock on the record that is current of the Player-Area area.
- KEEP EXCLUSIVE CURRENT WITHIN PLAYER-AREA. Sets an explicit exclusive lock on the record that is current of the Player-Area area.

EXPLICIT LOCK EXAMPLE

We will now look at what happens when two run units attempt to update the same record when explicit locks are used to protect the records. In Fig. 13.2, each run unit places, at retrieval time, an exclusive record lock on the Player record. This is now the sequence of events:

1. Run unit 1 retrieves the Player record.
2. Run unit 1 places an explicit exclusive lock on the Player record just retrieved.
3. Run unit 2 attempts to retrieve the record.
4. Since run unit 1 has already placed an exclusive lock on the Spitz record, run unit 2 waits.
5. Run unit 1 issues a MODIFY to update address information for the Spitz record.
6. Run unit 1 issues a FINISH, and IDMS/R releases the lock on the Spitz record.
7. Run unit 2 is now allowed to retrieve the Spitz record. Now that the address has been updated, the Zanesville manager will see the record with the latest address information and can make a determination as to whether the address should still be updated.

In this example, had run unit 2 retrieved the record before run unit 1 had placed its exclusive lock on it, a deadlock would have occurred. It is usually best to set the lock by coding the appropriate option in the OBTAIN statement as described earlier.

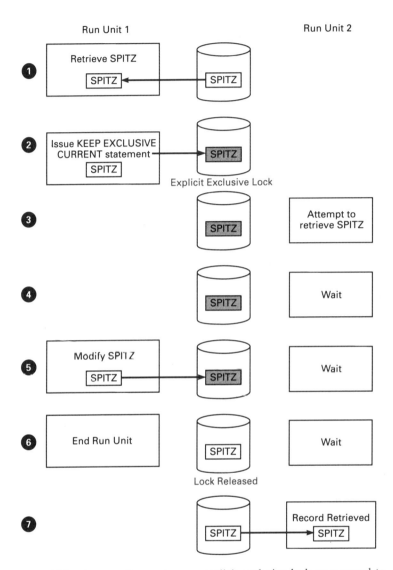

Figure 13.2   A run unit can place an explicit exclusive lock on a record to prevent any other run unit from retrieving it until the first run unit releases the lock.

DESIGNING LOCKS   The two examples we looked at showing the differences between using implicit versus explicit record locking illustrated that the needs of the individual application dictate the types of locks that are required to produce the desired results. Although in the cases we looked at, the two applications achieved similar results, in general, the system operates with less disruption when explicit locks are used.

If the probability is very low that the same record will be updated concurrently by two or more run units, implicit locks may give all the protection that is needed. A very occasional abend may not cause problems.

On the other hand, the probability is sometimes very high that contention problems will occur. Consider an airline reservations system where two agents may try to book a seat in the smoking section of first class on a crowded flight. Explicit record locks may be required for proper system operation.

In many cases, explicit locks may even be required to ensure data integrity. For example, a run unit can retrieve a record, retrieve other records of the same type, and then want to come back to the first record and update it. If the program expects the record to be unchanged from the time it was first accessed, the program must place an explicit lock on it at the time it is first retrieved. Implicit shared locks are maintained only until currency changes.

Choosing between implicit locks and explicit locks is an important design issue. In making this determination, the analyst or programmer needs to assess the probability of contention for one record and the degree of importance of ensuring data integrity in a given application.

SUMMARY   IDMS/R provides locking facilities to control access
                             to areas and records. Three levels of locking are provided. Area locks protect areas from being accessed by more than one IDMS/R central version or by more than one application running in local mode. Area usage modes control access to an area by the run units that are under the control of a single central version. Record locks protect individual records from concurrent update by more than one run unit running under the control of a single central version. Implicit record locks are set automatically by IDMS/R. Implicit shared locks allow different run units to retrieve, but not update, a record occurrence. Implicit exclusive locks prevent a run unit from even retrieving a record while some other run unit has a lock in effect. Explicit locks are locks that are set by a run unit by including a KEEP clause in a retrieval statement or by executing a KEEP DML statement. By using explicit locks, run units can better control locking to prevent system disruptions.

PART IV ADS/ONLINE

14 THE ADS/ONLINE ENVIRONMENT

The tools provided in the ADS/OnLine environment are designed to let the application developer efficiently design and implement the various components of an online application. ADS/OnLine can be used to rapidly build prototypes that can be tried out by the end users. The prototypes can be quickly refined, and when the users are satisfied with them, they can be converted to production systems. ADS/OnLine provides a complete environment for improving application development productivity. Following are some of the features incorporated by ADS/OnLine to simplify application development and execution:

- **Data dictionary integration.** ADS/OnLine is fully integrated with the *integrated data dictionary (IDD)*. ADS/OnLine applications and their data definitions and screen formats used in ADS/OnLine applications are stored in the data dictionary.

- **Modularity.** Each component of an ADS/OnLine application is defined and maintained separately and can be used in many different applications. ADS/OnLine applications are inherently modular because they are composed of discrete data-entry and response dialogs.

- **Online application definition.** ADS/OnLine applications are defined online using a terminal and can be executed immediately. The application developer is notified of errors and can correct mistakes before completing the definition.

- **High-level language facilities.** ADS/OnLine implements a high-level language that meets both simple and complex processing requirements.

- **Online screen formatting.** The application developer uses an online tool to design terminal screens. The system components that define screen formats are called *maps*. An online mapping facility allows screen maps to be quickly created and tailored to meet end-user requirements.

- **Automatic editing and error handling.** The application developer can supply criteria used to edit data and handle errors that occur during editing. ADS/On-

Line uses these criteria to format data for display and to verify that data entered by the terminal operator is valid.

- **Application design and prototyping.** ADS/OnLine's application design tools give the developer access to system-built menus, predefined processing procedures, and security mechanisms. Using these facilities, the application developer can create the application's structure and establish the flow of control without writing any processing code.

- **Security facilities.** Security controls can be enforced at multiple levels with ADS/OnLine. The application developer can prevent unauthorized users from signing on to the ADS/OnLine system and can restrict access to specific applications and functions. Data dictionary security facilities can also be used to restrict or limit access to data and ADS/OnLine facilities during application definition.

ADS/ONLINE DIALOGS

A segment of an application that relates to one screen display, or map, is called a *dialog*. Each dialog can be associated with a database subschema, and most applications consist of multiple dialogs that are hierarchically associated with one another. A dialog can be used in different places in one application and can be included in multiple applications.

The more complex processing logic of an application is handled with segments of procedural code. The procedural code is written with a flexible high-level process command language that has some similarity to COBOL but is easier to use. The ADS/OnLine process command language is described in Chapter 16. Functions developed outside of the ADS/OnLine environment, with other languages such as COBOL or PL/I, can be linked into the ADS/OnLine procedural code.

ADS/ONLINE DEVELOPMENT TOOLS

ADS/OnLine provides a set of three development tools that enable segments of the user terminal screen interaction to be built quickly. Each of the tools is used online at a terminal. With each of these tools, formatted screens guide the developer through the steps of the application development process. All of the tools share a common general format, which helps to make them easy to learn. Both fast and slow modes are supported to suit the needs of beginners as well as experienced developers. The three tools are discussed in detail in Chapters 15 and 17 and are briefly described here:

- **ADS/OnLine application generator (ADSA).** The developer uses ADSA to lay out the overall flow of control of a complete *application*. ADSA can be used as an automatic prototyping tool. (See Chapter 15.)

- **ADS/OnLine dialog generator (ADSG).** The developer uses ADSG to define individual *dialogs*, the application components that define the processing performed by the application. (See Chapter 17.)
- **IDMS-DC/UCF OnLine mapping facility (OLM).** The developer uses OLM to design and generate *maps*, the application components that define the format of the screens displayed by the application. (See Chapter 17.)

In addition to these three online tools, ADS/OnLine provides a *batch dialog generator* that the developer can use to create or modify ADS/OnLine applications in the batch mode. A *runtime system* is also provided to control online applications once they have been created. The ADS/OnLine runtime system is discussed in Chapter 17.

APPLICATION STRUCTURE

The basic building blocks of an ADS/OnLine application are end-user interactions that can be easily combined to form complex online systems. The structure of the application matches the flow of interactions within the system. This modular structure, in which the modules correspond to specific user interactions, is easy to understand, maintain, and enhance over the life of the system.

ADS/OnLine processing logic is not hidden in blocks of procedural code. Rather, each piece of procedural code is tied to a specific online transaction. The procedural logic is used to define the operation to be performed in each interactive dialog.

An ADS/OnLine *application* is a named set of system components that perform a specific business task. The main building blocks that make up an ADS/OnLine application are called *functions* and *responses*. Figure 14.1 illustrates the overall structure of a typical ADS/OnLine application. The boxes represent the functions that are performed by the application; the circles represent the possible responses that terminal operators can make to each function. Chapter 15 describes in detail how the overall structure of an ADS/OnLine application is specified using the ADS/OnLine application generator.

FUNCTIONS

Functions are named procedures that are performed by an application. Following are the six types of functions that ADS/OnLine supports:

- **Menu functions.** A menu function does no processing other than to display a screen that lists the options available to the terminal operator. Menu functions use system-defined screen maps that are built automatically by the ADS/OnLine runtime system.

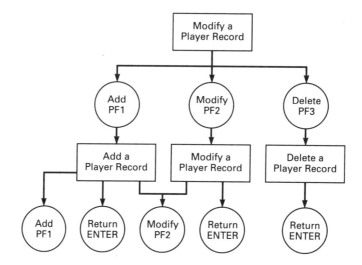

Figure 14.1   ADS/OnLine typical application structure.

- **Dialog functions.** A dialog function performs user-defined application processing, such as data retrieval or updating.
- **Menu/Dialog functions.** A menu/dialog function is a dialog that includes as part of its processing the display of a menu screen. Menu/dialog functions can use either system-defined or user-defined menu maps.
- **User Program functions.** A user program function is a program that is developed outside of the ADS/OnLine environment by using some other programming language, such as COBOL or PL/I.
- **Internal functions.** An internal function is a function performed within a dialog function.
- **System functions.** A system function is a function that is supplied with the ADS/OnLine software. Box 14.1 lists some commonly used system functions.

RESPONSES

Responses provide the means of navigating through an application. When each screen is displayed by an ADS/OnLine application, the screen may list the valid responses that can be entered. A response consists of pressing one of the terminal control keys, or typing in a particular value in a designated screen field.

DIALOG FUNCTIONS

An important type of function that can be performed by an ADS/OnLine application is a *dialog function,* or simply a *dialog.* A dialog is made up of ADS/OnLine procedural code written in the process command language that defines the

BOX 14.1   System functions

POP	Returns processing to the previous menu.
POPTOP	Returns processing to the highest-level menu.
TOP	Returns processing to the highest function.
RETURN	Returns processing to the next higher function in the application structure.
HELP	Displays the runtime help screen.
QUIT	Terminates processing of the current application.
SIGNON	Allows the terminal operator to execute a sign-on or sign-off function from within the application.
FORWARD	Allows the terminal operator to page forward in menu screens.
BACKWARD	Allows the terminal operator to page backward in menu screens.

processing to be performed by the dialog. Figure 14.2 shows a close-up of one part of an application and illustrates the structure of one of the application's dialog functions. Chapter 17 describes how each dialog that makes up an ADS/OnLine application is created using the ADS/OnLine dialog generator.

DIALOG COMPONENTS

Dialogs are constructed from a number of different components. Not all dialogs have all of the different components. Following are brief descriptions of each dialog component:

- **Maps.** A map defines the format of the screen displayed by the dialog. A dialog can have only one map associated with it. *Literal fields* on the map display constant information; *variable fields* are associated with fields in database records or fields in work records. Chapter 17 shows how the OnLine mapping facility is used to create maps.

- **Processes.** A process consists of ADS/OnLine procedural code that defines the processing to be performed by a part of the dialog. Processes are written in the process command language described in Chapter 16. A dialog can have one *premap process* (executed before the screen is displayed) and any number of *response processes* (executed after the terminal operator enters a response). The dialog in Fig. 14.2 has one premap process and one response process.

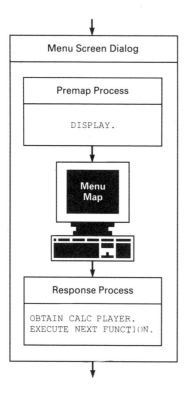

Figure 14.2 Typical ADS/OnLine dialog structure.

- **Subschemas.** A subschema provides the dialog with a view of the database. Each dialog can be associated with only one subschema.

- **Record Definitions.** Record definitions describe the data that the dialog accesses. Record definitions define three types of records: *subschema records, map records,* and *work records.* A subschema record defines fields in the database. A map record defines fields on the screen that are not in the database. A work record defines fields that are not stored in the database or displayed on the screen.

DIALOG PROCESSING   Applications developed with ADS/OnLine are composed of a series of interactions with the terminal user. Each dialog is a discrete unit of work oriented toward online transaction processing functions, that is, data-entry, data-editing, and data-update operations. A dialog in ADS/OnLine consists of the operations required to perform one interaction with the terminal user, including the processing associated with the interaction. The following are brief descriptions of the major categories of operation that a dialog can perform as it executes:

- **Premap Processing.** Premap processing is performed before a map is displayed to the terminal operator. For example, a premap process might retrieve a record that contains data to be displayed by the map.

- **Mapout.** A *mapout operation* uses the dialog's map to display a formatted screen on the terminal. Editing functions are performed as data is moved from storage to the terminal buffer. If a dialog has no premap process, the mapout operation is performed automatically when the dialog is invoked. If the dialog has a premap process, the dialog must end with a MAPOUT command for the map to be displayed.

- **Mapin.** A *mapin operation* causes data that the terminal operator entered in the screen to be moved from the terminal to variable storage. Editing functions are performed at this time also. The mapping operation is performed automatically when the terminal operator presses an appropriate terminal control key.

- **Response Process Selection.** Response process selection is performed automatically based on the response entered by the terminal operator.

- **Response Processing.** Response processing is performed by executing the code in the selected response process.

ADS/ONLINE PROCESSES

As mentioned earlier, ADS/OnLine procedural code is somewhat similar to COBOL code in its syntax. However, the similarity can be misleading. ADS/On-Line process code is much simpler to use and is quite concise compared to COBOL. All data is described outside of the process coding itself in descriptions of database records, map records, and work records. The process code itself is concerned only with the actual processing to be performed by the dialog.

A dialog's processes are added to the data dictionary by using the IDD data dictionary definition language (DDDL) before running ADSG to generate the dialog. The following is an example of an ADS/OnLine process:

```
MOVE MFLD-PLAYER-NAME TO PLAYER-NAME.
OBTAIN CALC PLAYER-REC.
IF DB-REC-NOT-FOUND THEN
    DISPLAY MSG TEXT IS 'PLAYER NOT FOUND'.

!
!          MOVE PLAYER INFORMATION
!
MOVE PLAYER-NAME      TO MFLD-PLAYER-NAME.
MOVE PLAYER-PHONE     TO MFLD-PLAYER-PHONE.
MOVE BATTING-AVERAGE TO MFLD-BATTING-AVERAGE.
MOVE DATE             TO MFLD-CURR-DT.
MOVE TIME             TO MFLD-CURR-TIME.
DISPLAY MSG TEXT IS 'ENTER ANOTHER PLAYER NAME'.

GOBACK.
```

This process performs similar functions as the COBOL program discussed in Chapter 9.

BOX 14.2 ADS/OnLine process commands

Arithmetic and Assignment Commands

ADD   Calculates the sum of two values.
COMPUTE   Evaluates an arithmetic expression.
DIVIDE   Divides values.
MOVE   Moves a value.
MULTIPLY   Calculates a product.
SUBTRACT   Subtracts values.

Conditional Commands

IF/THEN/ELSE   Performs conditional testing.
NEXT   Terminates an IF command.
WHILE   Executes commands repeatedly.
EXIT   Terminates a WHILE command.
DO/END   Executes a group of commands.

Subroutine Control Commands

CALL   Passes control to predefined subroutine.
DEFINE   Defines a subroutine.
GOBACK   Terminates a subroutine.
INCLUDE   Includes source code in a process.

Dialog Control Commands

INVOKE   Passes control to lower-level dialog.
LEAVE   Terminates an ADS/OnLine application.
LINK   Establishes a nested structure.
RETURN   Returns control to the calling dialog.
TRANSFER   Passes control to a dialog at same level.
EXECUTE NEXT
  FUNCTION   Terminates a response process.

Scratch and Queue Management Commands

DELETE QUEUE   Deletes queue records.
GET QUEUE   Retrieves queue records.
PUT QUEUE   Stores queue records.

BOX 14.2 *(Continued)*

DELETE SCRATCH	Deletes scratch records.
GET SCRATCH	Retrieves scratch records.
PUT SCRATCH	Stores scratch records.

Database Access Commands

ACCEPT	Retrieves database keys.
COMMIT	Writes checkpoints and releases locks.
CONNECT	Connects records in sets.
DISCONNECT	Disconnects records from sets.
ERASE	Erases records from the database.
FIND	Locates records in the database.
GET	Reads into storage a record located with FIND
KEEP	Places locks on records.
MODIFY	Modifies records in the database.
OBTAIN	Locates and retrieves database records.
READY	Specifies an area usage mode.
RETURN DB-KEY	Retrieves index entries.
ROLLBACK	Requests recovery operations.
STORE	Stores records in the database.
ON	Performs conditional testing.

Utility Commands

ABORT	Aborts the application.
ACCEPT	Retrieves runtime status information.
COMMIT TASK	Writes a checkpoint and releases locks.
INITIALIZE RECORDS	Reinitializes record buffers.
ROLLBACK TASK	Initiates task recovery procedures.
SNAP	Requests a snapshot dump.
WRITE PRINTER	Transmits data to a print queue.

Map Commands

DISPLAY	Passes control to premap process or map.
MODIFY MAP	Alters map options.

Box 14.2 lists the commonly used ADS/OnLine process commands by category and briefly describes the function of each command. Chapter 16 discusses many of these commands in detail.

SUMMARY   ADS/OnLine provides a set of three development tools: The application generator is used to define the overall flow of control of a complete application, the dialog generator is used to define individual dialogs, and the OnLine mapping facility is used to define maps that describe screen formats. An ADS/OnLine application is a named set of functions and responses that perform a specific business task. Functions are named procedures that are performed by an application. Responses provide the means of navigating through an application and consist of the terminal operator pressing one of the terminal control keys or typing in a particular value in a designated screen field. A dialog function is made up of ADS/OnLine procedural code written in the process command language that defines the processing to be performed by the dialog. Dialogs are constructed from a number of different components, including maps, processes, subschemas, and record definitions. A dialog relates to a single screen display, and most applications consist of multiple dialogs that are hierarchically associated with one another. The more complex processing logic of an application is handled with segments of procedural code. The procedural code is written with a flexible high-level process command language that is similar to COBOL but is easier to use.

15 APPLICATION GENERATION

We define the overall structure of an ADS/OnLine application at a terminal by running the ADS/OnLine application generator (ADSA). ADSA displays a series of screens that prompt us for information about the functions and responses that make up the application. ADS/OnLine stores the information that we supply in the data dictionary, and this information is later used by the ADS/OnLine runtime system to control the execution of the application.

An application generator session is started by entering the appropriate task code in response to the initial prompt displayed on the terminal. The task code used by most installations is ADSA. Six primary screens are available during an application generator session:

- Application Definition screen
- Security screen
- Global Records screen
- Task Codes screen
- Response Definition screen
- Function Definition screen

In addition to the six primary screens, five secondary screens can be accessed:

- Security screen
- Valid Responses screen
- Menu Specification screen
- Menu Response Sequence screen
- Program Parameter List screen

The Security screen can be accessed only when the Application Definition screen is displayed and the remaining four secondary screens can be accessed only when the Function Definition screen is displayed.

We can control the sequence in which screens are displayed during an ADSA session. When we are finished working with a screen, we select the next activity by entering a nonblank character in the appropriate place at the bottom of the screen where the activities are described. We can also select the next activity by pressing the control key associated with the activity to be performed. We will next describe and show examples of the various screens displayed by ADSA. Note that screen formats may vary somewhat depending on the system software your installation uses and the release level of the ADS/OnLine software.

APPLICATION DEFINITION SCREEN

The Application Definition screen, shown in Fig. 15.1, is the first screen displayed after we enter the ADSA task code. We use the Application Definition screen to give a name to the application and to describe its general characteristics. Using this screen, we give our application a name, in this case BPMMAINT, and enter a description of it. The bottom part of the screen lists the activities we can perform at this point. After completing

```
                        CULLINET SOFTWARE                    C8604M
        ADS/ONLINE REL 10.0          ***APPLICATION DEFINITION***


    ACTION:     (ADD/MOD/DEL)  DICT NAME: BPMSDICT    NODE:         MODE: UPDATE


    APPLICATION: BPMMAINT      VERSION:  1                      DATE FORMAT...
                                                             X  MM/DD/YY
    DESCRIPTION: BASEBALL PLAYER MAINTENANCE                  _  DD/MM/YY
                                                             _  YY/MM/DD
    MAXIMUM RESPONSES:  500    DEFAULT PRINT CLASS:           _  YY/DDD

    DEFAULT PRINT DESTINATION:              DEFAULT MODE: STEP (STEP/FAST)


    SELECT NEXT ACTIVITY:       _ TASK CODES          _ GLOBAL RECORDS
    _ HELP                      _ NEW FUNCTION        _ NEW RESPONSE
    _ DISPLAY                   _ OLD FUNCTION:       _ OLD RESPONSE:
    _ PRINT                                           _ SECURITY SPECIFICATIONS

    _ SUSPEND    _ QUIT
    _ GENERATE        _ SWITCH TASK:          (O-OLD/N-NEW)
```

Figure 15.1 Application Definition screen.

all application generation activities using the other screens, we can return to this one at any time to generate the completed application by choosing the GENER-ATE function.

A secondary screen that we can access only from the Application Definition screen is the Security screen.

SECURITY SCREEN   The Security screen, shown in Fig. 15.2, allows us to specify a *security class* for the application, to define a *sign-on function* to be executed at run time, and to provide *menu security information*. If we specify a security class, it is checked against the terminal operator's security class at runtime. The application is executed only if the terminal operator has an acceptable security class. If a sign-on function is specified, it is the first function executed at runtime. If sign-on is required, the application cannot execute until an acceptable sign-on sequence is entered. If sign-on is optional, the application can execute whether or not a sign-on sequence is requested. If the runtime menus are security-tailored, the menus list only those responses for which the terminal operator has an acceptable security class. For further information on how security classes are defined, consult the Cullinet documentation.

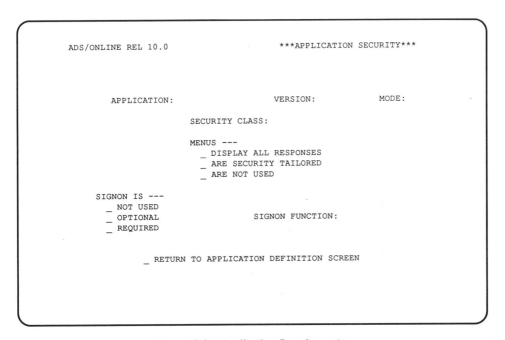

```
     ADS/ONLINE REL 10.0                    ***APPLICATION SECURITY***




           APPLICATION:                  VERSION:              MODE:

                           SECURITY CLASS:

                           MENUS ---
                             _ DISPLAY ALL RESPONSES
                             _ ARE SECURITY TAILORED
                             _ ARE NOT USED

         SIGNON IS ---
           _ NOT USED
           _ OPTIONAL                   SIGNON FUNCTION:
           _ REQUIRED


                _ RETURN TO APPLICATION DEFINITION SCREEN
```

Figure 15.2   Application Security screen.

```
        ADS/ONLINE REL 10.0                    ***APPLICATION GLOBAL RECORDS***



                APPLICATION:              VERSION:           MODE:

                        GLOBAL RECORDS:
            RECORD NAME          VER          RECORD NAME            VER




                                                              PAGE:



    SELECT NEXT ACTIVITY:       _  TASK CODES
      _  HELP                   _  NEW FUNCTION           _  NEW RESPONSE
      _  PRINT                  _  OLD FUNCTION:          _  OLD RESPONSE:
      _  SUSPEND      _  QUIT                             _  APPLICATION DEFINITION
      _  GENERATE
```

Figure 15.3   Global Records screen.

GLOBAL RECORDS SCREEN

The Global Records screen, shown in Fig. 15.3, is used to list the records that will be made available to all functions in the application. We must already have stored in the data dictionary definitions of global records before we begin generating the application.

TASK CODES SCREEN

The Task Codes screen, shown in Fig. 15.4, is used to name the task codes that terminal operators will enter at runtime to invoke the application. One or more task codes can be defined, and each task code specifies the name of the function that will be executed when that task code is entered. Multiple task codes provide multiple entry points into the application. On the Task Codes screen we also enter the function in the application that will be executed first when the application is invoked.

In an installation that runs ADS/OnLine under the control of the IDMS-DC telecommunications monitor, the DCMT command must be used to define to IDMS-DC the task codes that we define using this screen. If some other telecommunications monitor is being used, similar considerations may apply.

```
    ADS/ONLINE REL 10.0                     ***TASK CODES***



                                                          MODE: UPDATE
                                                                FAST
           APPLICATION: BPMMAINT        VERSION:   1

                    TASK CODES AND ASSOCIATED FUNCTIONS

           TASK CODE        FUNCTION             TASK CODE        FUNCTION
         : BPMA           : BPFMD001           :              :
         :                :                    :              :
         :                :                    :              :
         :                :                    :              :
         :                :                    :              :
                                                          PAGE:   1


      SELECT NEXT ACTIVITY:
      _  HELP                                  _ GLOBAL RECORDS
      _  PRINT                  _ NEW FUNCTION  X NEW RESPONSE
      _  SUSPEND    _ QUIT      _ OLD FUNCTION: _ OLD RESPONSE:
      _  GENERATE                              _ APPLICATION DEFINITION
```

Figure 15.4 Task Codes screen.

RESPONSE DEFINITION SCREEN

Responses direct the flow of control from one function to another within our application. The Response Definition screen, shown in Fig. 15.5, is used to add, modify, delete, and display information about the responses that terminal operators can enter while running the application. Each response in the application will be defined separately on this screen. A response can be *global* (acceptable from any screen) or *local* (acceptable only from a particular function). The Response Definition screen asks us to choose the control command that is to be used to pass control to the function associated with the response. The process code in a dialog function normally ends with the EXECUTE NEXT FUNCTION command. This command directs the runtime system to execute the control command associated with the response. An IDMS-DC security class can also be specified for a response. It is checked against the terminal operator's security class at run time. The response is accepted only if the terminal operator has an acceptable security class.

FUNCTION DEFINITION SCREEN

Functions are the building blocks that make up an application. They are named procedures that are associated with dialogs. The Function Definition screen, shown in Fig. 15.6, is used to add, modify, delete,

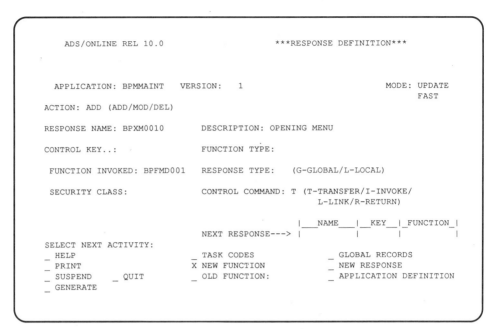

```
      ADS/ONLINE REL 10.0                    ***RESPONSE DEFINITION***


      APPLICATION: BPMMAINT   VERSION:   1                         MODE: UPDATE
                                                                         FAST
   ACTION: ADD (ADD/MOD/DEL)

   RESPONSE NAME: BPXM0010        DESCRIPTION: OPENING MENU

   CONTROL KEY..:                 FUNCTION TYPE:

    FUNCTION INVOKED: BPFMD001    RESPONSE TYPE:   (G-GLOBAL/L-LOCAL)

    SECURITY CLASS:               CONTROL COMMAND: T (T-TRANSFER/I-INVOKE/
                                                     L-LINK/R-RETURN)

                                                 |__NAME___|__KEY__|_FUNCTION_|
                                     NEXT RESPONSE---> |       |       |          |
   SELECT NEXT ACTIVITY:                          |       |       |          |
   _ HELP                   _ TASK CODES          _ GLOBAL RECORDS
   _ PRINT                  X NEW FUNCTION        _ NEW RESPONSE
   _ SUSPEND    _ QUIT      _ OLD FUNCTION:       _ APPLICATION DEFINITION
   _ GENERATE
```

Figure 15.5 Response Definition screen.

```
      ADS/ONLINE REL 10.0                    ***FUNCTION DEFINITION***



                                                             MODE: UPDATE
                                                                   FAST
      APPLICATION: BPMMAINT   VERSION:   1

   ACTION: MOD (ADD/MOD/DEL)

   FUNCTION NAME: BPFMD001             DESCRIPTION: MENU

   ASSOCIATED WITH : BPDMD001          TYPE.......:   (D-DIALOG/M-MENU/P-PROGRAM)

   DEFAULT RESPONSE: BPXMD001     USER EXIT DIALOG:



   SELECT NEXT ACTIVITY:        _ TASK CODES          _ GLOBAL RECORDS
   _ HELP                       _ NEW FUNCTION        _ NEW RESPONSE
   _ PRINT                      X NEW FUNCTION        _ NEW RESPONSE
   _ SUSPEND    _ QUIT          _ MENU SPECIFICATION  _ MENU RESPONSE SEQUENCE
   _ GENERATE                   _ PROGRAM PARM LIST   _ APPLICATION DEFINITION
```

Figure 15.6 Function Definition screen.

or display information about the functions executed by an application. When a function is displayed on the screen, it becomes the *current function* in the application generator session. Information entered on the secondary screens, described next, applies to the current function.

VALID RESPONSES SCREEN

The Valid Responses screen, shown in Fig. 15.7, is used to define responses for the current function. An alphabetical listing of all the responses that are valid for the application is displayed on the Valid Responses screen. When the Valid Responses screen is first displayed for a function, all global responses for the application and an optional default response are valid for the function. The default response is displayed in bright intensity for easy reference. Each additional valid response is selected by entering a nonblank character in the field before a response. A valid response can be deselected by overwriting the field before the response with a blank.

With this screen, we indicate all those responses that are valid for a particular function at hand, in this case our menu function, BPFMD001. We enter an 'x' by each one, since we want control to be able to pass from the menu to the inquiry, add, and update functions.

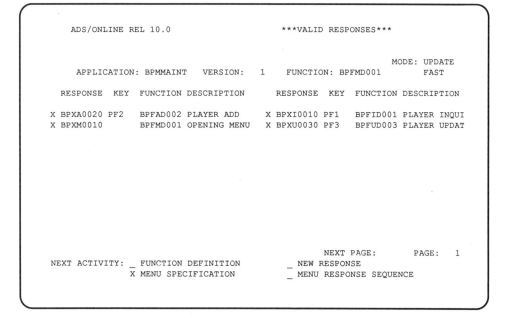

```
   ADS/ONLINE REL 10.0                     ***VALID RESPONSES***


                                                             MODE: UPDATE
      APPLICATION: BPMMAINT    VERSION:   1    FUNCTION: BPFMD001      FAST

     RESPONSE  KEY   FUNCTION DESCRIPTION      RESPONSE   KEY   FUNCTION DESCRIPTION

   X BPXA0020 PF2   BPFAD002 PLAYER ADD      X BPXI0010 PF1   BPFID001 PLAYER INQUI
   X BPXM0010       BPFMD001 OPENING MENU    X BPXU0030 PF3   BPFUD003 PLAYER UPDAT




                                                 NEXT PAGE:       PAGE:   1
     NEXT ACTIVITY: _ FUNCTION DEFINITION       _ NEW RESPONSE
                    X MENU SPECIFICATION         _ MENU RESPONSE SEQUENCE
```

Figure 15.7 Valid Responses screen.

MENU SPECIFICATION SCREEN

The Menu Specification screen, shown in Fig. 15.8, is used to define the characteristics of runtime menu screens that are displayed by the current function. We can specify whether the menu is a sign-on menu and whether the menu format is defined by the system or whether a custom menu is to be used. Heading text, to be displayed at the top of each menu page, can also be specified.

MENU RESPONSE SEQUENCE SCREEN

The Menu Response Sequence screen, shown in Fig. 15.9, is used to modify the sequence of responses displayed on runtime menu screens for the current function. The sequence of the displayed responses can be altered by overwriting the sequence number on the screen. Additionally, the display of a response can be suppressed by erasing or spacing over the sequence number, or by changing the sequence number to 0. Valid responses that are not displayed can still be selected at runtime by pressing the associated control key or by entering the response name in the response field.

This screen lists the valid responses that we previously selected for the menu function. They are shown in the order in which their descriptions will ap-

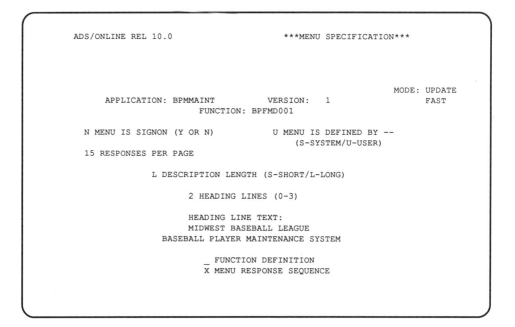

```
ADS/ONLINE REL 10.0                    ***MENU SPECIFICATION***




                                                      MODE: UPDATE
        APPLICATION: BPMMAINT        VERSION:   1           FAST
                     FUNCTION: BPFMD001

     N MENU IS SIGNON (Y OR N)          U MENU IS DEFINED BY --
                                           (S-SYSTEM/U-USER)
     15 RESPONSES PER PAGE


             L DESCRIPTION LENGTH (S-SHORT/L-LONG)


             2 HEADING LINES (0-3)


             HEADING LINE TEXT:
             MIDWEST BASEBALL LEAGUE
        BASEBALL PLAYER MAINTENANCE SYSTEM


                _ FUNCTION DEFINITION
                X MENU RESPONSE SEQUENCE
```

Figure 15.8 Menu Specification screen.

```
ADS/ONLINE REL 10.0                    ***MENU RESPONSE SEQUENCE***


                                                          MODE: UPDATE
        APPLICATION: BPMMAINT   VERSION:   1   FUNCTION: BPFMD001       FAST

     SEQUENCE   RESPONSE      SEQUENCE  RESPONSE      SEQUENCE  RESPONSE

          100   BPXA0020
          200   BPXI0010
          300   BPXM0010
          400   BPXU0030




                                              NEXT PAGE:        PAGE:   1
   NEXT ACTIVITY: _ UPDATE                 _ VALID RESPONSES
                  _ MENU SPECIFICATION     _ FUNCTION DEFINITION
```

Figure 15.9 Menu Response Sequence screen.

```
   ADS/ONLINE REL 10.0            ***PROGRAM PARAMETER LIST***


                                                        MODE:

        APPLICATION:                VERSION:

         FUNCTION:                  PROGRAM:

                     USING RECORDS:
      RECORD NAME                    RECORD NAME




                                                        PAGE:
            _ RETURN TO FUNCTION SCREEN
```

Figure 15.10 Program Parameter List screen.

pear on the actual menu screen when the application is run. To change that order, we can change the sequence numbers and select the UPDATE function.

PROGRAM PARAMETER LIST SCREEN

The Program Parameter List screen, shown in Fig. 15.10, is used to specify information about the record buffers and control blocks that are passed to the application at run time. When a function associated with a user program is started at runtime, the runtime system passes the data in the record buffers and control blocks that we specify using the Using Records List screen.

SUMMARY

The ADS/OnLine application generator is used to define the overall structure of an ADS/OnLine application. The six primary screens used by ADSA are the Application Definition screen, the Security screen, the Global Records screen, the Task Codes screen, the Response Definition screen, and the Function Definition screen. In addition to the six primary screens, the five secondary screens that can be accessed are the Security screen, the Valid Responses screen, the Menu Specification screen, the Menu Response Sequence screen, and the Program Parameter List screen.

16 DIALOGS AND THE PROCESS COMMAND LANGUAGE

In Chapter 14 we looked at the overall structure of an ADS/OnLine application and saw how it is made up of a number of functions that are executed depending on the responses that the system operator makes to menus that are displayed. We saw there that one type of function that an application can invoke is the *dialog* function. In this chapter, we discuss the structure of a dialog function and examine the process command language that is used to specify the processing that is performed in a dialog.

DIALOG STRUCTURE

Figure 16.1 shows the structure of a typical ADS/OnLine dialog function. A typical dialog begins with a premap process that performs some processing as soon as the dialog is invoked. The premap process ends by displaying the dialog's map. If a dialog has no premap process, the ADS/OnLine runtime system automatically displays the dialog's map when the dialog is invoked. After the terminal operator enters a valid response to the map, one of the dialog's response processes is executed.

PROCESS COMMANDS

The first step in constructing a dialog is to define the processing that is to be performed in the dialog's premap process (if it requires one) and the processing that is to be performed in each of the dialog's response processes. The processing to be performed by each of the processes of a dialog is defined by coding a set of commands using the ADS/OnLine process command language and storing

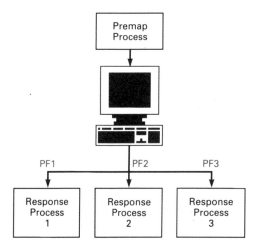

Figure 16.1 ADS/OnLine dialog structure.

those commands into the data dictionary. We will divide the ADS/OnLine process commands into four groups:

- Map display commands
- Dialog control commands
- Database access commands
- Process commands

DISPLAYING THE MAP   The DISPLAY command is used to display the dialog's map on the terminal screen. This process is called a *mapout* function. If a dialog has a premap process, the premap process must end by issuing the DISPLAY command:

```
DISPLAY.
```

If the premap process does not end by issuing a DISPLAY command, nothing will be displayed on the terminal screen.

The DISPLAY command can also be issued in a response process to redisplay the dialog's map, possibly after having modified the information that it displays. When a response process issues an unqualified DISPLAY command, the premap process is not reexecuted. If a response process would like the premap process reexecuted before the map is displayed, the CONTINUE parameter can be included:

```
DISPLAY CONTINUE.
```

A third form of the DISPLAY command can be issued to move a specified message to the map's message field prior to displaying the map:

```
DISPLAY MESSAGE TEXT IS
    'PLAYER RECORD NOT FOUND'.
```

DIALOG CONTROL COMMANDS

The dialog control commands are used to pass control between the various parts of an ADS/OnLine application. They determine the logic flow of the application. Using various dialog commands, a dialog can pass control between its various parts and also to other dialogs.

Each dialog executes at a particular level in the application structure depending on how control has been passed from one dialog to the next in the application structure. A dialog passes control to another dialog in the application structure by issuing an INVOKE, LINK, or TRANSFER command. A dialog passes control up in the application structure by issuing a RETURN command. A dialog can terminate the entire application by issuing a LEAVE command.

THE INVOKE COMMAND

The INVOKE command is used to pass control to another dialog in the application structure and creates a new, lower level in the application structure. Figure 16.2 shows three levels in the application structure. Dialog D1 invokes dialog D2, and dialog D2 invokes dialog D3. When one dialog invokes another, control is always passed to the invoked dialog's premap process. If the invoked dialog has no premap process, the dialog's map is displayed.

In coding an INVOKE command, we specify the invoked dialog by name, enclosing the name in quotes, or we can specify the name of the field that contains the name of the invoked dialog. Following are the two forms of INVOKE:

```
INVOKE 'BPMSPI01'.
INVOKE NEXT-PROGRAM.
```

When a dialog that was invoked by a higher-level dialog issues a RETURN, control is passed either to the premap process of the invoking dialog, or the invoking dialog's map is displayed, depending on parameters coded in the RETURN command. We will look at the RETURN command after we examine LINK.

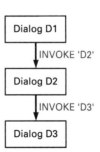

Figure 16.2 The INVOKE command can be used to pass control to another dialog that is lower in level in the application structure.

THE LINK COMMAND

As with INVOKE, when we pass control to another dialog using LINK, we create a new level lower in the application structure. The difference between IN-VOKE and LINK is in the way control is passed back upward when the invoked dialog executes a RETURN. With INVOKE, control always passes to the beginning of the invoking dialog, and either the map is displayed or the premap process is executed. With LINK, control is returned to the command immediately following the LINK command, thus implementing a form of subroutine call. Using the LINK command creates what is called a *nested application structure*.

The LINK command has several variations. In the following example, we are linking to a named dialog:

```
LINK TO DIALOG 'BPINQUIR'.
```

In the following example, we are passing control to the dialog whose name is contained in data field NEXT-DIALOG.

```
LINK TO DIALOG NEXT-DIALOG.
```

In the following example, we are passing control to an application program written in a conventional programming language, such as COBOL or assembler:

```
LINK TO PROGRAM 'BPUPDATE'
     USING (MAP-CONTROL
            SUBSCHEMA-CONTROL
            CALC-FIELDS).
```

The USING parameter specifies data that is to be passed from the dialog to the user program.

THE RETURN COMMAND

As we mentioned earlier, we use the RETURN command to pass control upward in the application structure. The way in which control is passed upward is determined by the parameters we code in the RETURN command and by the way in which control was originally passed downward.

In Fig. 16.3, dialog D1 issues a LINK to dialog D2. Dialog D2 then issues an INVOKE to dialog D3. When dialog D3 issues an unqualified RETURN command, control is passed upward to dialog D2, the dialog that invoked it. Since control was passed from dialog D2 to dialog D3 with an INVOKE command, the return causes control to be passed to the top of dialog D2 and its map is displayed. If dialog D3 issues a RETURN CONTINUE instead of an unqualified RETURN, control passes to the premap process of dialog D2 instead of the mapout operation.

When dialog D2 issues a RETURN, control is passed upward to dialog D1. Since dialog D1 passed control downward with a LINK, the RETURN

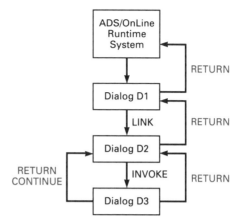

Figure 16.3 The RETURN command passes control back up a level in the application structure.

causes control to be passed to the process command immediately following the LINK. If a RETURN CONTINUE passes control to a dialog that issued a LINK, the CONTINUE keyword is ignored and control still passes to the process command following the LINK.

When dialog D1 issues a RETURN, control passes back to the runtime system.

If we do not wish to go back to the dialog that issued the INVOKE or LINK command that gave us this dialog control, we can specify the name of the higher-level dialog within the application structure to which we would like to pass control:

```
RETURN TO MENU01.
```

We can also use a variation of the RETURN command which passes control to the top of a nested structure or to the mainline dialog at the top of the application thread:

```
RETURN TO TOP.
```

THE TRANSFER COMMAND   The TRANSFER command passes control from the present dialog to another dialog that executes at the same level in the application structure level. The dialog issuing the TRANSFER becomes nonoperative, and the dialog given control logically replaces the issuing dialog in the application structure. We cannot issue a RETURN to a dialog that issued a TRANSFER; to execute it again, we must issue a LINK, INVOKE, or TRANSFER command.

Figure 16.4 shows an application structure containing a TRANSFER command. Dialog D3 issues a LINK to dialog D4. Dialog D3 thus establishes itself as the top of a nested application structure. Dialog D4 then issues a TRANSFER to dialog D5. Dialog D5 effectively replaces dialog D4 on the same level in the

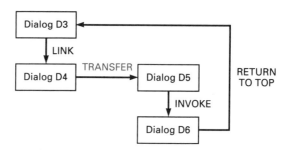

Figure 16.4 The TRANSFER command passes control to another dialog, which remains at the same level in the application structure.

application structure. Dialog D5 then issues an INVOKE to dialog D6, thus creating a new level in the application structure. Finally dialog D6 issues a RETURN TO TOP, which passes control to dialog D3, the top of the nested application structure.

In coding a TRANSFER command, we can specify the dialog name in either of the two ways as for the other dialog control commands:

```
TRANSFER TO 'BPMSPU02'.
TRANSFER TO NEXT-PROGRAM.
```

THE LEAVE COMMAND

We use LEAVE to terminate the application. There are four forms of the LEAVE command. With the following two forms of the LEAVE command, the application terminates and control is passed back to the ADS/OnLine runtime system:

```
LEAVE.
LEAVE APPLICATION.
```

With the following form of the LEAVE command, the application terminates and control is passed back to the telecommunications monitor:

```
LEAVE ADS/ONLINE.
```

With the following form of the LEAVE command, the application terminates and a new application begins execution with the named dialog:

```
LEAVE APPLICATION NEXT 'BPMSM000'.
```

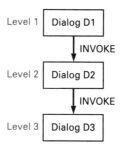

Figure 16.5   Levels in the application structure.

DATABASE CURRENCIES AND RECORD BUFFERS   At all points during the execution of an ADS/OnLine application, the runtime system maintains the locations of those records that are current of run unit, record type, set type, and area. Each process that accesses the database is a complete run unit and has available to it all the currency information normally associated with run units.

The particular level at which a dialog executes in the application structure determines the database currencies that are in effect and the availability of record buffers to the dialog. Whether the level changes or not depends on the dialog control command that was used to pass control to the dialog.

For example, in Fig. 16.5, dialog D1 at level 1 invokes dialog D2, which executes at level 2. The ADS/OnLine runtime system saves database currencies established by dialog D1. These currencies are now available to dialog D2. The record buffers used by dialog D1 are also passed down to dialog D2. Dialog D2 can now establish new currencies and can update the record buffers. If the second-level dialog in turn invokes another dialog, a third level is created. Now, the currencies and record buffers of dialog D2 are passed down to dialog D3. Dialog D3 can use these to establish new currencies and store new data values in the record buffers.

BOX 16.1   Database commands

- ACCEPT DB-KEY INTO SAVE-DB-KEY FROM CURRENCY. Moves the database-key value of the record that is current of run unit to the data element named SAVE-DB-KEY.

- COMMIT. Causes a checkpoint to be written to the journal file and releases database record locks.

- CONNECT PLAYER-REC TO TEAM-PLAYER. Establishes the current Player record occurrence as a member of the current Team-Player set occurrence.

(Continued)

BOX 16.1 *(Continued)*

- DISCONNECT PLAYER-REC FROM TEAM-PLAYER. Detaches the current Player record occurrence from the current occurrence of the Team-Player set.

- ERASE PLAYER-REC ALL MEMBERS. Deletes the current Player record occurrence from sets and/or removes it from the database. The specific action taken depends on the membership options of the sets to which it belongs. If the Player record is the owner of any nonempty sets, its members are erased as well.

- FIND NEXT PLAYER-REC WITHIN TEAM-PLAYER. Currency is established on the next occurrence of the Player record in the current Team-Player set occurrence. The record is not moved to the dialog's record buffer.

- GET PLAYER-REC. The record occurrence located as a result of the previous FIND command is moved to the dialog's record buffer.

- KEEP CURRENT PLAYER-REC. Places a lock on the current Player record occurrence.

- MODIFY PLAYER REC. Record element values in the dialog's record buffer are used to replace the values stored in the database for the current Player record occurrence.

- READY TEAM-AREA USAGE-MODE IS EXCLUSIVE UPDATE. The Team-Area area is prepared for access by the dialog. The dialog will be able to update records in the area, and no other run unit will be allowed to access or update records in that area.

- ROLLBACK. Causes the database to be restored to the condition that existed at the time the last checkpoint was written to the journal.

- STORE PLAYER-REC. The Player record element values in program variable storage are used to create a new occurrence of the Player record in the database.

DATABASE ACCESS COMMANDS
ADS/OnLine provides the same database retrieval and update functions that are available to the other programming languages supported by IDMS/R. Many of the database commands look the same as their DML counterparts. Box 16.1 shows examples of each database command that can be included in an ADS/OnLine process.

PROCESS COMMANDS

ADS/OnLine supports a full set of process commands. We will look at some of the more useful commands that fall into four general categories:

1. Map commands, including map attribute commands and MODIFY MAP
2. Procedural commands, including assignment and arithmetic commands, conditional commands, and subroutine control commands
3. Scratch and queue management commands
4. Utility commands

MAP COMMANDS

We use the online mapping facility to define a map for each dialog and to assign a set of attributes to each of the fields defined in the map. As an application executes, we may want to change the initial attributes assigned to one or more map fields. Map commands allow us to alter the attributes of map fields, either on a temporary basis—for a single mapout operation, or on a permanent basis—for as long as the dialog is operative.

Map Attribute Commands

We can use a map attribute command to change many of a map field's attributes, for example, to change a map field's intensity or to change a map field from protected to unprotected. Box 16.2 shows examples of map attribute commands.

BOX 16.2 Map attribute commands

- BRIGHTEN PLAYER-NAME. Causes the field to be displayed at bright intensity.
- DARKEN PLAYER-NAME. Causes the field to be displayed at dark intensity so it is not visible on the screen.
- NORMALIZE PLAYER-NAME. Causes the field to be displayed at normal intensity.
- PROTECT PLAYER-NAME. Causes the field to be protected so the operator cannot modify it.
- UNPROTECT PLAYER-NAME. Changes a protected field back to unprotected, allowing the operator to enter data into it.

The MODIFY MAP Command

Map attribute commands are useful for changing one map field attribute at a time. If we need to change several attributes or need to change an attribute that cannot be modified using a map attribute command, we can use the MODIFY MAP command. MODIFY MAP enables us to issue a single command to change any number of map attributes. The following MODIFY MAP command changes several attributes of the Player-Name map field:

```
MODIFY MAP FOR DFLD PLAYER-NAME
        ATTRIBUTES UNPROTECTED
                   BRIGHT
                   MDT.
```

In the following command, we are changing attributes of three map fields: Player-Name, Player-Phone, and Batting-Average:

```
MODIFY MAP FOR FIELD (PLAYER-NAME
                      PLAYER-PHONE
                      BATTING-AVERAGE)
        ATTRIBUTES PROTECTED
                   OPTIONAL.
```

PROCEDURAL COMMANDS

Procedural commands specify the processing an ADS/OnLine dialog is to perform and controls the flow of execution within a process. There are four types of procedural commands: assignment commands, arithmetic commands, conditional commands, and subroutine control commands.

Assignment Commands

An assignment operation is performed by issuing a MOVE command. MOVE replaces the contents of the second operand of the command with the contents of the first operand. The first operand may specify a data field, an arithmetic expression, or a literal value. The second operand must specify a data field. The following are three examples of the MOVE command:

```
MOVE COUNTER     TO OUT-FIELD.
MOVE COUNTER + 1 TO OUT-FIELD.
MOVE '00010'     TO OUT-FIELD.
```

Arithmetic Commands

With the arithmetic commands, ADD, SUBTRACT, MULTIPLY, and DI-VIDE, the first operand can be a data field, an arithmetic expression, or a numeric literal; the second field of the command must be a data field into which the result of the operation is stored. In the COMPUTE command, which allows evaluation of a complex arithmetic expression, the second field specifies an arithmetic expression to be evaluated and the first field specifies the data field in which to store the result. The following are arithmetic commands:

```
ADD COUNT-FIELD TO OUT-FIELD.
SUBTRACT COUNT-FIELD FROM OUT-FIELD.
MULTIPLY COUNT-FIELD BY OUT-FIELD.
DIVIDE COUNT-FIELD INTO OUT-FIELD.
COMPUTE OUT-FIELD = COUNT-FIELD * (STRIKE-CNT + BALL-CNT).
```

Conditional Commands

ADS/OnLine conditional commands allow both selection and iteration structures to be created. The conditional commands include IF, DO, and WHILE.

The IF Command

The following is an IF command:

```
IF TRAN-IN EQ '99'
THEN
      MOVE MSG99 TO DISPLAY-MESSAGE.
```

When interpreting a process command that includes a condition, ADS/OnLine begins by evaluating the conditional expression. If the condition is true, for example, if the Tran-In field in the example contains "99," the specified command is executed. If the conditional expression is not true, the THEN command in the IF statement is bypassed and the next command in the process is executed.

We can also include an ELSE keyword to specify a command to be executed if the conditional expression is not true. The following is an IF command that contains an ELSE clause:

```
IF TRAN-IN EQ 'ADD '
THEN
      MOVE ADD-MESS TO DISPLAY-MESSAGE.
ELSE
      MOVE INQ-MESS TO DISPLAY-MESSAGE.
```

Notice that only one of the two MOVE commands will be executed; never both.

The DO and END Keywords

To execute more than one command in a conditional structure, we can include the DO and END keywords. In Fig. 16.6 the DO and END keywords tell ADS/OnLine to execute all commands between the DO and the END if the conditional expression is true. ADS/OnLine executes the embedded IF statement if the first conditional expression is false.

Notice that the formatting conventions that we are using are not required but make the IF statement easy to read. A good set of formatting conventions is important, especially with nested IF statements.

```
IF TRAN-IN EQ 'ADD '
THEN
    DO.
        MOVE SPACE     TO PLAYER-NAME-OUT.
        MOVE ADD-MESS TO DISPLAY-MESSAGE.
    END.
ELSE
    IF TRAN-IN EQ 'INQ '
    THEN
        DO.
            MOVE PLAYER-NAME TO PLAYER-NAME-OUT.
            MOVE INQ-MESS    TO DISPLAY-MESSAGE.
        END.
```

Figure 16.6 The DO and END keywords.

The WHILE Command

The WHILE command is used to execute a set of commands repeatedly, as long as a conditional expression remains true. In the following example, a set of commands is executed repeatedly as long as the value of the Calc-Sub field is less than or equal to 10:

```
MOVE 0 TO CALC-SUB.
WHILE CALC-SUB LE 10 REPEAT.
    ADD 1 TO CALC-SUB.
    COMPUTE TOTAL(CALC-SUB) = (HITS(CALC-SUB) * GAMES).
END.
```

As with the IF command, we use the END keyword, on a line by itself, to signal the end of the set of commands to be repeated.

When ADS/OnLine executes a WHILE command, it evaluates the conditional expression first. If the condition is true, all the commands up to the END keyword are executed. The conditional expression is then evaluated again. If the condition is still true, the commands will be executed again. This operation continues until the condition is false. At that point, the command immediately following END is executed.

Subroutine Control Commands

In the last group of procedural commands are the subroutine control commands. These commands give us the ability to define a subroutine in a process and to call that subroutine from anywhere in the process. Figure 16.7 shows an example of a nested IF command. Because of the nested IF, the logic of this section of the process is not apparent. To make the logic easier to follow, we can use subroutine calls. This is shown in Fig. 16.8.

We place the commands that make up the subroutines at the end of the process. We use a DEFINE SUBROUTINE command to name each subroutine

```
IF TRAN-IN EQ 'ADD '
THEN
    DO.
        MOVE SPACE     TO PLAYER-NAME-OUT.
        MOVE ADD-MESS TO DISPLAY-MESSAGE.
    END.
ELSE
    IF TRAN-IN EQ 'INQ '
    THEN
        DO.
            MOVE PLAYER-NAME TO PLAYER-NAME-OUT.
            MOVE INQ-MESS     TO DISPLAY-MESSAGE.
        END.
```

Figure 16.7 Nested IF statement.

and define its beginning. The GOBACK command indicates the end of the sub-routine. It passes control back to the command following the CALL command.

MISCELLANEOUS COMMANDS

In the final three command categories are the scratch management commands, the queue management commands, and the utility commands.


```
IF TRAN-IN EQ 'ADD '
THEN
    CALL PLAYADD.
ELSE
    CALL PLAYINQ.
    .
    .
    .
DEFINE SUBROUTINE PLAYADD.

    MOVE SPACE     TO PLAYER-NAME-OUT.
    MOVE ADD-MESS TO DISPLAY-MESSAGE.
GOBACK.

DEFINE SUBROUTINE PLAYINQ.

    IF TRAN-IN EQ 'INQ '
    THEN
        DO.
            MOVE PLAYER-NAME       TO PLAYER-NAME-OUT.
            MOVE BATTING-AVERAGE TO PLAYER-AVERAGE-OUT.
        END.
GOBACK.
```

Figure 16.8 Subroutines.

Queue and Scratch Management Commands

Queue and scratch management functions allow us to write records to direct access storage, making these records available to other dialogs or user programs. These functions give us a convenient way to pass information between dialogs or user programs. IDMS-DC maintains scratch and queue records in their own area of the data dictionary.

Scratch records are typically used as nonpermanent storage and are available to all dialogs or user programs executed from the same terminal. We might use a scratch record to pass data from one dialog in an application to another without having to use main memory. Scratch records are cleared each time the system is started. We should use them only for storing transient data. We store a scratch record with the PUT SCRATCH command, retrieve a scratch record with the GET SCRATCH command, and delete a scratch record with the DELETE SCRATCH command.

Queue records are typically used as relatively permanent storage and are available to dialogs that are executed from any terminal and by user programs as well, including batch programs. Queue records are stored in the data dictionary as a member occurrence in a set owned by a queue header record. Queue records are maintained across system shutdowns, so they are used to maintain data for a relatively long time, such as one to a few days. We might use a queue record to pass data from a dialog invoked from one terminal to a dialog invoked from another terminal.

The queue commands are similar to the ones we use for scratch records. We add a queue record to the data dictionary with the PUT QUEUE command, retrieve a queue record with the GET QUEUE command, and delete a queue record with the DELETE QUEUE command.

Utility Commands

In addition to all the other commands we have discussed, ADS/OnLine provides a set of utility commands. We can use the INITIALIZE RECORD command to reinitialize one or more of our dialog's record buffers to its original value. The ACCEPT command allows us to retrieve system-maintained information such as the current user id, dialog name, and logical- and physical-terminal identifiers. The SNAP command is helpful in debugging and is used to request a dump of any or all of the main storage locations maintained by the application. Finally, the WRITE PRINTER command is used to send data to a printer.

SUMMARY

A typical dialog is made up of a premap process, a map, and one or more response processes. The process commands that are used to specify the processing that premap and response processes perform can be divided into four categories: map display commands, dialog control commands, database access commands, and process commands. Map display commands cause the screen defined by the dialog's map to be displayed for the terminal operator. Dialog control commands are used to pass control between a dialog's component parts and between the various dialogs that make up an application. Database access commands provide the same database retrieval and update functions that can be requested using the data manipulation language in a conventional application program. Process commands include map commands that allow a dialog to modify map attributes; procedural commands that include assignment and arithmetic commands, conditional commands, and subroutine control commands; queue and scratch management commands that allow the programmer to pass information between dialogs; and utility commands that provide an assortment of miscellaneous functions.

17 MAP, DIALOGS, AND THE RUNTIME SYSTEM

As we have seen, we begin developing an ADS/OnLine application by defining the overall structure of the application using the ADS/OnLine application generator. We then define all the processes that make up each dialog and store the process code for each into the data dictionary. Our next steps are to use the On-Line mapping facility (OLM) to generate the maps that the dialogs use, execute the ADS/OnLine dialog generator (ADSG) to generate the dialogs, and then run the completed application using the ADS/OnLine runtime system. We will discuss each of these steps in this chapter.

THE ONLINE MAPPING FACILITY

We use the OnLine mapping facility to define the maps that our dialogs will display. A map definition determines what the terminal display screen will look like, associates map fields with data elements, and defines specific attributes for each map field. We will next look at examples of the screens that the OnLine mapping facility displays:

- Initial Definition screen
- Format screen
- Field Selection screen
- Field Edit screen
- Extended Field Edit screen

We gain access to the OnLine mapping facility by entering the transaction code for the OnLine mapping facility, generally "OLM," after signing onto the system.

The Initial Definition Screen

The first screen that OLM displays is shown in Fig. 17.1. The Initial Definition screen allows us to add, modify, or delete a map. From this screen, we can create an entirely new map, or we can copy information from an existing map if there is one that is similar to the one we are creating. Using this screen, we also list the work records that are associated with this map. A work record is a record that we must define in the data dictionary that contains data elements that we will tie to screen fields defined in the map. The *ADSO-Application-Global-Record* is a universal work record that can be used to pass information between dialogs. We have shown another work record that we have created to define data elements that will be specific to our map.

By entering "Y" after EDIT (Y/N) we can specify automatic editing and error handling for one or more fields. These features shift much of the detail work involved in editing fields from the application program to the ADS/OnLine runtime system. Refer to the Cullinet documentation for detailed information about automatic editing and error handling.

The Format Screen

The Format screen begins as a totally blank screen if we are defining a map from scratch. If we have copied some already existing map, the map we copy

```
                        CULLINET SOFTWARE                          C8604M
        IDMS-DC ONLINE MAPPING REL 10.0      *** INITIAL DEFINITION *** FAST


   ACTION:    MAPNAME: BBMUD002 VER: 1     DICTNAME: BPMSDICT   DICTNODE:
   EDIT(Y/N): Y                                               PAGING(Y/N): N
                              USING RECORDS
            RECORD NAME              VER           ROLE NAME            DEL
   : ADSO-APPLICATION-GLOBAL-RECORD   1
   : BBRUD002                         1
   :
   :
   ---------------------------------------------------------------------------
   DEVICES    24X80 (Y/N): Y   32X80 (Y/N): Y   43X80 (Y/N): Y   27X132 (Y/N): Y
                   X    DIMENSION (Y/N):    FILE..(Y/N):
   ---------------------------------------------------------------------------
   COPY FROM MAPNAME:       VER:         DICTNAME:        NODENAME:
           COPY ACTION (ALL/FMT):
   ---------------------------------------------------------------------------
   WRITE CONTROL CHARACTER        UNLOCK KEYBOARD.....: Y      RESET MDT: Y
                                  START PRINT.........: N      ALARM....: N
                                  NEWLINE(NL/40/64/80):
   ---------------------------------------------------------------------------
                                     DECIMAL POINT IS COMMA (Y/N): N
```

Figure 17.1   Initial Definition screen.

will be displayed on the Format screen. We use the Format screen to initially "paint" an image of what we want the screen to look like when this map is displayed. Figure 17.2 shows a screen that we have created for the Baseball Player Maintenance System. After we have initially created our screen fields, we use other OLM screens to perform field selection and editing to describe the characteristics of each field in the map. We can call up the Format screen at any time during the OLM session to see what the map looks like and mark specific fields for changing. We can then use the other screens to adjust field attributes as required.

The Field Selection Screen

The Field Selection screen allows us to select by group those fields that we would like to edit. An example of the Field Selection screen is shown in Fig. 17.3. This screen allows us to assign attributes to fields in groups and to copy attributes from one field to another.

The Field Edit Screen

The Field Edit screen, shown in Fig. 17.4, is used to define attributes for the screen fields that we select using the Field Selection screen. The top half of the screen displays the top half of the map; the bottom half shows the editing options available for the first field, which is highlighted to show us which field we

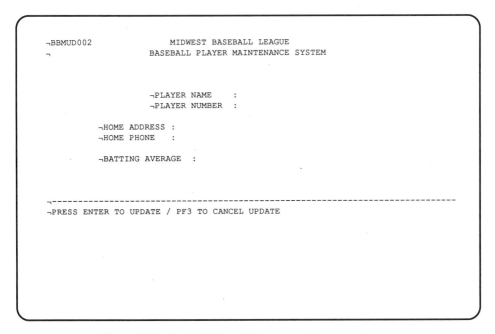

Figure 17.2   Baseball Player Maintenance System main menu.

```
        IDMS-DC ONLINE MAPPING REL 10.0              *** FIELD SELECTION ***
     DC353001 * 011 FIELDS REMAIN TO BE UPDATED IN DICTIONARY  PROCEED TO FIELDS
   ED
   ITS TO COMPLETE MAP UPDATE*
   MAP: BBPMD002 VER:   1
   FAST


              ACTION:    E    (E-EDIT/D-DELETE/C-COPY/F-FINISH/G-GENERATE)
                         COPY ACTION: N      (OCCURS Y-YES/N-NO/#-INCR)
                                      C      (BY R-ROW/C-COL)

              GROUPING: N  (N-NEW/A-ALL)

              TYPE    : A  (A-ALL/D-DATA/L-LITERAL)

              FROM ROW: 1    COL:   1
              TO ROW  : 24   COL:  80

              DEFAULT EXTENDED SCREEN: N   (Y/N)
```

Figure 17.3 Field Selection screen.

```
     BBMUD002                    MIDWEST BASEBALL LEAGUE
                            BASEBALL PLAYER MAINTENANCE SYSTEM



                      ¬PLAYER NAME    :
                      ¬PLAYER NUMBER  :

               ¬HOME ADDRESS :
               ¬HOME PHONE   :

               ¬BATTING AVERAGE  :
   ...5...10...15...20...25...30...35...40...45...50...55...60...65...70...75...80
       LITERAL   AT  ROW: 1 COL:  1    _ (DELETE Y/N)    ** FIELD EDIT **
   FAST
   N (A-ALPHA/N-NUM)          S (S-SKIP/N-NOSKIP)        N (Y-MDT/N-NOMDT)
   N (D-DETECT/N-NONDETECT)   P (U-UNPROT/P-PROTECT)     D (D-DISP/B-BRIGHT/K-DARK)




                                              _  (EXT SCRN Y/N)
```

Figure 17.4 Field Edit screen.

```
BBMUD002                    MIDWEST BASEBALL LEAGUE
                       BASEBALL PLAYER MAINTENANCE SYSTEM



                    ¬PLAYER NAME    :
                    ¬PLAYER NUMBER  :

            ¬HOME ADDRESS :
            ¬HOME PHONE    :

            ¬BATTING AVERAGE  :

...5...10...15...20...25...30...35...40...45...50...55...60...65...70...75...80
      LITERAL   AT  ROW: 1 COL:  1     _  (DELETE Y/N)    ** FIELD EDIT **
FAST
  N (BLINK Y/N)        N (N-NORMAL VIDEO/R-REVERSE VIDEO)    N (UNDERSCORE Y/N)
  N (B-BLUE/R-RED/P-PINK/G-GREEN/T-TURQUOISE/Y-YELLOW/W-WHITE/N-NOCOLOR)
```

Figure 17.5 Extended Field Edit screen.

are working on. We work through all the fields that we have selected for editing, one at a time. When we begin working on fields that are defined in the bottom half of the map, the two halves of the screen will be reversed.

The Extended Field Edit Screen

The Extended Field Edit screen is shown in Fig. 17.5. This screen is invoked from the Field Edit screen when we must specify certain field attributes that are not defined for all types of terminal screens, such as colors, underscores, and normal or reverse video.

GENERATING THE MAP

Once we have successfully edited all of the fields that we have defined in the map, OLM redisplays the Field Selection screen. Here we can generate our completed map by choosing the GENERATE function.

ADS/ONLINE DIALOG GENERATOR

After we have generated all the maps that our dialogs require, we next run the ADS/OnLine dialog generator (ADSG) to generate all the dialogs in the application. As with the other online tools, ADSG displays a series of screens that prompt us for information about each dialog function. The dialog generator uses the information that we supply to generate executable code for the dialog. The executable code is maintained in the data dictionary and is executed at runtime by the ADS/OnLine runtime system.

Before we initiate an ADSG session, we must already have stored the process code for all the processes that make up each dialog that we will generate. In using the ADS/OnLine development tools to create a prototype of a working application, we can store very simple versions of each process into the data dictionary before starting the ADSG session. For example, the initial version of each dialog might simply display the dialog's map. Such simple versions of each dialog will allow the end user to get a feel for how the system will operate. After we have a working prototype, we can then begin creating the actual processes that will make up the final system.

We start an ADSG session by entering the appropriate task code in response to the initial prompt, in most cases "ADSG." Five primary screens are available during a dialog generator session:

- Dialog Definition screen
- Dialog Options screen (not discussed in this chapter)
- New Copy/Work Record screen
- Premap Process Definition screen
- Response Process Definition screen

Four secondary screens that display information about a dialog can also be displayed:

- Map Display screen
- Dialog Summary Report screen (not discussed in this chapter)
- Process Command List screen (not discussed in this chapter)
- Process Error List screen (not discussed in this chapter)

Following are descriptions of some of the screens displayed by ADSG.

DIALOG DEFINITION SCREEN

The Dialog Definition screen is the first screen displayed at the beginning of an ADSG session. The Dialog Definition screen, shown in Fig. 17.6, is used to give the dialog a name, tie it to a map, and name the schema and subschema that will be used by the dialog.

```
                                 CULLINET SOFTWARE                        C8604M
              ADS/ONLINE REL 10.0 DIALOG GENERATOR        ***DIALOG DEFINITION***
         DC151035 NO ERRORS DETECTED



           ACTION: MOD   (ADD/MOD/DEL)  DICTNAME: BPMSDICT DICTNODE:          MODE: UPDATE
                                                                                   STEP
           DIALOG....:  BBDUD002        VER...:   1       MAINLINE: NO    (YES/NO)

           SUBSCHEMA.: SUBBASE          SCHEMA: SCHBASE    VERSION:   1

           MAPNAME...: BBMUD002         VER...:   1

           AUTOSTATUS: YES  (YES/NO(    RECORD: ADSO-STAT-DEF-REC                 VER:   1


           SELECT NEXT ACTIVITY:        X PREMAP PROCESS          _ NEW RESPONSE
           _ RESPONSE:                                            _ NEW COPY/WORK RECORD
           _ DISPLAY                    _ DISPLAY MAP             _ UPDATE MAP
           _ PRINT
           _ DISPLAY RECORD:                                     VER:
           _ GENERATE                   _ QUIT                    _ SUSPEND
           _ DIALOG OPTIONS
```

Figure 17.6   Dialog Definition screen.

NEW COPY/WORK RECORD SPECIFICATION SCREEN

The New Copy/Work Record Specification screen, shown in Fig. 17.7, is used to describe how the runtime system should initialize buffers while the dialog is executing and to define work records for the dialog. This screen is also used to name work records, map records, and subschema records that are to be used by the dialog. We can also specify the names of map records or subschema records that are to be given new, initialized record buffers at runtime. Subschema and map records that are associated with the dialog's map are already known to the dialog, so we need not list them on this screen unless we want a new record buffer for the record. However, work records that are not associated with the dialog's map must be defined using this screen.

PREMAP PROCESS DEFINITION SCREEN

The Premap Process Definition screen, shown in Fig. 17.8, is used to describe a premap process for a dialog. The source code for the premap process must already exist in the data dictionary before the generator session is begun. When we define a premap process for the dialog, the dialog generator compiles the premap process source code and generates executable code for it. If the process

```
        ADS/ONLINE REL 10.0 DIALOG GENERATOR          ***NEW COPY/WORK RECORD***




DIALOG: BBDUD002    MAPNAME: BBMUD002    SUBSCHEMA: SUBBASE         MODE: UPDATE
                                                                         FAST
                         RECORD NAME                VERSION   NC   WK
              1   BBGUD001-GLOBAL                       1           X
              2   BBM-DEBUG                             1           X
              3   BBWUD101                              1           X
              4
              5
              6
              7
              8

SELECT NEXT ACTIVITY:          _ PREMAP PROCESS            _ NEW RESPONSE
_ RESPONSE:                                                _ NEW COPY/WORK RECORD
                               _ DISPLAY MAP
                               _ DIALOG
_ DISPLAY RECORD:                                      VER:
_ GENERATE                     _ QUIT                      _ SUSPEND
_ DIALOG OPTIONS
```

Figure 17.7 New Copy/Work Record screen.

```
         ADS/ONLINE REL 10.0 DIALOG GENERATOR      ***PREMAP PROCESS DEFINITION***




DIALOG: BBDUD002   MAPNAME: BBMUD002    SUBSCHEMA: SUBBASE         MODE: UPDATE
                                                                        FAST
DELETE:      (Y/YES)

PREMAP PROCESS NAME: BBDUD002-PM                        VERSION:    1




SELECT NEXT ACTIVITY:          _ PREMAP PROCESS            _ NEW RESPONSE
_ RESPONSE:                                                _ NEW COPY/WORK RECORD
_ DISPLAY                      _ DISPLAY MAP
_ PRINT                        _ DIALOG                    _ UPDATE PROCESS
_ DISPLAY RECORD:                                      VER:
_ GENERATE                     _ QUIT                      _ SUSPEND
_ DIALOG OPTIONS
```

Figure 17.8 Premap Process Definition screen.

does not compile successfully, the dialog generator issues error messages. The source code for the premap process can then be viewed by selecting DISPLAY or PRINT as the next activity.

RESPONSE PROCESS
DEFINITION SCREEN
The Response Process Definition screen, shown in Fig. 17.9, is used to define a response process.

The screen prompts us for a control key and a response field value used to pass control at runtime to the response process. The response process source code must already exist in the data dictionary before the generator session is begun.

This screen also allows us to specify if the response process should be executed even if input errors were detected in the map, or if automatic editing should redisplay the map, thus allowing the terminal operator to correct the input errors before output is passed to the response process.

As for a premap process, the dialog generator compiles the source code for a response process and generates executable code. ADSG assumes that multiple response processes will be defined and allows us to define as many response processes as are required. The source code for a response process can be viewed by selecting DISPLAY or PRINT.

```
     ADS/ONLINE REL 10.0 DIALOG GENERATOR   ***RESPONSE PROCESS DEFINITION***



  DIALOG: BBDUD002   MAPNAME: BBMUD002   SUBSCHEMA: SUBBASE      MODE: UPDATE
                                                                      FAST
  DELETE:       (Y/YES)

  RESPONSE PROCESS NAME..: BBDUD002                    VERSION:   1
  CONTROL KEY............: PF3
  RESPONSE FIELD VALUE...:
  EXECUTE ON EDIT ERRORS.: YES    (YES/NO)



  SELECT NEXT ACTIVITY:      _ PREMAP PROCESS         _ NEW RESPONSE
  _ RESPONSE:                                         _ NEW COPY/WORK RECORD
  _ DISPLAY                  _ DISPLAY MAP
  _ PRINT                    _ DIALOG                 _ UPDATE PROCESS
  _ DISPLAY RECORD:                                   VER:
  _ GENERATE                 _ QUIT                   _ SUSPEND
  _ DIALOG OPTIONS
```

Figure 17.9 Response Process Definition screen.

**MAP DISPLAY
SCREEN**

The Map Display screen, shown in Fig. 17.10, is used to display a dialog's map to see how it will look to the terminal operator at runtime. A map can be displayed by selecting DISPLAY MAP as the next activity from any primary screen. Map modifications defined in process code associated with the dialog are not in effect when the screen is displayed. Map data fields do not contain any values when the Map Display screen is displayed.

**EXECUTING THE
APPLICATION**

After we have finished with ADSG, we can use the ADS/OnLine runtime system to execute the application. We pass control to the ADS/OnLine runtime system by entering the task code that is assigned to it, generally "ADS." We can then initiate a particular ADS/OnLine application by entering the task code that we have assigned to it or by specifying the name of a dialog to which we would like to pass control. The runtime system loads the required load modules, sets up control blocks and record buffers for the application, and displays the first screen of our sample application.

When each dialog is executed by our prototype application, it simply displays the dialog's map. This will allow the end user actually to operate the system, even though no process code exists and no data will be displayed in the variable fields in the maps.

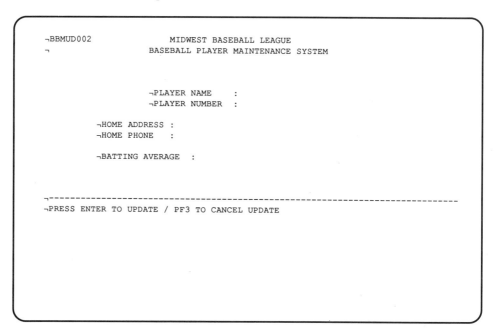

Figure 17.10 Map Display screen.

SUMMARY   The OnLine mapping facility is used to define maps that control the format of the screens that are displayed by the online application. A map definition determines what the terminal screen will look like, associates map fields with data element types, and defines attributes for each map field. The screens that OLM displays include an Initial Definition screen, a Format screen, a Field Selection screen, a Field Edit screen, and an Extended Field Edit screen. The ADS/OnLine dialog generator is used to generate executable code that controls the processing that is performed by the online application. The screens that ADSG displays include a Dialog Definition screen, a Dialog Options screen, a New Copy/Work Record screen, a Premap Process Definition screen, a Response Process Definition screen, a Map Display screen, a Dialog Summary Report screen, a Process Command List screen, and a Process Error List screen. The ADS/OnLine runtime system is used to control the execution of the online system once the maps and dialogs have been generated.

18 THE LOGICAL RECORD FACILITY

IDMS/R provides two methods for providing programmers and end users with a relational view of the data stored in an IDMS/R database: the Logical Record Facility (LRF) and the Automatic System Facility (ASF). In this chapter, we examine the Logical Record Facility. The Logical Record Facility allows a database administration staff member to define logical records that describe quasi-relational views of the data stored in a network-structured database. These quasi-relational views of the data allow application programmers to access an IDMS/R network-structured database without being aware of its actual set structure. The Automatic System Facility (ASF), discussed in Chapter 19, provides a means by which end users can create and maintain data in the form of relational tables.

LOGICAL RECORD FACILITY OPERATION
Figure 18.1 shows a program's subschema view, and Fig. 18.2 shows the database record occurrences that the program works with. To code a conventional program to access these records, we have to be aware of the set relationships that exist between the three record types. The Logical Record Facility allows the database administration staff to create a single *logical* record that contains data element values from all three record types. Figure 18.3 shows an example of a logical record that we are calling Player-Data. It combines into a single logical record selected data elements from the Team, Player, and Position records.

The application program can then request the retrieval of a particular occurrence of the Player-Data logical record by supplying one or more record selection criteria. In satisfying each retrieval request, the Logical Record Facility retrieves the appropriate occurrences of the Team, Player, and Position records from the database and constructs the required occurrence of the Player-Data log-

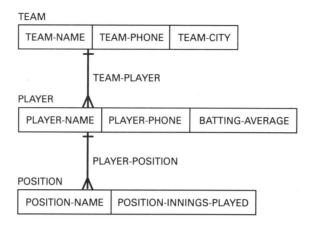

Figure 18.1   Program's subschema view.

ical record. The logical record is then placed in the program's variable storage.

The program views Player-Data logical records as if they were stored in a conventional file, as shown in Fig. 18.4. Keep in mind, however, that IDMS/R does not store the data in the database in this way; that would require that a good deal of redundant data be stored in the database. Instead, the Logical Record Facility creates each logical record occurrence as required by retrieving the appropriate database records from the database, extracting the required data element values from them, and combining them to construct the required logical record.

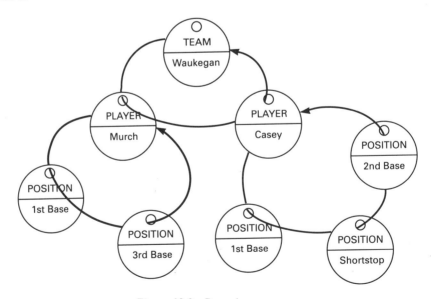

Figure 18.2   Record occurrences.

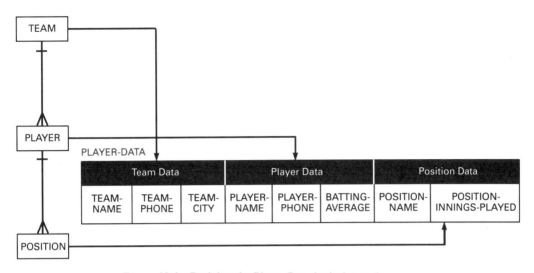

Figure 18.3   Deriving the Player-Data logical record.

DATABASE
NAVIGATION

To construct an occurrence of the Player-Data logical record occurrence, IDMS/R must perform the same database navigation that we perform in a conventional application program. However, the programmer need not know that the database navigation is taking place. Let us assume that the application program makes a request for the first occurrence of the Player-Data logical record that has a Player-Name data element value of Casey. LRF satisfies this request by first asking IDMS/R to retrieve the Player record for Casey. It next asks IDMS/R to retrieve the owner of the Casey record to locate the appropriate team information. Finally, it retrieves the next occurrence of the Position record in the Player-Position set.

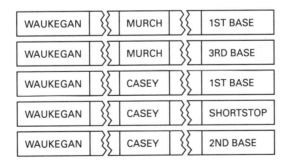

Figure 18.4   Application program view of the Player-Data logical record occurrences.

LRF combines data elements that it extracts from the Player, Team, and Position record occurrences to form the requested occurrence of the Player-Data logical record. Notice that in this example, LRF issued three separate retrieval requests, but the programmer made only one request for a single Player-Data logical record.

Although the detailed instructions for navigating the database do not appear in the application program, they must, of course, be specified somewhere. We will see later in this chapter that they are specified in the subschema DDL.

LOGICAL RECORD RETRIEVAL PROGRAM Figure 18.5 contains a complete listing of an application program that takes advantage of the Logical Record Facility and retrieves occurrences of the Player-Data logical record. We will next look at those parts of the program that make use of the logical record facility.

As we can see by examining the beginning of the program, the program performs the MAINLINE-RTN paragraph repeatedly until end-of-file is detected on the input file. This program does not issue a READY statement. We are expecting IDMS/R to issue the appropriate READY automatically.

The following code in the program performs all the processing that is required to retrieve an occurrence of the Player-Data logical record for each record it reads from the input file:

```
MOVE INPUT-PLAYER-NAME TO PLAYER-NAME.

OBTAIN FIRST PLAYER-DATA
    WHERE PLAYER-NAME EQ PLAYER-NAME OF LR.

IF LR-STATUS = 'NO-PLAYER'

    MOVE '** NO PLAYER RECORD  **' TO TEAM-NAME
    PERFORM WRITE-PLAYER-LINE-RTN

ELSE IF LR-STATUS = 'LR-FOUND'

    PERFORM WRITE-PLAYER-LINE-RTN
    PERFORM WRITE-POSITION-INFO-RTN
        UNTIL LR-STATUS = 'NO-MORE-POS'.
```

Notice that the OBTAIN FIRST PLAYER-DATA statement supplies a *selection criterion* that LRF uses to retrieve the desired Player-Data logical record. IF statements that follow the OBTAIN statement test various status conditions that the Logical Record Facility might return in the LR-STATUS field.

The database administration staff must define the path status conditions NO-PLAYER and NO-MORE-POS when the Player-Data logical record is defined in the subschema. We will see an example of how this is done after we finish looking at the application program. The LR-FOUND status is a system-supplied path status name that indicates that the required logical record has been found.

```
ID DIVISION.
PROGRAM-ID.      LRFPROG.
ENVIRONMENT DIVISION.
IDMS-CONTROL SECTION.
PROTOCOL.
    MODE IS BATCH DEBUG
    IDMS-RECORDS WITHIN WORKING-STORAGE SECTION.
INPUT-OUTPUT SECTION.
FILE-CONTROL.
    SELECT REPORT-FILE ASSIGN UT-S-SYSPRINT.
    SELECT INPUT-FILE  ASSIGN UT-S-SYSIN.
DATA DIVISION.
SCHEMA SECTION.
DB  SUBLRF  WITHIN SCHBASE.
FILE SECTION.
FD  REPORT-FILE
    RECORDING MODE IS F
    LABEL RECORDS ARE STANDARD
    RECORD CONTAINS 133 CHARACTERS.
01  REPORT-REC          PIC X(133).

FD  INPUT-FILE
    RECORDING MODE IS F
    LABEL RECORDS ARE STANDARD
    RECORD CONTAINS 80 CHARACTERS.
01  INPUT-REC.
    05  INPUT-PLAYER-NAME  PIC X(20).
    05  FILLER             PIC X(60).

WORKING-STORAGE SECTION.

01  EOF-SWITCH          PIC X     VALUE 'N'.
    88  END-OF-FILE     VALUE 'Y'.

01  PLAYER-LINE.
    05  FILLER             PIC X(22) VALUE ' POSITIONS FOR PLAYER '.
    05  RPT-PLAYER-NAME    PIC X(20).
    05  FILLER             PIC X(11) VALUE ' FROM TEAM '.
    05  RPT-TEAM-NAME      PIC X(20).
01  POSITION-LINE.
    05  FILLER             PIC X(22) VALUE '        POSITION NAME '.
    05  RPT-POSITION-NAME  PIC X(20).
    05  FILLER             PIC X(14) VALUE 'INNINGS PLAYED'.
    05  RPT-INNINGS-PLAYED PIC ZZ9.
```

Figure 18.5 Logical record retrieval program.

(Continued)

```
PROCEDURE DIVISION.

BEGIN-PROGRAM.

    OPEN OUTPUT REPORT-FILE    INPUT INPUT-FILE.
    COPY    IDMS SUBSCHEMA-BINDS.
    PERFORM IDMS-STATUS.
    READ     INPUT-FILE
             AT END MOVE 'Y' TO EOF-SWITCH.
    PERFORM  MAINLINE-RTN
       UNTIL END-OF-FILE.

    FINISH.
    PERFORM IDMS-STATUS.

    CLOSE   REPORT-FILE
            INPUT-FILE.
    STOP RUN.

MAINLINE-RTN.

    MOVE INPUT-PLAYER-NAME TO PLAYER-NAME.

    OBTAIN FIRST PLAYER-DATA
        WHERE PLAYER-NAME EQ PLAYER-NAME OF LR.

    IF LR-STATUS = 'NO-PLAYER'

        MOVE '** NO PLAYER RECORD  **' TO TEAM-NAME
        PERFORM WRITE-PLAYER-LINE-RTN

    ELSE IF LR-STATUS = 'LR-FOUND'

        PERFORM WRITE-PLAYER-LINE-RTN
        PERFORM WRITE-POSITION-INFO-RTN
            UNTIL LR-STATUS = 'NO-MORE-POS'.

    READ INPUT-FILE
        AT END MOVE 'Y' TO EOF-SWITCH.

WRITE-PLAYER-LINE-RTN.
    MOVE PLAYER-NAME      TO  RPT-PLAYER-NAME.
    MOVE TEAM-NAME        TO  RPT-TEAM-NAME.
    WRITE REPORT-REC FROM PLAYER-LINE
        AFTER ADVANCING 2 LINES.

WRITE-POSITION-INFO-RTN.
    MOVE  POSITION-NAME             TO RPT-POSITION-NAME.
    MOVE  POSITION-INNINGS-PLAYED TO RPT-INNINGS-PLAYED.
    WRITE REPORT-REC FROM POSITION-LINE
        AFTER ADVANCING 2 LINES.
    OBTAIN NEXT PLAYER-DATA
        WHERE PLAYER-NAME EQ PLAYER-NAME OF LR.

IDMS-ABORT.
IDMS-ABORT-EXIT.
    EXIT.

COPY IDMS IDMS-STATUS.
```

Figure 18.5 (Continued)

After a Player-Data logical record has been retrieved, the program performs the WRITE-PLAYER-LINE-RTN paragraph to write the player and position information on the output report. It then executes the WRITE-POSITION-INFO-RTN paragraph repeatedly.

The first time through, the WRITE-POSITION-INFO-RTN paragraph writes out the position information that has already been retrieved in the first occurrence of the Player-Data logical record:

```
        PERFORM WRITE-POSITION-INFO-RTN
            UNTIL LR-STATUS = 'NO-MORE-POS'.
                              .
                              .
                              .
WRITE-POSITION-INFO-RTN.
    MOVE   POSITION-NAME            TO RPT-POSITION-NAME.
    MOVE   POSITION-INNINGS-PLAYED TO RPT-INNINGS-PLAYED.
    WRITE REPORT-REC FROM POSITION-LINE
        AFTER ADVANCING 2 LINES.
    OBTAIN NEXT PLAYER-DATA
        WHERE PLAYER-NAME EQ PLAYER-NAME OF LR.
```

The program then attempts to retrieve the next occurrence of the Player-Data logical record for the same player. The process is repeated until the NO-MORE-POS status indicates that all Player-Data logical record occurrences for the requested player have been retrieved. Notice that we are testing the NO-MORE-POS condition in the statement that performs WRITE-POSITION-INFO-RTN.

In the preceding discussion, there is nothing in the program logic that requires a knowledge of the existence of Team, Player, and Position records. Nor is there any reference in the program to set relationships. The application program needs to know only the field structure of the Player-Data logical record and the meanings of the NO-PLAYER, NO-MORE-POSITIONS, and LR-FOUND conditions. The meanings of these condition names are normally documented in the form of comments in the subschema definition.

SUBSCHEMA LOGICAL RECORD DEFINITION

We will next look at the statements in the subschema DDL that define database navigation instructions that permit the logical record facility to construct occurrences of the Player-Data logical record. Figure 18.6 shows the complete subschema for the application program from Fig. 18.5. The following ADD LOGICAL RECORD statement from the subschema defines the Player-Data logical record:

```
        ADD    LOGICAL RECORD  PLAYER-DATA
               ELEMENTS ARE     TEAM-REC
                                PLAYER-REC
                                POSITION-REC.
```

```
ADD    SUBSCHEMA          SUBLRF
       OF SCHEMA          SCHBASE
       DMCL               DMCLBASE
       USAGE              LR.


ADD    AREA               TEAM-AREA.
ADD    AREA               POSITION-AREA.


ADD    RECORD             TEAM-REC
       ELEMENTS ARE          ALL.

ADD    RECORD             PLAYER-REC
       ELEMENTS ARE          PLAYER-NAME
                             PLAYER-PHONE.


ADD    RECORD             POSITION-REC
       ELEMENTS ARE          POSITION-NAME
                             POSITION-INNINGS-PLAYED.


ADD    SET                TEAM-PLAYER.
ADD    SET                PLAYER-POSITION.


ADD    LOGICAL RECORD     PLAYER-DATA
       ELEMENTS ARE          TEAM-REC
                             PLAYER-REC
                             POSITION-REC.


ADD    PATH-GROUP         OBTAIN PLAYER-DATA
       SELECT FOR FIELDNAME-EQ PLAYER-NAME
            OBTAIN PLAYER-REC
                 WHERE CALCKEY EQ PLAYER-NAME OF REQUEST
                 ON 0326 RETURN NO-PLAYER
            OBTAIN OWNER WITHIN TEAM-PLAYER
            OBTAIN EACH POSITION-REC WITHIN PLAYER-POSITION
                 ON 0307 RETURN NO-MORE-POS.

GENERATE.
```

Figure 18.6   Logical record retrieval program subschema.

These statements name the Team, Player, and Position records as *elements* of the Player-Data logical record. The ADD LOGICAL RECORD statement defines the structure of the logical record.

The ADD PATH-GROUP statement from the subschema defines the DML statements that the Logical Record Facility will issue to IDMS/R in constructing each logical record occurrence:

```
ADD    PATH-GROUP         OBTAIN PLAYER-DATA
       SELECT FOR FIELDNAME-EQ PLAYER-NAME
            OBTAIN PLAYER-REC
                 WHERE CALCKEY EQ PLAYER-NAME OF REQUEST
                 ON 0326 RETURN NO-PLAYER
            OBTAIN OWNER WITHIN TEAM-PLAYER
            OBTAIN EACH POSITION-REC WITHIN PLAYER-POSITION
                 ON 0307 RETURN NO-MORE-POS.
```

Notice that the individual instructions in the path group definition resemble the DML statements that are coded in application programs. The first DML statement in the path group definition is similar to an OBTAIN CALC statement. The OBTAIN statement is followed by an OBTAIN OWNER statement for a Team record. The last one is an OBTAIN EACH WITHIN SET statement for retrieving Position records. ON clauses in two of the OBTAIN statements are used to inform the application program of certain conditions. As we have already seen, the application program can test the NO-PLAYER and NO-MORE-POS conditions.

DATABASE UPDATING   Any DML functions that can be performed by conventional OBTAIN, STORE, MODIFY, and ERASE functions can also be performed by the Logical Record Facility. The database administration staff can define logical records that allow application programs to easily perform database updating functions as well as database retrievals. The programmer, if given an appropriate subschema, can issue DML statements that add new logical records and replace or delete existing ones. Again, these updating functions can be performed without a knowledge of the structure of the database.

We will next look in more detail at the DML statements that are used in the sample logical record retrieval program.

THE OBTAIN FIRST PLAYER-DATA STATEMENT   As we have seen, a request by a program to retrieve a logical record is handled by statements included in the subschema the program uses. In setting up the subschema, the database administration staff defines a number of different *path groups* in the subschema. LRF uses the logical record that is being accessed and the type of DML statement that was issued to choose a path group to satisfy a logical record request. Notice that the logical record retrieval statement from the sample program requests the first Player-Data record where the value of the Player-Name data element is equal to the value stored in the record work area:

```
MOVE INPUT-PLAYER-NAME TO PLAYER-NAME.

OBTAIN FIRST PLAYER-DATA
    WHERE PLAYER-NAME EQ PLAYER-NAME OF LR.

IF LR-STATUS = 'NO-PLAYER'

    MOVE '** NO PLAYER RECORD  **' TO TEAM-NAME
    PERFORM WRITE-PLAYER-LINE-RTN

ELSE IF LR-STATUS = 'LR-FOUND'

    PERFORM WRITE-PLAYER-LINE-RTN
    PERFORM WRITE-POSITION-INFO-RTN
        UNTIL LR-STATUS = 'NO-MORE-POS'.
```

Once LRF has chosen a path group, it then uses the information specified in the program's WHERE clause to choose a specific *path* from within that path group. To satisfy the request in our example, a path gives specific instructions for navigating the database and locating the occurrences of the Team, Player, and Position records that are required to construct the requested Player-Data logical record.

We will next show how the WHERE clause can be coded to specify record selection criteria.

THE WHERE CLAUSE

As we have seen, a WHERE clause can be included in a logical record DML statement to specify logical record selection criteria. We can select a logical record in two ways: by coding a keyword defined in the subschema or by coding an explicit comparison statement. We can also combine these two techniques by using the Boolean operators AND, OR, and NOT in a WHERE clause. We have already seen an example of a comparison statement. The WHERE clause that we looked at in the previous example selects a record *where* the Player-Name data element contains a specific value.

SUBSCHEMA-DEFINED KEYWORDS

Suppose the database administration staff wanted to make it easy for application programmers to retrieve Player-Data logical-record occurrences based on the values of the Team-Name and Position-Name data elements. Assume the database administration staff has assigned the keyword CHIC-SHORTSTOP to a path that contains database navigation instructions for constructing Player-Data record occurrences where the Team-Name value is Chicago and the Position-Name value is Shortstop. We cause LRF to choose this particular path by coding the subschema-defined keyword in a WHERE clause in our request for a logical record retrieval:

```
OBTAIN NEXT PLAYER-DATA WHERE CHIC-SHORTSTOP.
```

In processing the OBTAIN request, LRF selects the CHIC-SHORTSTOP path and uses the database navigation instructions it finds there to retrieve an occurrence of Player-Data constructed from a Team record that has a Team-Name data element value of Chicago and a Position record that has a Position-Name data element value of Shortstop.

WHERE CLAUSE COMPARISONS

We will next examine in more detail the kinds of comparison statements that can be specified in a WHERE clause. The subschema indicates the types of comparisons that can be made and tells the names of the logical record data element values that can be referenced in comparisons. Here, we will discuss the general rules that must be followed in coding comparison statements. The following statement shows a WHERE clause with a comparison statement:

```
OBTAIN NEXT PLAYER-DATA
     WHERE POSITION-NAME = POSITION-NAME OF LR.
```

In the example, the application program supplies a Position-Name data element value. LRF selects an appropriate path and uses the supplied Position-Name value in constructing an appropriate occurrence of Player-Data. Comparison statements can use all the conventional comparison operators:

- EQ (IS) (=)   Equal to
- NE (N) (#)   Not equal to
- GT (H) (>)   Greater than
- LT (L) (<)   Less than
- GE (>=) (=>)   Greater than or equal to
- LE (<=) (=<)   Less than or equal to

In addition to the foregoing operators, we can also use the MATCHES and CONTAINS operators.

The following example shows a WHERE clause that uses the MATCHES operator:

```
OBTAIN NEXT PLAYER-DATA
     WHERE POSITION-NAME MATCHES '@@@@@@@@@@@@@@@@@@@'.
```

When the MATCHES operator is used, the operand on the right serves as a mask that is used in controlling the comparison. Each character in the operand on the left is compared against the corresponding character in the operand on the right. The following three special characters can be included in the mask to control the results of the comparison:

@   Matches any alphabetic character
#   Matches any numeric character
*   Matches any numeric or alphabetic character

In the previous example, the WHERE clause selects a Player-Data record occurrence that has a Position-Name data element value that consists of all alphabetic characters.

The following example shows a WHERE clause that includes the CONTAINS operator:

```
OBTAIN NEXT PLAYER-DATA
    WHERE POSITION-NAME CONTAINS ' '.
```

In the example, LRF selects a Player-Data logical record that has a Position-Name data element value that contains one or more spaces.

A WHERE clause can contain more than one comparison and/or specify more than one subschema-defined keyword; they can be connected with the Boolean operators, AND and OR. The NOT operator can also be used in conjunction with AND or OR. In the following example, the WHERE clause includes an AND operator:

```
OBTAIN NEXT PLAYER-DATA
    WHERE CHIC-SHORTSTOP AND PLAYER-NAME = PLAYER-NAME OF LR.
```

In the example, the WHERE clause tells LRF to use the subschema-defined keyword CHIC-SHORTSTOP in selecting an appropriate path *and* to select a Player-Data logical record that has a specified Player-Name data element value.

THE ON CLAUSE

As with conventional DML statements, we can use an ON clause, when the AUTOSTATUS protocol is in effect, to test for the path status that is returned by LRF. We can also test for a specific path status by means of a conventional COBOL IF statement, as in the sample program we have been examining. The following OBTAIN statement includes an ON clause to test for a specific path status:

```
OBTAIN NEXT PLAYER-DATA WHERE CHIC-SHORTSTOP
    ON LR-NOT-FOUND
        PERFORM NOT-FOUND-ROUTINE.
```

PATH-STATUS NAMES

The Logical Record Facility allows the database administration staff to define, in the subschema, any number of path-status names. In addition to path-status names that the database administration staff defines in the subschema, LRF supplies the following three standard path-status names that can be referenced in DML statements that access logical records:

- LR-FOUND. The requested logical record has been successfully retrieved and is available in variable storage.

- LR-NOT-FOUND. The requested logical record cannot be found.
- LR-ERROR. An error has occurred in the processing of the selected path.

UPDATING LOGICAL RECORDS

In the previous examples, we have been using the OBTAIN statement to illustrate WHERE and ON clause options. If the subschema allows updating of the logical records it defines, the database can be updated using the following DML statements:

- STORE
- MODIFY
- ERASE

Since the Logical Record Facility makes sets transparent to the application program, the connect, disconnect, and if functions are not used with logical records. The find and get functions are also not supported. The logical record updating statements can also include WHERE clauses to select the logical records to update and ON clauses to test the results of the operation.

THE STORE STATEMENT

The STORE statement is used to create a new occurrence of a logical record. The store function does not necessarily create new occurrences of each of the database records that make up the new logical record. For example, suppose we create a new occurrence of the Player-Data logical record with the following statements:

```
PERFORM BUILD-PLAYER-DATA-RTN.

STORE PLAYER-DATA WHERE PLAYER-NAME = PLAYER-NAME OF LR
    ON NO-TEAM PERFORM NO-TEAM-RTN.
```

LRF may determine that appropriate occurrences of the Player and Team records already exist in the database. In that case, only a new Position record will actually be added to the database.

THE MODIFY STATEMENT

The MODIFY statement is used to replace logical record data element values with new values. As with conventional DML MODIFY statements, the logical record must first be retrieved before it can be updated using a MODIFY statement. The following example shows how a MODIFY statement can be used to update a logical record:

```
OBTAIN PLAYER-DATA WHERE CHIC-SHORTSTOP
     ON LR-FOUND PERFORM REPLACE-ROUTINE.
                      .
                      .
                      .
     REPLACE-ROUTINE.
          MOVE NEW-DATE TO POSITION-DATE.
          MODIFY PLAYER-DATA.
```

THE ERASE STATEMENT

The ERASE statement is used to delete an occurrence of a logical record. The ERASE function does not necessarily erase all the database records that make up the logical record being erased. For example, suppose we erase a particular Player-Data logical record using the following ERASE statement:

```
ERASE PLAYER-DATA WHERE CHIC-SHORTSTOP
    AND PLAYER-NAME = PLAYER-NAME OF LR.
```

The Team record may not be erased if it still has Player and Game member records associated with it. The Player record may not be erased if it still has other Position member records associated with it. Even the Position record may not be erased if it is still associated with a Game owner record.

SUMMARY

The Logical Record Facility allows a database administration staff member to define logical records that describe quasi-relational views of the data stored in a network-structured database. The application program can then request the retrieval of a logical record without having to be aware of the record and set structure of the database. LRF combines data elements that it extracts from database records to form the requested occurrence of the logical record. The DML statements that define the database navigation that is required to construct an occurrence of the logical record are specified in path definitions in the subschema rather than in the application program.

19 THE AUTOMATIC SYSTEM FACILITY

The Automatic System Facility (ASF) is a menu-driven system that allows users to define database records and automatically generate all supporting structures, including data definitions, screens, and documentation. The relationship between ASF and other IDMS/R components is shown in Fig. 19.1. ASF allows an end user to create simple applications with very little training in its use.

ASF uses a relational database structure rather than a network-structured database. In a relational database, all relationships between data are represented in the form of simple two-dimensional tables in which data elements are arranged in columns and rows. ASF supports two types of tables: *stored* tables and *derived* tables. Derived tables are also called *views*. Stored tables are physically stored in the database, while views are derived from the information in the stored tables.

The top half of Fig. 19.2 shows a representation of a typical stored table. The Player table stores the same data that we have been maintaining in a Player record in a network-structured database. Each row in the table stores the data for one player. Each column contains all the data element values for a particular data element.

In a relational database, we apply relational operators to previously defined stored tables or views to create new views of those tables. ASF provides three relational operators that can be applied to stored tables or views that we have already defined:

- The Select operator is used to include only certain rows from an existing table or view in creating a new view.

- The Project operator is used to include only certain columns from an existing table or view in creating a new view.

- The Join operator is used to combine tables based on common data element values in one or more columns in creating a new view.

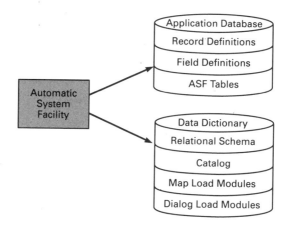

Figure 19.1 Automatic System Facility components.

Player Table

Player-Name	Player-Phone-Number	Batting-Average
SHORT	(312) 555-6161	.222
CONNORS	(815) 555-1031	.317
MITCHELL	(606) 555-4198	.104
WILSON	(312) 555-1425	.193
MILLER	(815) 555-8152	.087
JACKSON	(815) 555-8881	.100

Select All Players Whose Batting Average
is Greater than .200.

Project Player-Name, Batting-Average

High Batting Average Table

Player-Name	Batting-Average
SHORT	.222
CONNORS	.317

Figure 19.2 The Select and Project relational operators can be used to create a new view of a table.

In the bottom portion of Fig. 19.2 we see an example that uses the Select and Project operations to create a new view that we have named the High Batting Average table. First, we selected for our rows all players whose batting average is higher than .200. Then, we projected for our columns the Player-Name and Batting-Average columns. The resulting High Batting Average table displays the player name and batting average for each player whose batting average is higher than .200.

Figure 19.3 shows another table, the Team All-Star table. It is composed of team name, city name, and the names of all players designated as all-stars. We can use the Join operator to create a view that combines columns from both the Player table described earlier and the Team All-Star table, based on the common Player-Name column. By using the Join operator, we can create a new view that combines data from both tables as if it all resided in the same table.

Player Table

Player-Name	Player-Phone-Number	Batting-Average
SHORT	(312) 555-6161	.222
CONNORS	(815) 555-1031	.317
MITCHELL	(606) 555-4198	.104
WILSON	(312) 555-1425	.193
MILLER	(815) 555-8152	.087
JACKSON	(815) 555-8881	.100

Team All-Star Table

Team-Name	Team-City	Player-Name
PURPLES	WAUKEGAN	SHORT
PURPLES	WAUKEGAN	WILSON
TORNADOS	LOCKPORT	MILLER
SLUGGERS	WAUKEGAN	JACKSON

Join Player, Team.

All-Star Player Table

Player-Name	Player-Phone-Number	Batting-Average	Team-Name	Team-City
SHORT	(312) 555-6161	.222	PURPLES	WAUKEGAN
WILSON	(312) 555-1425	.193	PURPLES	WAUKEGAN
MILLER	(815) 555-8152	.087	TORNADOS	LOCKPORT
JACKSON	(815) 555-8881	.100	SLUGGERS	WAUKEGAN

Figure 19.3 The Join relational operator can be used to create a view that combines columns from two or more tables.

The result of joining the two tables is the All-Star Player table. It shows all of the all-star players found on the Team All-Star table but with additional player information listed.

AUTOMATIC SYSTEM FACILITY FUNCTIONS

There are four major functions that ASF provides:

- **Table definition functions.** These functions include such tasks as defining ASF tables and views, storing new tables in the system, and deleting existing tables.
- **Data manipulation functions.** These functions include loading data into tables, selecting data for display, and changing or deleting data.
- **Passkey functions.** These functions control security.
- **Administrative functions.** These functions allow authorized personnel to control and maintain the ASF system.

In this chapter, we will concentrate on the first two sets of ASF functions, table definition and data manipulation. Refer to the Cullinet documentation for information about the passkey and administrative functions.

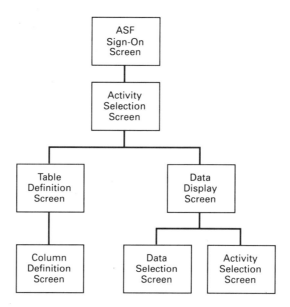

Figure 19.4   Hierarchy of ASF screens.

AUTOMATIC SYSTEM FACILITY SCREENS

ASF is a menu-driven system. Figure 19.4 shows the hierarchy of the most commonly used screens that ASF displays. We will next examine the screens used in the table definition and data manipulation functions.

The ASF Sign-on Screen

Figure 19.5 shows the first screen we see after we call up ASF, the ASF Sign-on screen. This screen asks us to supply a password and the name of a catalog.

The Activity Selection Screen

Figure 19.6 shows the Activity Selection screen. We will primarily be interested in the define table, display/change data, and select data functions.

The Table Definition Screen

The Table Definition screen is shown in Fig. 19.7. In this example, we are defining a Player-Team view that uses a Join operation to combine columns from the Player and Team tables that we defined previously. In the table derivation section, we enter Player as the first source table name and Team as the second. The next step is to name the columns from each table that will participate in the

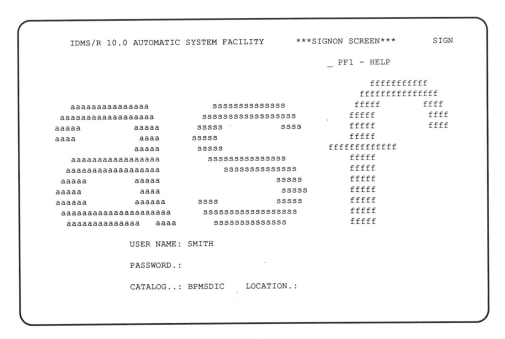

Figure 19.5 ASF Sign-on screen.

```
                            CULLINET SOFTWARE                              C8407G
          IDMS/R 10.0 AUTOMATIC SYSTEM FACILITY     ***ACTIVITY SELECTION***   ASEL
DC560004 SELECT A TABLE

USER NAME: SMITH

 _  PF1 - HELP                  _  PF6  - POPULATE DATA      _  PF14  - SIGNON
 _  PF2 - DEFINE TABLE          _  PF7  - PAGE BACKWARD      _  PA1   - PRIOR LEVEL
 _  PF3 - LOAD DATA             _  PF8  - PAGE FORWARD       _  CLEAR - LEAVE ASF
 _  PF4 - DISPLAY/CHANGE DATA   _  PF9  - PASSKEY
 _  PF5 - SELECT DATA           _  PF13 - QUERY

TABLE NAME.: PLAYER TEAM
TABLE OWNER: SMITH

                                                              PAGE:  1  OF   1

 _  PLAYER
 _  TEAM
```

Figure 19.6 Activity Selection screen.

```
       IDMS/R 10.0 AUTOMATIC SYSTEM FACILITY     ***TABLE DEFINITION***     TDEF
DC560203 TABLE UNDEFINED
TABLE NAME.: PLAYER TEAM
TABLE OWNER: SMITH                           DEFN NUMBER:
VIEW/STORED: STORED                             STATUS.....: NEW
COMMENTS...:

        _  PF1 - HELP                 _  PF4 - EXTENDED TABLE DEFINITION
        _  PF2 - DEFINE COLUMNS       _  PF5 - DELETE TABLE DEFINITION
        _  PF3 - GENERATE             _  PF6 - MESSAGE SCREEN

                        TABLE DERIVATION
SOURCE TABLE #1
 TABLE NAME.: PLAYER
 TABLE OWNER: SMITH

SOURCE TABLE #2
 TABLE NAME.: TEAM
 TABLE OWNER: SMITH

COLUMN #1: PLAYER NAME
COLUMN #2: TEAM MEMBER NAME                WHERE COLUMN #1 EQ COLUMN #2
```

Figure 19.7 Table Definition screen.

Join operation. In this case, the Player-Name column from the first table will be joined with Team-Member-Name column from the second table. Notice that in the upper lefthand corner of the screen ASF has displayed "STORED" as its default. We will overtype "STORED" with "VIEW" when generating a view.

The Column Definition Screen

We next use the Column Definition screen shown in Fig. 19.8 to list the columns in the new table. For each column, we provide the field length (called *width* by ASF) and type of data. Player-Phone and Batting-Average are described as 'n' for numeric; the others are 't' for text data. Finally, we establish one field, the Player-Name field, as a unique key. After defining our columns, we can return to the Table Definition screen to generate the table. Generation stores the definition, creates an application for the table, and makes it available for use.

The Data Display Screen

An all-purpose screen for adding, changing, deleting, and displaying our table entries is the Data Display screen pictured in Fig. 19.9. We reach this screen from the Activity Selection screen by selecting the load data or display/change data functions. Our table columns are listed on the left side of the screen. To

```
    IDMS/R 10.0 AUTOMATIC SYSTEM FACILITY      **COLUMN DEFINITION**      CDEF
  DC560306 NO FIELDS DEFINED FOR TABLE
  TABLE NAME.: PLAYER TEAM

  _  PF1 - HELP                        _  PF3 - EXTENDED SELECTION DEFINITION
  _  PF2 - EXTENDED COLUMN DEFINITION  _  PF4 - EXTENDED KEY DEFINITION

     PAGE:  1  OF  1


                                              UNIQUE  FROM      THRU     DISPLAY
          COLUMN NAME            WIDTH   TYPE  KEY     VALUE     VALUE    SEQ EXT
     player name                  30     t      x
     player phone                 10     n
     batting average               3     n
     team name                    20     t
     team address                 40     t
```

Figure 19.8   Column Definition screen.

```
                              CULLINET SOFTWARE
            PF1 = ADD; PF2 = CHANGE; PF3 = DELETE; ENTER = NEXT; CLEAR = EXIT
            PLAYER TEAM

            PLAYER NAME

            PLAYER PHONE

            BATTING AVERAGE

            TEAM NAME

            TEAM ADDRESS
```

Figure 19.9   Data Display screen.

load data, we enter values corresponding to the columns and press the PF1 key. Pressing ENTER clears the screen of data, but not the column names, so we can continue to enter rows into our table. Changing and deleting table entries is done in a similar fashion, using the PF keys listed at the top of the screen.

The Data Selection Screen

Having defined our table and loaded it with data, we can use relational operators to select table rows and columns that we want to display. ASF allows two basic approaches to formatting commands: fixed format and free form. We will introduce ASF facilities using fixed-format commands. Figure 19.10 illustrates the general structure of ASF fixed-format commands. Each command consists of two operands separated by a conditional operator. The first operator is one of the table's columns. The second operator can be another table column, an arithmetic expression, a decimal number, or a quoted string. A range of values can also be expressed using the THRU keyword, or a choice of values can be specified by separating a series of expressions with commas.

Figure 19.11 shows the Data Selection screen on which we have entered our display request. Note that all of the columns in the Player-Team table are listed under Field Name and each has been assigned an ID number. We have

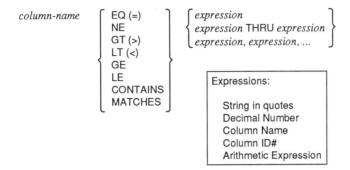

Figure 19.10   Structure of ASF fixed-format commands.

keyed in our commands under the Selection Criteria heading. In this particular example, we are asking for a display of players whose batting averages are greater than .300.

On the Data Display screen shown in Fig. 19.12 we see the result of our request. The entry for Connors is displayed, with data from two tables merged. If desired, we can keep pressing the ENTER key to walk through all the selections that meet our search criteria.

```
      IDMS/R 10.0 AUTOMATIC SYSTEM FACILITY    *** DATA SELECTION ***    DSEL
   DC560603 ENTER SELECTION CRITERIA
   RECORD NAME: PLAYER TEAM
           _ PF1 - HELP      _ PF2  - MESSAGE SCREEN        PAGE:   1  OF   1

    ID          FIELD NAME                   SELECTION CRITERIA
   0001 PLAYER NAME
   0002 PLAYER PHONE
   0003 BATTING AVERAGE            gt  .300
   0004 TEAM NAME
   0005 TEAM ADDRESS
```

Figure 19.11   Data Selection screen.

```
                              CULLINET SOFTWARE
        PF1 = ADD; PF2 = CHANGE; PF3 = DELETE; ENTER = NEXT; CLEAR = EXIT
        PLAYER TEAM

        PLAYER NAME                     CONNORS

        PLAYER PHONE                    (815) 555-1031

        BATTING AVERAGE                 .317

        TEAM NAME                       TORNADOS

        TEAM CITY                       LOCKPORT
```

Figure 19.12   Data Display screen.

AUTOMATIC SYSTEM   ASF maintains all the various application data-
FACILITY OPERATION   bases that users create and also accesses the data
                         dictionary. ASF uses the data dictionary to store
relational schemas. A relational schema contains definitions of *relational definition records* that are used to define tables. Relational definition records are
stored in the application database itself. Box 19.1 lists the different types of relational definition records that ASF creates. The application database also contains the tables themselves.

The data dictionary contains, in addition to the relational schema, a *catalog,* which serves as a directory of users and tables. As ASF uses tables, it references the catalog. The dictionary also stores the map and dialog load modules
that are used by ASF in formatting the screens that it displays.

When we use the Table Definition screen to create a new table, ASF performs the following functions:

- Assigns a table definition number to the table.
- Adds an occurrence of the Record Definition record using the table definition
  number to identify the table.
- Stores the table name and number in the catalog.
- Adds a Field Definition record for each column in the table.
- Adds a key header record for each index defined for the table.

BOX 19.1   Relational definition records

- **Record definition record.** Defines a table.
- **Field definition record.** Defines columns in a table.
- **Element definition record.** Describes internal characteristics of a column.
- **Record derivation record.** Used to connect columns in views to their source tables.
- **Join record.** Provides information ASF uses to build the logical record path used in accessing source records in a view.
- **Record selection record.** Holds the selection criteria used in building logical record path DML statements.
- **Key header record.** Defines the index key for a table.
- **Key element record.** Defines the elements contained in an index key.

Figure 19.13 shows the internal structure of a stored table. A special-purpose database record is the owner of an indexed set that has table data records as members. Each occurrence of a member record is a row in the table. The Player record for Short is row 1, the record for Connors is row 2, and so forth. To access the table, ASF walks the indexed set and obtains all data records.

When we generate a stored table, ASF adds record and element definitions that describe the table rows and columns to the dictionary. Then, record and set

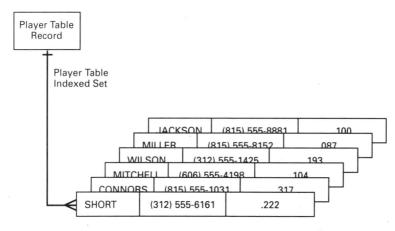

Figure 19.13   Player table physical storage structure.

descriptions are added to the relational schema. When generating a view, a new subschema is created that defines a logical record with paths that allow the various DML manipulation activities. Then, a map is generated using the defined columns as data fields. Finally, a dialog is generated that uses the subschema and map and allows online access of the table.

INTEGRATION WITH OTHER IDMS/R PRODUCTS   The Automatic System Facility is integrated with many other related Cullinet products. We will briefly describe how ASF relates to some of the other major IDMS/R components.

- **Integrated Data Dictionary (IDD).** As we have seen, ASF uses IDD to store relational schemas, the ASF catalog, and map and dialog load modules.
- **OnLine Query (OLQ).** OLQ is a database retrieval system that is closely linked to ASF. It allows the user to call up OLQ while using ASF to display a data table. OLQ can create data tables for use within ASF as well as perform relational operations on ASF tables. See Appendix I for a brief introduction to OLQ.
- **ADS/OnLine (ADSO).** ADS/OnLine applications can access ASF data tables within dialogs, and ADS/OnLine facilities can be used to modify dialogs that ASF generates.
- **OnLine mapping facility (OLM).** OLM can be used to modify maps that ASF generates. Also, model maps can be created using OLM that can be used by ASF for the screens that it generates for data tables.
- **Data manipulation language (DML).** IDMS/R application programs written in conventional programming languages can be used to access ASF tables by using the Logical Record Facility described in Chapter 18.

SUMMARY   The Automatic System Facility allows users to define relational databases that can be accessed online using a terminal. ASF provides a series of screens that enables the user to perform relational operations on tables, including an ASF Sign-on screen, an Activity Selection screen, a Table Definition screen, a Column Definition screen, a Data Display screen, and a Data Selection screen. ASF works in conjunction with IDD and stores user data in application databases. ASF automatically generates data definitions, maps, and documentation. A relational database represents data in the form of two-dimensional tables. A user can access stored tables or views, which are derived from stored tables. Views can combine data from two or more tables and can provide security by limiting access to certain rows and columns. Relational processing involves three relational operators: *Select,* to limit a view to only certain rows; *Project,* to limit a view to only certain columns; and *Join,* to create a view that combines columns from two or more tables.

PART **VI** APPENDICES

▌ RELATED PRODUCTS

Cullinet offers IDMS/R users additional products that enhance the capabilities of IDMS/R. Some of these complementary products can stand alone; others must be integrated with IDMS/R. We will briefly describe some of the more important products. Reference materials are available for each product that describe in greater detail the features of the product.

TRANSFER CONTROL FACILITY

The Transfer Control Facility (TCF) of IDMS/R provides windowing facilities that can be used by other Cullinet products. TCF allows the user to interact with many different sessions concurrently and enables the user to jump from one session to another. The main menu of TCF, shown in Fig. I.1, lists the tools available to the user. A secondary menu containing a list of all currently active suspended sessions is built dynamically during a TCF session, including multiple sessions with the same tool. Within a TCF session a user can jump from one tool directly into another without going through the main menu.

INFORMATION DATABASE

The Information Database product (IDB) allows data to be extracted from IDMS/R databases, from conventional files, and from databases organized using other database management systems. The files thus extracted can be accessed by users at personal computers. The product allows files to be moved back and forth between the mainframe and the personal computer workstations. Cullinet software also markets a number of applications that run on personal computers of the IBM and IBM-compatible variety that interface directly with the Information Database product. Links to data on hardware such as DEC, Data General,

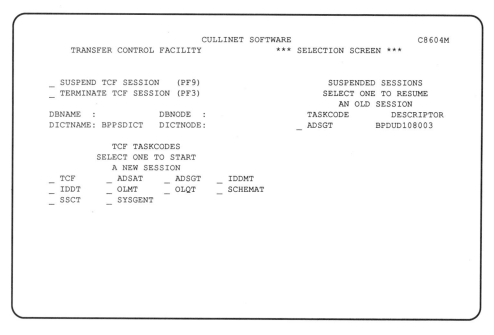

Figure 1.1 Transfer Control Facility selection screen.

and Wang are available as are links to Lotus personal computer software products, such as 1-2-3 and Symphony.

Rather than allowing PCs to read production databases directly, IDB organizes data in logical units called objects. Specific objects are transmitted to a personal computer on request. Another function of IDB is to provide a unified network for PCs, allowing them to communicate with each other and share information. A user can easily share objects with other PCs in the network. Users interact with IDB through catalogs that are managed by Goldengate, Cullinet's integrated software for personal computers. IDB is integrated with IDMS/R, which allows the database administration staff to manage both IDB and IDMS/R as a single system. IDB works with the DML compiler as well as the Automatic System Facility, and it supports access by CULPRIT, OnLine query, and ADS/OnLine.

DISTRIBUTED DATABASE SYSTEM

The Distributed Database System allows multiple IBM computers to share a common IDMS/R database by allowing the installation to define a network of such systems. It supports application programs at remote sites and allows them to access a central database with complete user transparency and full data integrity. A single network node can process a data-

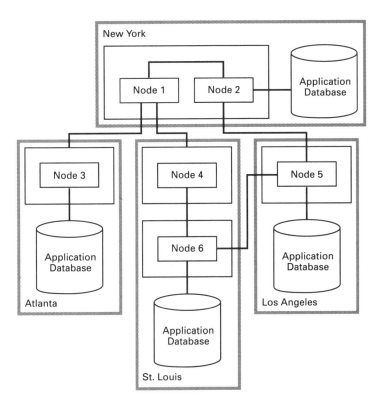

Figure I.2   With the distributed database system processors can be interconnected in a variety of ways. In this example, two nodes in the same system, two nodes in different processors at the same location, and nodes in processors at different locations are all interconnected to form a single network.

base retrieval request either by accessing a database under its control or by acting as a *host* and passing the request on to the node that controls the appropriate database. The *target* node, upon receiving the routed request, performs the database service and returns the results to the host node. Figure I.2 shows a possible DDS configuration that shows various ways in which nodes can be interconnected.

UNIVERSAL COMMUNICATIONS FACILITY   The Universal Communications Facility (UCF) allows IDMS-DC applications to run under the control of telecommunications monitors other than IDMS-DC. With UCF, programmers don't have to know the characteristics of the telecommunications monitor they are actually using. IDMS-DC applications can control terminals connected to CICS, SHADOW II,

Intercom, Westi, Task/Master, and others. UCF allows users with an investment in programs written under other telecommunications monitors to continue operating those systems while using IDMS-DC for new applications. UCF can also serve as a transition aid for installations that are converting to IDMS-DC from some other telecommunications monitor. Like IDMS-DC, UCF is fully integrated with IDMS/R and shares modules, storage, backup and recovery facilities, and dictionary/directory resources with the database system.

APPLICATION DEVELOPMENT SYSTEM/BATCH

The Application Development System/Batch (ADS/Batch) is a facility that simplifies and standardizes the development of IDMS/R batch application programs. Like its online counterpart, ADS/OnLine, ADS/Batch simplifies the programming effort by automatically handling input editing, database control and update functions, and error reporting and correction.

Figure I.3 shows the steps involved in using ADS/Batch. In step 1, the developer defines to IDD the input documents and messages to be used by the application. In step 2, the developer codes the application logic using a high-level, free-form language called the application development language (ADL). This source code is maintained by IDD. The ADL statements are processed by a language translator, which generates executable code. In step 3, the transaction processor is executed to run the completed batch application.

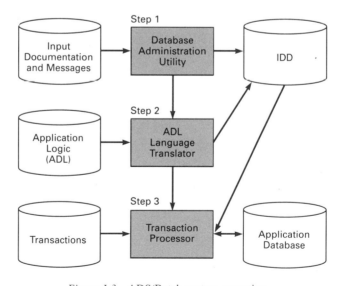

Figure I.3 ADS/Batch system operation.

CULPRIT is a report generator that can be used to produce complex reports with relatively simple coding. It can access files in a variety of formats, including sequential files and IDMS/R databases. CULPRIT offers the following features:

- Integration with IDD. CULPRIT copies record definitions for the file or database from the IDD dictionary database.
- Ability to retrieve automatically any number of record occurrences following set relationships defined for the subschema in use.
- Selective record retrieval based on CALC-, index-, or database-key values.
- Selective record retrieval based on the value of data contained in work areas or database records previously retrieved.

Figure I.4 shows the CULPRIT code that accesses the baseball database to produce a simple player salary report. Each line begins with an identifier that tells what type of information is contained on that line. For example, REC identifies input field elements; SORT determines the order of the report. Other lines start with 01 to identify them as belonging to report 01 and are followed by additional characters or numbers that further identify their purpose: A number in the third column indicates a parameter type. A line with a parameter of 5 defines a work field; a parameter of 7 specifies program logic. EDP AUDITOR is a re-

```
IN 200 F 400 PS(TAPE)
REC   PLAYER-NAME           5     25
REC   PLAYER-CAREER-START  30     34
REC   PLAYER-SALARY         50      7   3    DP=2
01OUT D
01SORT PLAYER-NAME
010 COUNT
013 PLAYER SALARY REPORT
0151*010   PLAYER-NAME    SZ=20   HH 'PLAYER' 'NAME'
0151*020   PLAYER-CAREER-START  HH 'CAREER' 'STARTING YEAR'
0151*030   AMOUNT      SZ=10   F$
0161*040   'NUMBER OF PLAYERS'
0161*050   COUNT
017010     MOVE PLAYER-SALARY TO AMOUNT
017020     COUNT + 1 COUNT
```

```
Report No.  01      PLAYER SALARY REPORT        08/10/88     Page 1

          Player           Career                  Salary
          Name             Starting Year

          Anderson         1980                    $50,000.00
          Booker           1986                    $95,400.40
          Maldin           1986                    $77,700.11

                                            Number of Employees    3
```

Figure I.4 CULPRIT program and the report it generates.

lated product that combines the capabilities of CULPRIT with a special library of audit routines. Also, IDD uses a version of CULPRIT to produce various dictionary reports.

ONLINE ENGLISH   OnLine English (OLE) is a version of the INTELLECT product developed by the Artificial Intelligence Corporation. OnLine English is a natural language inquiry system designed for use by users who have no background in computers. Operating with a large, flexible dictionary, this system has an outstanding ability to respond to conversational questions. OnLine English interprets and responds to questions concerning the contents of a data file. OLE builds an extract file from an IDMS/R database using a version of CULPRIT. The extract file is then accessed by the OLE user. The following is an OnLine English query:

```
Query: how many teams has Lefty Skinner played on?
Response: 4
Query: what are they?
Response: BROOKFIELD BULLS
         MADISON BLUEBIRDS
         DENVER PIKERS
         OMAHA SLUGGERS
Query: what is his batting average?
Response: .252
```

ONLINE QUERY   OnLine Query (OLQ) is an interactive information retrieval system. It is fully integrated with IDMS/R and requires no programming in order to use it. OLQ can be used by nontechnical users to retrieve information from an IDMS/R database. The terminal user requests that OLQ retrieve and display records by issuing retrieval commands that perform similar functions as the FIND and OBTAIN functions of IDMS/R. The user can retrieve database records to produce formatted reports. The OLQ language includes comparison operators (greater than, less than, etc.) and Boolean logic (and, or, and not operations) which can be combined in any desired manner. The user can store often-run queries in the data dictionary and run them at any time.

The following is an example of a typical OLQ query. It displays the name of the player whose CALC key is equal to Henderson:

```
GET PLAYER(PLAYER-NAME) WHERE(CALCKEY=HENDERSON)
```

INTERACT   INTERACT is a document processing system that supports program development, remote job processing, text editing, and word processing. It provides many of the same functions as IBM's TSO. INTERACT provides the terminal user with ready access to data such as documents, programs, and JCL, and makes them available for viewing and editing.

INTERACT allows the user to enter text from a terminal or through batch methods. Once entered, data can be manipulated by a full complement of INTERACT commands. INTERACT displays revised text as changes are applied. Text can be saved on direct access storage and can later be retrieved at the terminal. An automatic formatting facility of INTERACT can be used to create various types of documents.

GOLDENGATE　　　　　　GOLDENGATE is an integrated software package for IBM and IBM-compatible personal computers. GOLDENGATE provides support for word processing, local database management, spreadsheet, graphics, and data communications. The product provides split-screen capability, macro facilities, combined text and graphics output, data importing directly into ASCII, DIF, and dBASE formats, relational database management, sorting, and IBM 3270 terminal emulation.

Various types of utility programs are available to the database administration staff. These utility programs can be grouped into three categories:

IDMS/R
UTILITIES

Various types of utility programs are available to the database administration staff. These utility programs can be grouped into three categories:

- Dictionary utilities
- Backup/recovery utilities
- Database maintenance utilities

Following is a brief description of some of the more useful utility programs provided with IDMS/R.

DICTIONARY UTILITIES

- IDMSDIRL. The Directory Load utility loads the system schema and sub-schema into a dictionary.
- IDMSRPTS. The Data Dictionary Reports utility produces reports that summarize data dictionary contents.

BACKUP/RECOVERY UTILITIES

- IDMSAJNL. The Archive Journal utility offloads the disk journal to the archive tape.
- IDMSJFIX. The Journal Fix utility rewrites the tape journal file in use during a system failure.

- IDMSRBCK. The Rollback utility restores the database using before images recorded on the journal file.

- IDMSRFWD. The Rollforward utility restores the database using after images from the journal file.

- IDMSRSTR. The Restore utility restores the database from a backup file created by IDMSDUMP.

- RHDCFIXK. The Storage Key Fix utility resets pages in the IDMS-DC partition to the primary storage protect key after a system failure.

- RHDCPRLG. The Print Log utility prints the system log file.

- RHDCTJIN. The Transaction Log File Initialization utility initializes the system log file.

- JOURNAL REPORTER. The Journal Reporter produces reports summarizing the contents of the archive journal file.

- IDMSDUMP. The Database Dump utility creates a backup copy of a database.

DATABASE UTILITIES

- IDMSUNLD. The Database Unload utility creates a backup copy of a database for use with IDMSDBLU.

- IDMSDBLU. The Database Load utility loads a database for the first time or reloads a database using a backup copy created by IDMSUNLD.

- IDMSINIT. The Initialize utility initializes a database, transaction log, or disk journal file.

- IDMSLDEL. The Logical Delete utility physically erases logically deleted database records.

- IDMSRADM. The Relational Database Administration utility exports and imports relational tables to and from a sequential file.

- IDMSRSTU. The Restructure utility modifies database records in place, allowing global changes in record length, format, and set relationships.

- IDSMXPAG. The Expand Page utility increases the size of database pages.

- IDMSPFIX. The Page Fix utility prints and alters contents of database pages.

- IDMSDBAN. The Database Analysis utility examines and reports on pages, line indexes, records, and sets.

Appendix

III   NORMALIZATION

Normalization theory was first described by E. F. Codd and is used in practice to aid in database design. Normalization theory can be described in rigorous mathematical terms. However, its underlying ideas are simple and have much to do with ordinary common sense. In this appendix, we will rely on simple explanations and examples to show how the normalization process can be used to help stabilize the design of either network-structured or relational databases.

The overall goals of the normalization process are to

- Arrange data so that it can be represented in tabular form where each row-column position contains a single data element (no repeating groups).
- Ensure that data elements are associated with the correct keys, and thereby minimize data redundancy.

Normalization involves a series of steps that change the structure of the various records that make up a database by placing the data into a series of different forms called *first normal form, second normal form,* and so on. The normalization process that we discuss here can be applied to the tables that make up a relational database or to the records that make up a network-structured database.

FIRST NORMAL FORM

The first step of the normalization process is to place the data into *first normal form*. This involves the removal of repeating groups. We remove repeating groups by simply creating a separate record for each of the elements in the repeating group. Suppose we begin with the following employee data:

Here, a given record stores information about a number of different projects that a particular employee has worked on.

To represent this data in tabular form, we generate a separate record for each project by repeating the employee information in each record. Here is how the data would look in tabular form; each row represents a separate record occurrence:

Employee

Employee-#	Employee-Name	Job-Code	Job-Title	Project-#	Completion-Date	Hours-Worked
120	Jones	1	Programmer	01	7/17	37
120	Jones	1	Programmer	08	1/12	12
121	Harpo	1	Programmer	01	7/17	45
121	Harpo	1	Programmer	08	1/12	21
121	Harpo	1	Programmer	12	3/21	107
270	Garfunkel	2	Analyst	08	1/12	10
270	Garfunkel	2	Analyst	12	3/21	78
273	Selsi	3	Designer	01	7/17	22
274	Abrahms	2	Analyst	12	3/21	41
279	Higgins	1	Programmer	01	7/17	27
279	Higgins	1	Programmer	08	1/12	20
279	Higgins	1	Programmer	12	3/21	51
301	Flannel	1	Programmer	01	7/17	16
301	Flannel	1	Programmer	12	3/21	85
306	McGraw	3	Designer	12	3/21	67

It is generally useful to define a unique key that identifies each record occurrence. In some cases, it is possible to identify a single data element that uniquely identifies each record; in other cases, two or more data elements must be combined to form a *concatenated key*. In this case, we must use both the Employee-# and Project-# data elements as a concatenated key that uniquely identifies each record:

Employee

Employee-#	Project-#	Employee-Name	Job-Code	Job-Title	Completion-Date	Hours-Worked
120	01	Jones	1	Programmer	7/17	37
120	08	Jones	1	Programmer	1/12	12
121	01	Harpo	1	Programmer	7/17	45
121	08	Harpo	1	Programmer	1/12	21
121	12	Harpo	1	Programmer	3/21	107
270	08	Garfunkel	2	Analyst	1/12	10
270	12	Garfunkel	2	Analyst	3/21	78
273	01	Selsi	3	Designer	7/17	22
274	12	Abrahms	2	Analyst	3/21	41
279	01	Higgins	1	Programmer	7/17	27
279	08	Higgins	1	Programmer	1/12	20
279	12	Higgins	1	Programmer	3/21	51
301	01	Flannel	1	Programmer	7/17	16
301	12	Flannel	1	Programmer	3/21	85
306	12	McGraw	3	Designer	3/21	67

One of the goals of normalization is to reduce data redundancy. At this point, it appears that we have instead increased data redundancy by placing the data into first normal form; job code and job title data elements are repeated many times, and the same completion dates are stored multiple times as well.

This increase in data redundancy is an important argument for why further normalization steps are required to produce a stable design. A record type that is in first normal form only and has not been further normalized may have many undesirable characteristics, of which data redundancy is only one. We will see how subsequent steps in the normalization process will reduce the redundancy that we have introduced and how additional normalization steps improve the data structure in other important ways as well.

SECOND NORMAL FORM

The second step in the normalization process places the data into *second normal form*. Second normal form involves the idea of *functional dependence*.

Functional Dependence

In general a given data element, say, data element B, is functionally dependent on some other data element, say, data element A, if for any given value of data element A there is a single value of data element B associated with it. Saying that data element B is functionally dependent on data element A is equivalent to saying that data element A *identifies* data element B. Notice that there are three record occurrences that have an Employee-# value of 121, but in each of those records, the Employee-Name data element value is the same—Harpo:

Employee

Employee-#	Project-#	Employee-Name	Job-Code	Job-Title	Completion-Date	Hours-Worked
120	01	Jones	1	Programmer	7/17	37
120	08	Jones	1	Programmer	1/12	12
121	01	Harpo	1	Programmer	7/17	45
121	08	Harpo	1	Programmer	1/12	21
121	12	Harpo	1	Programmer	3/21	107
270	08	Garfunkel	2	Analyst	1/12	10
270	12	Garfunkel	2	Analyst	3/21	78
273	01	Selsi	3	Designer	7/17	22
274	12	Abrahms	2	Analyst	3/21	41
279	01	Higgins	1	Programmer	7/17	27
279	08	Higgins	1	Programmer	1/12	20
279	12	Higgins	1	Programmer	3/21	51
301	01	Flannel	1	Programmer	7/17	16
301	12	Flannel	1	Programmer	3/21	85
306	12	McGraw	3	Designer	3/21	67

A similar relationship exists between the Employee-# and Employee-Name data elements in the other record occurrences that have the same Employee-# value. Therefore, as long as we assume that no two employees can have the same employee number, Employee-Name is functionally dependent on Employee-#. We can use the same argument to show that Job-Code and Job-Title are also functionally dependent on Employee-#.

Full Functional Dependence

In some cases, a data element will not be functionally dependent on a single data element but will be functionally dependent on a *group* of data elements. For example, Hours-Worked is functionally dependent on the combination of

Employee-# and Project-#. This leads to the idea of *full functional dependence*. A data element can be said to be fully functionally dependent on some collection of other data elements when it is functionally dependent on the entire set but not on any subset of that collection. Hours-Worked is fully functionally dependent on Employee-# and Project-#. However, Completion-Date is not fully functionally dependent on Employee-# and Project-#, since Completion-Date is functionally dependent on Project-# alone.

To place into second normal form a group of data elements that is in first normal form, we identify all the full functional dependencies that exist and create a separate record for each set of these. We begin by identifying a likely key—in this case Employee-#—and determining which other data elements are fully functionally dependent on that key. Employee-Name, Job-Code, and Job-Title are functionally dependent on Employee-#, so we move them to a separate Employee record type that has Employee-# as its primary key:

Employee

Employee-#	Employee-Name	Job-Code	Job-Title
120	Jones	1	Programmer
121	Harpo	1	Programmer
270	Garfunkel	2	Analyst
273	Selsi	3	Designer
274	Abrahms	2	Analyst
279	Higgins	1	Programmer
301	Flannel	1	Programmer
306	McGraw	3	Designer

Of the remaining data elements, Completion-Date is dependent on Project-#, so we move the Project-# and Completion-Date data elements to a separate Project record type that has Project-# as the primary key:

Project

Project-#	Completion-Date
01	7/17
08	1/12
12	3/21

This leaves the Hours-Worked data element. Hours-Worked is fully functionally dependent on the concatenated key that consists of Employee-# and Project-#. So we create a third record type called Hours that consists of Employee-#, Project-#, and Hours-Worked. The key of the Hours record type consists of Employee-# and Project-#:

Hours

Employee-#	Project-#	Hours-Worked
120	01	37
120	08	12
121	01	45
121	08	21
121	12	107
270	08	10
270	12	78
273	01	22
274	12	41
279	01	27
279	08	20
279	12	51
301	01	16
301	12	85
306	12	67

We can now say that our set of data elements is in second normal form because it is in first normal form and every nonkey data element is fully functionally dependent on the primary key of its record type.

Notice that we have repeated the Employee-# data element in two of the records and that we have repeated the Project-# data element in two of the records:

Employee

Employee-#	Employee-Name	Job-Code	Job-Title
120	Jones	1	Programmer
121	Harpo	1	Programmer
270	Garfunkel	2	Analyst
273	Selsi	3	Designer
274	Abrahms	2	Analyst
279	Higgins	1	Programmer
301	Flannel	1	Programmer
306	McGraw	3	Designer

Project

Project-#	Completion-Date
01	7/17
08	1/12
12	3/21

Hours

Employee-#	Project-#	Hours-Worked
120	01	37
120	08	12
121	01	45
121	08	21
121	12	107
270	08	10
270	12	78
273	01	22
274	12	41
279	01	27
279	08	20
279	12	51
301	01	16
301	12	85
306	12	67

Duplicating data element types is perfectly valid and often occurs when converting records to second normal form. With a relational database, these duplicate data element types implement the relationships that exist between the record types. With a network-structured database, these data element duplications can later be removed and the relationships between record types can be implemented using sets.

Notice that placing the data into second normal form has reduced much of the redundancy that existed in the original set of first normal form records. Job-

Code and Job-Title data element values now appear only once per employee, and Completion-Date data element values appear only once per project.

Now that we have our data in second normal form, we can point out another undesirable characteristic of a record type that is in first normal form only. When our data was in first normal form, we had a single record type whose primary key consisted of Employee-# and Project-#. With that structure, we needed to have valid values for both Employee-# and Project-# in order to create a new record occurrence. This means that we would be unable to store a record occurrence for an employee that is currently not assigned to a project unless we used a null Project-# value. Similarly, we would be unable to store a record occurrence for a project that currently has no employees assigned to it without using a null Employee-# value.

With our data elements in second normal form, we can add a new employee by adding only an Employee record occurrence. After the new employee has been assigned to a project and has logged some time on that project, we can add an Hours record occurrence to describe the project assignment and the number of hours logged. In a similar manner, we can add only a Project record occurrence to describe a new project.

THIRD NORMAL FORM

The third step in the normalization process involves the idea of *transitive dependence*. Suppose we have a record type with data elements A, B, and C:

A	B	C

If data element C is functionally dependent on data element B, and data element B is functionally dependent on data element A, then data element C is functionally dependent on data element A:

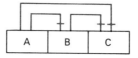

If similar dependencies are not true in the opposite direction (i.e., data element A is not functionally dependent on data element B or data element B is not functionally dependent on data element C), then data element C is said to be transitively dependent on data element A:

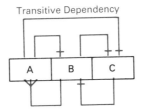

Transitive Dependency

We said earlier that Job-Code and Job-Title were functionally dependent on Employee-#:

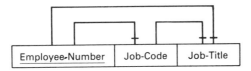

Assuming there is only one job title associated with a given job code, Job-Title is functionally dependent on Job-Code:

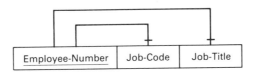

In the reverse direction Job-Code is functionally dependent on Job-Title as long as a given job title is associated with only one job code. However, many employees may have the same job code. So Employee-# is not functionally dependent on Job-Code. This means that Job-Title is transitively dependent on Employee-#:

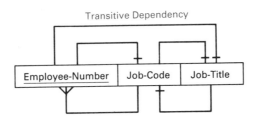

Transitive Dependency

To place our data into third normal form, we must remove transitive dependencies. This is done by placing the Job-Title data element in a separate record type called Jobs with Job-Code as its primary key. The following shows the data after it has been placed into third normal form:

Employee

Employee-#	Employee-Name	Job-Code
120	Jones	1
121	Harpo	1
270	Garfunkel	2
273	Selsi	3
274	Abrahms	2
279	Higgins	1
301	Flannel	1
306	McGraw	3

Jobs

Job-Code	Job-Title
1	Programmer
2	Analyst
3	Designer

Project

Project-#	Completion-Date
01	7/17
08	1/12
12	3/21

Hours

Employee-#	Project-#	Hours-Worked
120	01	37
120	08	12
121	01	45
121	08	21
121	12	107
270	08	10
270	12	78
273	01	22
274	12	41
279	01	27
279	08	20
279	12	51
301	01	16
301	12	85
306	12	67

A record type is said to be in third normal form if it is in second normal form and every nonkey data element is nontransitively dependent on the primary key. We can give an informal definition of third normal form by saying that in third normal form, all the data elements of a record type are functionally dependent on the key, the whole key, and nothing but the key.

Placing data into third normal form eliminates additional potentially undesirable characteristics of data that is in only first or second normal form. The preceding set of records shows that a job title associated with a given job code now appears in only one place instead of appearing for each employee that has that job code. This makes it easier to change a job title, since the change has to be made in only one place. Also, we can now add a new job code with its associated job title even though no employee has yet been assigned that job code. And we will not lose the job title if we temporarily have no employees assigned a given job code.

FOURTH NORMAL FORM

In the great majority of cases, placing data into third normal form provides a sufficient level of normalization. Higher levels of normalization are possible, however, and it is occasionally beneficial to place data into *fourth normal form*.

Suppose that an employee can be assigned to several projects concurrently. Also suppose that an employee can possess a series of skills. If we record this information in a single record type, we need to use all three data elements as the key, since no other data element grouping produces unique record identification.

Employee-Project-Skill

Employee-#	Project-#	Skill
120	01	Design
120	01	Program
120	01	Document
120	08	Design
120	08	Program
120	08	Document

Using a single record type, like the foregoing one, is not desirable because values have to be repeated, which could cause consistency problems when updating. However, since there are no data elements in this record that are not part of the key, the record is in third normal form. We can represent the relationships in this record in a simpler manner if we split them into the following two separate all-key record types:

Employee-Project

Employee-#	Project-#
120	01
120	08

Employee-Skill

Employee-#	Skill
120	Design
120	Program
120	Document

These record types are in fourth normal form. Fourth normal form involves the idea of *multivalued dependencies*, in which a given value for a single data element identifies multiple values of another data element. A multivalued dependency is defined in terms of the set of values of one data element type that is associated with a given pair of values from two other data element types. Look again at our original three data element record occurrences:

Employee-Project-Skill

Employee-#	Project-#	Skill
120	01	Design
120	01	Program
120	01	Document
120	08	Design
120	08	Program
120	08	Document

The relationship between Employee-# and Project-# is a multivalued dependency because for each pair of Employee-#/Skill values, the associated set of Project-# values is determined only by Employee-# and is independent of Skill. Similarly, the relationship between Employee-# and Skill is a multivalued dependency, since the set of Skill values for an Employee-#/Project-# pair is independent of Project-#. Conversion to fourth normal form involves decomposing the original record type into multiple record types so that the multivalued dependencies are eliminated.

Notice that the two individual record types better represent the true relationships between the data elements because there is no real relationship between projects and skills. Also, there is less redundant data when we use two separate records, and the update behavior of the database is better as well. For example, if an employee acquires a new skill, we simply add a new Employee-Skill record occurrence. With the single record type, we would have to add multiple record occurrences, one for each of the projects the employee is assigned to.

Another way of looking at fourth normal form is that it gives us a good way of handling multiple repeating groups. We could view the original set of data in the following manner, where Project-# and Skill each takes the form of a repeating group:

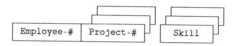

Placing the data into fourth normal form simply eliminates the repeating groups by placing each of them into separate record types. In actual practice, the earlier steps of normalization often identify such repeating groups and remove them, thus producing third normal form records that are already also in fourth normal form.

FIFTH NORMAL FORM

Fifth normal form is of interest mainly to users of relational database management systems that will be performing relational operations on the tables that make up the database. The relational operations that are concerned with fifth normal form are quite simple, so this discussion of fifth normal form can be understood even if the reader has no background in the relational database architecture.

In all the normalization steps we have discussed thus far, we have split record types into their constituent parts by performing what is essentially a relational *project* operation. A *project* operation produces a new set of record occurrences that contains all the original record occurrences but only a subset of the data elements from them. Any record occurrences that contain exactly the same values as some other record occurrence are then eliminated from the result. For example, let us begin with the following set of record occurrences that we looked at previously:

Employee-Project-Skill

Employee-#	Project-#	Skill
120	01	Design
120	01	Program
120	01	Document
120	08	Design
120	08	Program
120	08	Document

One projection of this set of records would produce a new set with only Employee-# and Project-# data elements:

Employee-Project

Employee-#	Project-#
120	01
120	01
120	01
120	08
120	08
120	08

Eliminating redundant record occurrences, the final result would be:

Employee-Project

Employee-#	Project-#
120	01
120	08

In all the previous examples, we were able to split a set of record occurrences into a set of its projections that together contain all the original data elements while still retaining all the data contained in the original set of records. In other words, we were able to recombine the constituent sets of record occurrences to exactly re-create the original set of records.

There exist, however, some sets of records, whose record types are in fourth normal form and that contain three data element types but cannot be split into two projections and then recombined to form the original set of record occurrences. This phenomenon occurs because of the particular combination of data element values that exists in the records and is the result of the inherent relationships in the data. Consider the following set of records:

Employee-Project-Skill

Employee-#	Project-#	Skill
120	01	Design
120	08	Program
120	01	Program
205	01	Program

In the preceding set of records, an employee is assigned to one or more projects and uses one or more skills on each project. However, in this case the particular combinations of data element values implies that there is a relationship not only between employees and skills (an employee has a particular skill) but also between projects and skills (certain skills are employed by each project). We can interpret these relationships to mean that an employee *uses* a skill that he or she possesses on a project only if that skill is *employed* by that project. This means that employees may *have* skills that are not *used* on projects to which they are assigned.

At first glance, the foregoing set of records seems to have the same characteristics as the records we looked at when examining fourth normal form. However, suppose we split the above set of records into two of its projections as we did earlier:

Employee-Project

Employee-#	Project-#
120	01
120	08
205	01

Employee-Skill

Employee-#	Skill
120	Design
120	Program
205	Program

Since we have two sets of records that together contain all the data elements from the original set of records, it appears as though these two new sets of records are equivalent to the original set of records. Let us now perform a relational join operation in an attempt to re-create the original records. A relational join operation combines two sets of records and results in a new set that combines all the data element types from both sets of records. The join operation is based on data element values that are common between the two sets of records. In this case, the resulting set of records is formed by matching up the Employee-# values from both sets of records. By performing the join we get the following result:

Employee-Project-Skill

Employee-#	Project-#	Skill
120	01	Design
120	08	Design
120	01	Program
120	08	Program
205	01	Program

Notice that there is now an extra record occurrence that the original set of records did not have (the second record occurrence). Project 08 now appears to use design skills when the original data shows no employee performing design tasks for that project. The reason this occurs is that the two new sets of records we created by performing *project* operations on the original set of records do not accurately represent all the associations inherent in the original records. In this case, the original combination of data element values implies that there *does* exist a relationship between projects and skills; each project only uses certain types of skills. This relationship is lost when we decompose the records into the two projections shown.

It is interesting to note that the original set of records does *not* contain multivalued dependencies and thus is already in fourth normal form. The set of Project-# values associated with each Employee-Skill pair *is* dependent on both Employee-# and Skill and not just on Employee-#. Similarly, sets of Skill values are dependent on both Employee-# and Project-#. Thus, it is not correct to separate the set of records into only *two* projections. One of the relationships is lost by doing so.

This record can, however, be further normalized by placing the data into *fifth normal form*. This involves decomposing the set of records into *three* projections, thus retaining all three relationships that exist between the various data elements:

Employee-Project

Employee-#	Project-#
120	01
120	08
205	01

Employee-Skill

Employee-#	Skill
120	Design
120	Program
205	Program

Project-Skill

Project-#	Skill
01	Design
08	Program
01	Program

To rejoin the three sets of records, we first perform a relational join on the first two sets to form an intermediate result. We then join the intermediate set with the third set of records to form the final result of the three-way join operation. The result of the first join operation in this case corresponds to an intermediate result that shows all the skills that *might* be used on projects:

Employee-Project-Skill

Employee-#	Project-#	Skill
120	01	Design
120	08	Design
120	01	Program
120	08	Program
205	01	Program

The third set of records specifies the skills that each project *actually* uses. We then join the intermediate set with the third set:

Employee-Project-Skill

Employee-#	Project-#	Skill
120	01	Design
120	08	Design
120	01	Program
120	08	Program
205	01	Program

Project-Skill

Project-#	Skill
01	Design
08	Program
01	Program

In performing this join, we match up sets of both Project-# and Skill data element values. Because values for both Project 08 and Skill Design do not exist in both sets of records, the spurious record is eliminated, and we get a result that is identical to our original set of record occurrences:

Employee-Project-Skill

Employee-#	Project-#	Skill
120	01	Design
120	08	Program
120	01	Program
205	01	Program

The projections from the previous example, which *can* be rejoined to produce the original set of records, are in fifth normal form. This constraint on which projections can be validly rejoined is called a *join dependency*.

A set of records that is in fourth normal form but not in fifth normal form has strange update behavior. Consider the following two record occurrences that show an employee using design skills on one project and programming skills on another project:

Employee-Project-Skill

Employee-#	Project-#	Skill
120	01	Design
120	08	Program

Suppose we added a new Employee record occurrence for an employee who uses programming skills on Project 01:

Employee-Project-Skill

Employee-#	Project-#	Skill
120	01	Design
120	08	Program
205	01	Program

The addition of that record occurrence on first glance seems to be valid. But let us now again decompose this new set of records into its three fifth normal form projections:

Employee-Project

Employee-#	Project-#
120	01
120	08
205	01

Employee-Skill

Employee-#	Skill
120	Design
120	Program
205	Program

Project-Skill

Project-#	Skill
01	Design
08	Program
01	Program

We now rejoin the three preceding sets of records, producing the following result:

Employee-Project-Skill

Employee-#	Project-#	Skill
120	01	Design
120	08	Program
120	01	Program
205	01	Program

Notice that we have an extra record occurrence that did not exist in the set of records that we began with. This result at first seems intuitively wrong. Does this mean that the three projections are not in fifth normal form? No, it means that it is not valid to add only that one record occurrence to the nonfifth normal form set of records. By adding the one new record to the nonfifth normal form set of records, we are actually stating three facts:

1. Employee 205 has been assigned to Project 01.
2. Employee 205 has programming skills.
3. Project 01 now uses programming skills.

By analyzing the contents of the original set of records, together with the foregoing facts, we can see that when we add the new record for Employee 205, Project 01, and the programming skill, then we must also add a new record for Employee 120, Project 01, and the *programming* skill. This is because Employee 120 already had the programming skill and was already assigned to Project 01; thus, Employee 120's programming skill is now available to Project 01, which, when we added the first record, we stated that Project 01 is now using.

The join dependencies that exist in the single set of records that is not in fifth normal form create constraints on the updating of the database. If the records are left in fourth normal form, then we must sometimes add two records at a time instead of only one. There can be similar problems with deletions. It is often quite difficult to determine when these updating anomalies occur. Such arcane relationships are impossible for mere mortals to discern during normal update operations. But, by using the three individual record types (in fifth normal form) rather than the composite record type, we can be sure that all three facts are reflected properly and completely in the database. When the data is in fifth normal form, we can add the Employee 205 data in a straightforward manner by simply adding a new record occurrence of each of the three record types. The two new records will then automatically appear in the result if we rejoin the three fifth normal form individual sets of records.

Placing the data into fifth normal form also allows us to add data that couldn't be added when using the composite record type. For example, we can show an employee having a particular skill by adding an Employee-Skill record occurrence, even though no project currently uses that skill. This information cannot be added to the set of composite records without using a null Project-# value.

Research is continuing on normalization, and even higher forms of normalization have been identified. However, it can be shown that fifth normal form is the highest form of normalization that is possible with respect to the relational operations of projection and join, and fifth normal form is the highest form of normalization that is generally required in practice.

INDEX

.